R. g. Edward.

HELPING DRUG USERS

Helping Drug Users

Social work, advice giving, referral and training services of three London 'street agencies'

NICHOLAS DORN
Assistant Director
NIGEL SOUTH
Research Sociologist
Institute for the Study of Drug Dependence,
London

Gower

Published by Gower Publishing Company Limited, Gower House, Croft Road, Aldershot, Hants GU11 3HR England

Gower Publishing Company, Old Post Road, Brookfield, Vermont 05036, U.S.A.

British Library Cataloguing in Publication Data

Dorn, Nicholas
    Helping drug users : social work, advice-giving, referral
    and training services of three London 'street agencies'.
    1. Narcotic addicts --Rehabilitation--
    England--London 2. Social service--
    England--London
    I. Title II. South, Nigel
    362.2'938'09421   HV5840.G72L6

Library of Congress Cataloguing in Publication Data

Dorn, Nicholas
    Helping drug users
    Bibliography: p.
    1. Drug abuse--treatment--England--London--case studies.
    2. Drug abuse counselling--England--London--case studies.
    I. South, Nigel. II. Title.
    HV5840.G72D67 1985   362.2'9386'09421   84-18875

    ISBN 0-566-00797-5

Printed and bound in Great Britain by
Biddles Ltd, Guildford and King's Lynn

Contents

Contents

Preface

During a thirteen month period ending in July 1983 we were able to carry out an intensive study of the work of three London 'street agencies'. The Blenheim, Hungerford, and Community Drug Projects provide a variety of services to statutory and to non-statutory agencies in the specialist drugs field and beyond, and to clients facing a variety of problems related to use of illegal and prescribed drugs and homelessness, poverty, criminality, sexual oppression and violence, loneliness, and ill-health.

This book describes the historical origins of the agencies in the 1960/70s, their present day working practices, the referral system that they inhabit, and the possibilities for future work. It will be of value to all those who - as either health, welfare or social work practitioners in the statutory or non-statutory sector, or as members of self-help and other community groups - want to be able to respond more constructively to drug users.

The views expressed in this book are those of the authors and do not necessarily reflect the views of the DHSS (who funded the study) nor of staff members or management of the three agencies concerned. We are most grateful to all those who helped us and we hope that by making their experience available in this form, others will become more confident and competent in helping drug users. Our thanks are due not only to the DHSS, and to the staff of the Blenheim, Hungerford and Community Drug Projects, but also to the staff of sixty-one other agencies (statutory and non-statutory) who helped with our enquiries by agreeing to visits and interviews, and other persons who discussed our work with us as it developed. We also wish to thank Karolina Frey, Hilarie Kerr and Susan Marrows who typed interview transcripts and sections of this report. Lastly, we thank Jasper Woodcock, who read the draft and made several suggestions.

ND and NS

ISDD (Institute for the Study of Drug Dependence)

London

1 Introduction and overview

INTRODUCTION TO A STUDY OF THREE LONDON 'STREET AGENCIES'

This book describes the work of three London 'street agencies' providing a variety of services to people with drug-related problems (including problems related to legal drugs). The three agencies described are:

The Hungerford Drug Project, Craven Street, in the West End of Central London. This agency is closest in its practice to the idea conveyed by the term 'street agency', doing some detached work in and around the Piccadilly area, and having a relatively high proportion of its clients calling at its reception desk (i.e. as opposed to being telephone referrals).

The Blenheim Project, in North Kensington, i.e. north-west of the metropolis, but still within the inner city area. Of the three agencies, this one has probably most consistently placed drug-related problems in a context of other problems, such as housing shortages and lack of provision to meet women's particular needs. The Blenheim strives to offer to every client a range of options for his or her self-help and recovery.

The Community Drug Project (CDP), in Camberwell, south-east London (and relatively cut-off, socially as much as geographically, from the inner city centre). This agency began as an attempt to keep addicts attending local drug clinics off the streets, then emphasised intensive psycho-therapeutic counselling of drug users, and currently spends nearly as much time on advising and training professionals, and working with probation projects and in prisons, as it does in face-to-face client contact on its own premises. Since this study was completed, CDP has moved from Camberwell to premises near the Elephant and Castle.

This book describes the origins, development, current prac-tices, inter-relations, and place within the broader social welfare system of each of these three agencies. Chapter 1 gives some background on the development of drug policies and problems for the benefit of those readers who may lack such essential 'contextualising' information. Chapters 2 to 6 go on to describe the neighbourhood, premises, staffing, philosophies, daily work and special concerns of each agency, and their collaboration on a London-wide basis. Whilst each has a focus of work (the Hungerford with street multi-drug users, the Blenheim with self-help and women's needs, the CDP with probation work and training other agencies), each agency also responds to the broad range of problems present-ed by other agencies (seeking referral advice), by families and friends of users, and by drug users referred by self or by other helping agencies.

THE POTENTIAL VALUE OF THE STUDY FOR SOCIAL WORK POLICY AND PRACTICE

Social work practice in the drugs field is something that is imbued with a certain mystique. It occupies what must be a fairly unique position within the range of forms of social work practice, generic or specialised.

To other social workers outside the drugs field, as well as to other professional and lay observers, social work with drug users is not part of their province and surely requires specialised skills and training.

For social work and allied staff within the drugs agencies this perception represents both a myth and a reflection of one of the things that they see as seriously wrong - the absence of training in dealing with drug-related social work problems, not merely for generic social workers, but also for the so-called 'specialists'. For these specialist workers, 'expertise' has developed principally through immersion in the job. This leads to their conviction that there is nothing 'special' about social work with drug users, that anybody within the statutory or non-statutory care and welfare sectors could do it - and that, furthermore, apart from clearly difficult cases where experience would be necessary, such workers should be taking drug users as part of their caseload. But, of course, the point is that there are difficult cases demanding the lessons of experience, and street agency social workers have developed into specialist workers with specialised expertise.

On balance, it is probably true that generic social workers could and, in order to demystify the issue, should take on more (if not all) drug-related case work. It is unlikely in present circumstances, however, that their existing caseloads would actually allow such additional, problematic weight. Hence such problems will continue to remain outside their province - as much because of the need to reduce work-loads to tolerable levels by any feasible manner (such as referral to specialist facilities), as because of any particular difficulty in coping with drug-related problems (which are not necessarily more intractable than many other social work problems). And there may well continue to be a certain proportion of drug-related social work cases that will benefit from the attention of a seasoned drug worker, whether that attention is direct and long term counselling of the client, or 'indirect' (e.g. advising the generic social worker who is handling the case).

So, although a description of 'specialist' drug-related social work may at first sight seem to reify the practice instead of demystifying it for others, we have to acknowledge that there is a demand for this sort of service, and that the agencies do respond to this demand. The important point is that they do not respond to this demand in a purely passive manner, but negotiate in terms of referral, advice-giving, consultancy, training and other forms of support with the generic agencies making the demands. In doing so, the street agencies offer to the careful observer three valuable sets of lessons:

(a)   lessons about the appropriateness and inappropriateness of various kinds of referral to a range of specialist drug agencies (advice and counselling agencies, crisis intervention, rehabilitation, etc.) as well as to non-drug specialist agencies (e.g. for basic medical care, housing advice, etc.);

(b)   lessons about ways in which the generic agencies themselves can (within limits of available time, staffing, policies, etc.) cope with many social work cases in which drug/alcohol/solvent-related problems are present as a part of the broader picture;

(c)   lessons about the practical workings of the complex system of inter-locking institutions (statutory/non-statutory, specialist/non-specialist, health/social welfare/education/etc.) that make up the referral network through which individual persons with drug-related problems pass, and lessons about the possibility of better coordination between agencies, new approaches to handling these cases, policy implications of the experience gained by street agency staff, and so on.

It is from this perspective that the history and present practices of the three London street agencies hold valuable lessons for social work and allied policy and practice.

HOW WE CAME TO WRITE THIS BOOK

The origins of this book lie in a decision by the Department of Health and Social Security to give temporary financial support to three London street agencies. As part of that support, it was agreed that some kind of exercise of description, assessment or evaluation would be carried out. The aims of the exercise seem - as far as can be discerned by the authors - to include accounting for the money spent by the Department; to collect information that would aid further decisions on funding by a range of potential funders (e.g. at national, regional, or local levels); to generate a description of the social work practice of the agencies that might be useful for other social work and allied agencies (drug-specialist and non-specialist); to generate information that might be useful in throwing light on drug-related problems in general; and to increase 'value for money'.

The Department's draft written *Brief* for the exercise said that:

> The principal aims of the exercise will be to obtain basic descriptive information about the work of these street agencies and the contribution which they make to the overall response to the problems of drug mis-users. We understand that these agencies are also approached by clients with problems arising from solvent misuse and would like information about this at the same time.

The reader will notice the specific reference to solvent sniffing, which reflects concerns that were coming to the fore at that time. The street agencies deal with sniffing 'cases' as they arise in their work, and sniffing does some-times form part of a broader picture of use of legal and illegal drugs by some clients. As suggested by the inclusion in the *Brief* of problems related to the use of and intoxication by means of a range of psychotropic substances, the scope of this report spans 'licit' and 'illicit' drugs (including medi-cines, where these are the concern of the agencies). We also attempt to describe the work of the agencies in relation to other problems which are mentioned in the *Brief* - 'housing, alcohol problems, drug misuse problems, solvent misuse, legal difficulties or a combination of these' - as represented in the day-to-day work of the street agencies.

This is very definitely a book for practitioners, students and parents involved in the related fields of social welfare, health, probation, education and youth work, and in preparing it for publication we have therefore removed any technical material on methodologies and the like. Readers wishing to learn more of such matters are welcome to visit ISDD's London reference library, wherein can be found a fuller version of our report, including a number of appendices:

Draft DHSS 'Brief' for information-gathering exercise.

ISDD submission.

Methodology, and List of Interviewees.

Formal aims of the three agencies.

Records routinely kept by the three agencies.

Selective annotated bibliography of some relevant reports.

In the following pages, however, we omit the more academic appendices, and remain firmly in the vernacular.

OVERVIEW OF THE FOLLOWING CHAPTERS

Following this introductory chapter, we turn in chapter 2 to an account of the origins and development of the street agencies in the 1970s. Each of the three was set up in response to aspects of social problems that came to be publicly recognised as such: homeless and rootless young drifters in the case of the Blenheim (then administered by Notting Hill Social Council); street users of illicit drugs in the case of the Hungerford (which operates near Piccadilly); and persons attending local drug clinics and finding them-selves at a loose end, in the case of the Community Drug Project (which was and is still located outside the city centre, and in the vicinity of two clinics attended by persons prescribed opiates). Thus, all three agencies were initially concerned with drug users, but varied in the extent to which they focussed upon drug users - the Blenheim least of all, whilst CDP focussed upon opiate addiction, and the Hungerford on street use of drugs in general.

During the mid-1970s, the agencies became more alike insofar as each operated as a Day Centre for injecting drug users; each had a protracted crisis involving a struggle between staff and attenders for the 'ownership' of its Day Centre; and each finally closed its Day Centre in the mid 1970s and subsequently re-opened as a 'Street Agency' to which drug users were admitted only in limited numbers and for limited purposes (excluding the consumption of any drugs or alcohol on the premises). Each street agency then developed in particular ways, the Blenheim emphasising detached work in local streets and squats, and developing campaign work on issues related to homelessness, whilst the CDP focussed on a psychotherapeutically-orientated approach to counselling drug users individually on its premises, and the Hungerford combined counselling and detached work with 'multi-drug users' and referral to residential rehabilitation facilities. This brief summary of 1970s social work practice in each of the three agencies may draw distinctions more clearly than they existed in practice; whilst the general outlines were as described, each of the three agencies was involved in each of these types of work. Chapter 2 describes these three histories in some detail, and places them within the context of broader developments during the 1970s.

In chapters 3 to 6, we describe the philosophies, staffing and working practices of each of the three agencies, and their working relations with each other and with other agencies at the time of our study. Let us now preview the main themes that arise out of our observations of the work of each agency.

In chapter 3, the Hungerford's recent work with inner-city street drug users is described, with particular reference to this agency's position within an informal referral system of statutory and non-statutory agencies, and to its continuing detached work. The Project sees persons with a variety of drug-related problems, amongst which homelessness and general ill-health are predominant. It is possible to distinguish between older users using the agency, and groups of younger and often 'chaotic' drug users, and the chapter concludes with short accounts of the viewpoints of two clients of the agency that illustrate aspects of the agency's work.

Chapter 4 describes CDP's recent work, drawing attention to its involvement not only in advising other agencies on a London-wide basis (a role it increasingly shares with the other two agencies), but also in the provision of more formal in-service training. CDP also works with the probation service, illustrating a more general trend for drug agencies to engage health services on the one hand (e.g. drug clinics), and the criminal justice system on the other.   CDP's face-to-face and street-level work with clients is correspondingly less than that of the Hungerford, and on average probably equals that of the Blenheim.

The Blenheim's recent work with drug users, described in chapter 5, spans a variety of drug-related problems arising from several contexts (such as homelessness, loneliness, problems of women as defined by them). The agency also emphasises its publications, designed for use by drug users and their families and friends. This chapter also explores (in greater depth than those preceding) the ways in which systems of referral and advice-giving and support (to users and to the staff of non-drug specialist agencies) are evolved.

There are elements of work which are common to each of the three agencies described in this report - for example an increasing interest in helping generic services (social work, probation) to cope better with 'non-crisis' drug users; to encourage provision that is more adequate to the needs of women; and to influence policy developments, both within the umbrella organisation, SCODA, (Standing Conference on Drug Abuse) and more directly (e.g. by joint press releases, responses to official reports, etc.).   At the same time, each of the three has developed its own particular practices - e.g. detached work, women-only outreach and attendance times (Blenheim) - and each agency will refer clients to the others as appropriate in any particular case. We describe this aspect of the agencies' joint work as complementarity; as a (still developing) form of co-operation on a London-wide (regional) basis.   Chapter 6 discusses this aspect of the street agencies, and outlines some directions for possible future development for the street agencies and for other agencies involved in responding to drug-related problems in the metropolis.

2 The 1970s in retrospect

'This is an area where the alternative society was centred, but no longer. It's everybody for himself in the accommodation crisis.' (ex-street agency worker)

'There is little incentive for "polydrug" abusers to attend clinics, for there is little likelihood of receiving a prescription.' (street agency annual report, 1978)

'I felt at times that some or certain members of staff were using and implementing a very conventional approach, i.e. "I'm OK, you are not OK".' (1976 internal staff paper)

INTRODUCTION

This chapter briefly overviews the development of social work and allied practices in three London street agencies dealing with homelessness, drug-related and other welfare problems of young people in the 1970s. The three quotations above identify three problems - changes in the housing market, changing patterns in drug use and provision, and problems of how to respond in a social work setting

- that then confronted the three street agencies (whose recent circumstances we discuss in chapters 3, 4 and 5).

In the paragraphs that now follow, we first outline the circumstances surrounding the formation and early history of each of the three agencies, observing how each initially operated a 'drop-in' day centre, and was obliged to close it in favour of more structured and 'professional' social work approaches. We then examine the broader developments in the drug policy and housing fields which impacted so heavily upon the street agencies and their clients; and finally note the severe problems that arose from attempts to operate small and under-resourced residential houses in these circumstances. The chapter as a whole attempts to provide the reader with information and a perspective within which he or she can appraise the value of the various social work and welfare approaches attempted by the three agencies during the 1970s, and to lay the groundwork for a more detailed description of day-to-day practice in the 1980s.

The histories of the three street agencies are undoubtedly complex, and largely enscribed in the shifting memories of those who then worked in the agencies. Relatively little was written down at the time. Interpretation of the information that is available is made more difficult by the fact that there have been, and continue to be, considerable differences of opinion within the drugs field. Some of these differences are articulated in this chapter, and some in subsequent sections of this book. Such differences in perspective affect one's view of what 'counts' as evidence, and how to describe it. This being so, it is best for us to describe the perspective which we have adopted in this report.

After study of surviving printed material produced by the three street agencies in their early years, discussions with persons who worked in the street agencies or were otherwise familiar with them in the 1960s and 70s, review of the available general drug literature and of the literature on some types of innovative social care/health services for drug and alcohol users, we have adopted a particular perspective. This is illustrated in the form of a Venn diagram (*From 'Day Centres' in the 1960s to 'Street Agencies' in the 1970s*: influences on the agencies, p.12). Here the reader will see that we have identified the following areas as important for an understanding of the history of the street agencies: the drug abuse control and care system, and drug cultures interacting with that system; housing and (less importantly) the employment situation; developments in the generic field of social work; and the financial resources available to the three agencies. This perspective will be elucidated in subsequent sections of this chapter. The point of introducing it here is that it illustrates the four main factors that have - in varying degrees, at different times - been important in providing a context for the development of each of the three street agencies. Each agency has its own starting point and trajectory within this broader set of influences.

THE ORIGINS AND DEVELOPMENT OF THE HUNGERFORD, COMMUNITY DRUG AND BLENHEIM PROJECTS

A potted history of the Hungerford Project

The Hungerford opened as a Day Centre in 1970, under the management of the Helping Hand Organisation (now Turning Point, and still the managing agency). Then followed a history that is probably the most turbulent of the three agencies studied.

Initially, there were three staff, 'hospital trained and therapeutic community oriented' (i.e. nurses), and they introduced principles of negotiating rules with the centre's initial clients. Some of the earliest clients seemed to wish to use the centre to dissociate themselves from the drug scene and these few clients helped the staff to adopt a 'peer modelling' approach to other clients. But a larger number gave the impression that they wanted the centre to be 'a Dilly with a roof, where they could fix and score freely'.

After the 'good' clients left, the centre descended into a 'chaotic and depressed state', and the situation seems to have been highly variable until 1974 (when the centre closed for some time). In the absence of 'good' role models, the staff focussed upon attempts to involve clients in 'one-to-one counselling'. On average in this period (1970-73) there seem to have been between three and nine attenders per day, with the most common attendance

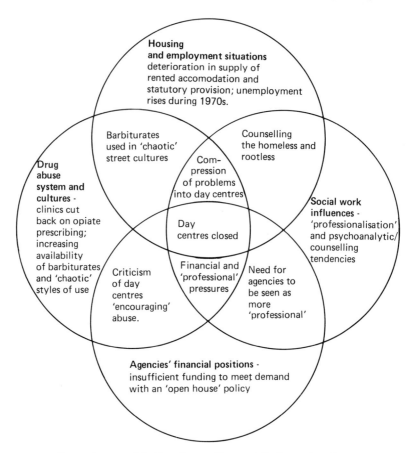

Within the diagram (from outside inwards):

Housing
and employment situations
deterioration in supply of
rented accomodation and
statutory provision; unemployment
rises during 1970s.

Barbiturates
used in 'chaotic'
street cultures

Counselling
the homeless and
rootless

Com-
pression
of problems
into day centres

Drug
abuse
system and
cultures -
clinics cut
back on opiate
prescribing;
increasing
availability
of barbiturates,
and 'chaotic'
styles of use

Social work
influences -
'professionalisation'
and psychoanalytic/
counselling
tendencies

Day
centres closed

Criticism
of day
centres
'encouraging'
abuse.

Financial and
'professional'
pressures

Need for
agencies to
be seen as
more
'professional'

Agencies' financial positions -
insufficient funding to meet demand
with an 'open house' policy

Notes on how to read the Venn diagram: Please read this diagram **from the
outside** (ie. from the four inter-connected 'systems' around drug abuse, housing,
social work, and finance - represented by the four circles), **inwards.**
Overlapping systems/circles produce particular results; eg. the combination
of increasing homelessness, and increasing multi-drug use, results in an
increasingly 'chaotic' street drug scene. Street agency staff, influenced
by trends in social work practice, attempted various approaches to
counselling these 'chaotic' users;

The centre of the diagram represents the response which each of the three
street agencies finally made to increasingly difficult circumstances - they
closed their day centres, and subsequently attempted to develop as 'street
agencies' (see text). This diagram is intended as an heuristic aid, to
accompany the text, for those readers who find such visual summary useful:
it is not intended to represent a full analytic account of the circumstances
in the late 1960s and early 1970s.

Diagram 2.1   From 'day centres' in the 1960s to 'street
                  agencies' in the 1970s: Influences upon
                  the agencies from professional social
                  work, the drug abuse control system,
                  the housing market, and available agency
                  funding.

pattern being that a person would attend between three and nine times (though some attended only once, and a few nearly every day). Formal social work approaches were not very practical in these circumstances:

> Case work as such rarely takes place, nor do we see the clients at fixed or regular intervals. Emphasis is therefore placed on immediacy of response and efforts to meet the addicts presenting needs, particularly in the initial stage of contact. Case work tends to take the form of informal discussion groups. (1972 Hungerford report).

The approach adopted was a modified social work approach, with practical advice and support, a degree of counselling focussed more upon the clients' present circumstances than upon the past, cheap meals and various practical activities (including cleaning oneself and one's clothes), and building various things (such as a radio). During this period (1971-2) the 'clinic room' (fixing room) was quite infrequently used, 'and is obviously not the main attraction for addicts attending the centre'. It would appear from this that the agency was being patronised by persons who largely satisfied whatever 'drug-focussed' needs they may have had elsewhere.

But from 1973 onwards, the staff experienced increasing difficulties in their attempts to maintain an atmosphere in which counselling could be given and 'worthwhile' (i.e. non-drug focussed) activities engaged in - partly because of increasing barbiturate use amongst clients, and a building that was difficult to supervise. Increasing police activity against drug users in the vicinity, greater use of barbiturates (especially marked after Ritalin was scheduled under the Misuse of Drugs Act, causing a shift from this stimulant to the sedative, barbiturate), and a general escalation of overdoses, aggression and violence seriously alarmed both staff and some of the older, relatively stable opiate users. As one heroin user reportedly said, 'You'd better watch out, letting those barbed-up people in here - you'll have all sorts of riff-raff in'. These difficulties cannot be understood in isolation - they relate to changes in drug users' housing circumstances, to changes in the drug control system, and to agency funding problems (e.g. understaffing and staff burn-out); circumstances which we describe in greater detail later in the book. For our present purposes, however, suffice it to say that there was 'a crisis' that the agency could not endure, and that it closed down for about eighteen months.

In 1975, Helping Hand began to hire new staff, and these staff undertook a three-month assessment of the situation before attempting to re-open the Hungerford. In the document *Drug use in London - and responses to it* they described the crisis as being not restricted to the Hungerford Day Centre, but as more widespread: 'It quickly became evident that there was a widespread move on the part of day centre staff, both in London and in the provinces, to modify the ways in which their projects worked.' (Helping Hand, n.d., p.4.)

The circumstances within which and processes whereby this 'widespread move' occurred are discussed in later sections of this chapter. The result was simply the abandonment of the idea of having a 'day centre' (i.e. premises with little or no restriction on entry, and with facilities for 'fixing' drugs). In the case of the Hungerford, this abandonment was total and permanent (whilst in the case of the Community Drug Project, described in the next section, there was considerable uncertainty amongst the staff, and an attempt to open a Day Centre for part of each day). Slowly and reluctantly, the Hungerford adopted a policy whereby clients were not allowed to enter the premises at will, were not allowed to use drugs on the premises, were generally sent away if they arrived intoxicated, and were met by staff either 'on the street' (detached work) or at the reception desk, where they would be encouraged to make an appointment if longer-term support, counselling or follow-up was indicated.

The Hungerford thus began as a Day Centre (the non-medical equivalent to a day ward in a hospital), and went through a period of crisis and closure, to re-emerge as a Street Agency (or 'drop-in' centre) for giving advice and counselling (the non-medical equivalent to a General Practitioner's surgery, or health centre). This change was so fundamental - and the previous history perhaps so disagreeable - that subsequent project reports refer to the Hungerford as having 'opened' in 1976. The 1977-8 Annual Report refers to the 'more formal social work' approach then adopted, without elaborating on past difficulties.

Whilst a report describes the 'new' Hungerford as a 'detached work project and advice centre, offering counselling and referral facilities', we understand from the then senior social worker that the detached street work was, in practice, secondary in importance to the project based advice and counselling (and so it has remained). Subsequent develop-ments were less fundamental, once the day centre 'problem' had been resolved by closure. (We describe the recent work-ing practices of the Hungerford in chapter 3.)

A potted history of the Community Drug Project

The Community Drug Project opened as an independent agency - though with the active encouragement and support of persons at the Institute of Psychiatry - in 1968 (i.e. two years before the Hungerford). It, too, went through a crisis and a closure, and re-opened without its previous day centre facility, but the circumstances and manner of CDP's transition from 'day centre' to 'street agency' have their own specific features, different from those of the Hungerford or the Blenheim projects.

Summarising very greatly, we can say that these differences are related to the CDP's location (not in the centre of the metropolis), clientele, and interests of staff (the development of which cannot have been unrelated to the agency's location and clients). There are, however, some common features - an increasing housing shortage (affecting clients of all three agencies), increasing use of barbiturates in the 1970s, trends in generic ('professional') social work practice, and agency funding problems - which affected CDP as much as the Blenheim and the Hungerford.

CDP is the only agency to have the word 'community' in its title, and this reflects the concern of Griffith Edwards and others around the Addiction Research Unit of the University of London's Institute of Psychiatry to relate to broader trends in health and social policy, towards 'community medicine' and 'community care', that had been encouraged by successive governments since 1962. It is within this 'community' perspective - one sensitive to the unapproachability of some forms of statutory services - that the accessibility of the day centre was emphasised in the first Annual Report:

> One of the strengths of CDP is that it is available - it is in the community. No appointments or formalities stand between the addict who wants help, and that help. He can walk in at the door for the first time even before he has worked out what he needs. (Edwards, in CDP Annual Report, 1969)

This statement contains a contradiction that was later to become manifest - i.e., that between the client being able to walk in and use the facility, and the agency's perception that the client doesn't know what he or she needs (and hence needs to be told, or at least to be steered in a direction tolerable to the staff).

Initially, CDP opened as an evening club offering 'reality based social work help', and within a few months moved to permanent premises, and opened every afternoon. A fixing room was agreed upon, since the absence of such a facility 'would result in a continued use of the public lavatories and telephone boxes for injections, which was already causing a great deal of disquiet in the area'. The first project report notes (similarly to that of the Hungerford) that the most 'constructive' users, i.e. those who wish 'to get away from the drug world', were encouraged to move to hospital and after-care facilities - leaving the most drug-focussed persons behind in the centre. Another problem was that local people - 'the community' - agitated to remove CDP and its attenders from their midst, forcing a move. Activities in the new premises revolved around fixing (each day upon arrival), improving the structure and facilities of the house, and discussing 'the difficulties to the continuing use of drugs' (First Annual Report, p.11). Other activities were attempted, including 'dress making as a means of encouraging the girls to be more conscious of their appearance...'. There was a stream of outside enquiries, and liaison with a range of referral agents. In this period, it is clear that the attenders were script-receiving opiate addicts, between thirty-five and fifty reportedly coming in each day. The project was evidently considered sufficiently exemplary to be visited by H.R.H. the Duke of Edinburgh.

By 1969, however, the staff and management became concerned that their success in attracting attenders might be undermined by 'the junkie ethic (appearing) to be stronger than the value(s) of the Centre'. Following scrutiny of replies given to a questionnaire sent to all the London drug clinics, and prolonged staff discussion, the activities of attenders were curtailed. Henceforth they had to arrive before 11.00 am (or not be admitted), when they could use the fixing room; then they had either to join in a house meeting and communal activities, or leave.

> The effect of introducing rules was to acknowledge the reality that in effect two groups existed within the centre, attenders and staff. The values of the staff group were reflected in the demands and expectations required from those who came. (CDP, Third Report

The immediate result of the new structure (which was slightly modified in 1971) was that attenders decreased in numbers by two thirds; and by the end of 1971 attenders 'polarised' into two groups - one of which came in only for a short while in the mornings to fix, whilst others remained in the house for longer periods and were subject to the conflicting influences of the morning visitors on the one hand, and the staff on the other. During the 1970s, CDP also developed its external activities (involvement in training, lobbying for facilities for the homeless and for drug users, liaison with other agencies), partly in an attempt to compensate for the loss of its original clients and functions.

In 1972, the departure of two senior members of staff, who had been particularly interested in the circumstances of the clients, led to changes in working methods that laid more emphasis upon the importance of engaging his or her intra-psychic state, values, attitudes and motivation. By the end of 1975, new staff (supported by a largely new management committee, the moving spirits in setting up CDP having mostly retired) were engaged in the acquisition of groupwork and counselling skills, attending courses and being advised in collective methods of work by a groupwork consultant. Staff morale appears to have been low in the mid-1970s, and the atmosphere in the dayroom 'often seemed chaotic and amorphous' (Sixth Report). Attempts were made to appraise attenders of their 'responsibilities' by way of individual counselling, and the centre was closed at mid-day to 'decrease the dependence the addict had on the centre, expecting it to be open at their convenience'. Lunch was dropped, except on Wednesday. Attendance was low - approximately fourteen persons attending 'regularly', according to one month's selected figures. More consultancy was provided (this time from the Consortium Action Research Team) to help with conflicts within the staff team.

In 1978, following an increasing tendency amongst attenders to favour 'turning up stoned, barbed up (i.e. intoxicated by barbiturates) and using CDP as a "crashing out pad" ', which resulted in 'a struggle between social workers and attenders as to the project's philosophy and "ownership" ', the staff closed the fixing room. The closure was felt to be justified not only because the behaviour of barbiturate users was alternatively aggressive and comatose, but because 'it is virtually impossible to engage in meaningful communication with these people...' (Seventh Report). Staff found that multi-drug use (unlike 'traditional' heroin use) 'reduces them (staff) to the roles of policemen and nurses, roles which they were not employed for in the first place, and in general a marked lack of motivation for these role adaptions was experienced' (ibid).

The closure of the day centre was a contentious matter for staff (as well as for attenders). Whilst one view was that a day centre and fixing room 'colludes' with the culture of the drug scene and/or with the 'medical model' of the clinics, a contrasting staff view was that the project had relinquished its responsibilities to clients and to the founding notion of 'community', and that the attempt to develop a role centering upon psychological counselling (plus some detached work) was counterproductive:

> In March '78 it became evident that CDP's role and function was in desperate and drastic need of re-evaluation and critical self-examination. The team had been concentrating on 'therapy' (using Freudian and Jungian, mixed with Laingian theories and other heavy friends) and on therapeutic counselling...
>
> In my opinion the more obvious achievement counselling or therapy revealed was that the individuals (clients) concerned became better equipped with the technical terms and therefore much more powerful in the

game of manipulation.   (Project Director, internal report.)

This shift in emphasis was the result of a shift in method from a community orientated social work approach to a therapeutic counselling approach. This shift suited the needs of the staff far more than those of the clients.   The amount of time and resources spent on counselling courses and psychoanalysis support this argument.   Eventually the clients voted with their feet hence the dramatic decline in attendance figures.   When I arrived in 1978 we had longterm contact with about six addicts at the outside. (Staff member, internal paper.)

It is not known whether disaffected ex-attenders of CDP were responsible for the fire that burnt it down, a few months after they lost effective 'ownership' of the project. The fire brought the work of the project to a halt for a number of months.
In 1979, new staff were appointed, and the project re-opened in Camberwell.   (Since we completed this study it has again moved to a more convenient location near the Elephant and Castle.)   A new role was now envisaged for the project:

(a)   giving advice, information and counselling - by telephone, or in the office by appointment only (a condition subsequently somewhat relaxed);

(b)   doing detached work (i.e. advice etc. on the street);

(c)   working with members of particular social groups (principally women, and divertees from the criminal justice system).

It may be considered, in retrospect, that this orientation does indeed correspond quite closely to the original aim of a 'community' approach, since it involves working with members of social groups who have circumstances (and sometimes perspectives) in common, and may be able to support each other in achieving the changes that they desire. The extent to which this direction of work has been developed by CDP in their recent practice is described in chapter 4.

A potted history of the Blenheim Project

Whereas the initiating spirit of the Hungerford Project
was 'Rehabilitation' (i.e. in the shape of the Helping Hand
Organisation), and of CDP was 'Community Psychiatry'
(Institute of Psychiatry), that of the Blenheim Project
was rescue work with young 'drifters' (organised by the
Notting Hill Social Council).

The Blenheim was (and is) situated near railway stations
connecting London to the Midlands, the North and South-
West of England, Scotland and Ireland, and a continuing
interest in helping young 'drifters' has influenced its
development, staff attitudes, and working practices.
The most pressing and obvious needs of these 'drifters'
were for accommodation, employment or social security
benefits, and companionship and advice.

The particular concerns of the Blenheim project -
especially the focus upon housing problems - were articulated
within the more broadly experienced context of increasing
barbiturate use, trends in social work, funding problems,
etc., to produce the Blenheim's characteristic approach.
Perhaps partly because the Blenheim's origins were already
relatively close to the social work model towards which
all three street agencies moved during the 1970s, this
agency had a rather smoother 'ride' from the early 1960s
to the late 1970s, although it did close for a while during
1980 (largely because of a financial crisis). We now examine
this agency's history in some detail, noting how it draws
our attention to the ways in which housing problems
may underlie some drug-related problems.

The Blenheim Project developed out of the appointment of
a social worker 'to look into the possibility of working with
drifting young people' in 1964. This person began doing
detached work, was then given a room as a base, and in 1967
a self-contained flat. In 1969 the Project - as it had then
become - moved into a house in the Portobello Road. A 1974
report retrospectively described the rationale as follows:

> For many years Notting Hill has been a centre for
> young drifters. They are people who come to London
> for one reason or another but cannot fit into the
> society they find there. They have no regular income,
> most of them are homeless and some have taken
> to drugs. They are attracted by the anonymity of
> the streets round Ladbroke Grove and Portobello

Road where all kinds of people come together and most eccentricities of dress and behaviour go unremarked. The attraction of Notting Hill has been enhanced by its association with groups who talked of building an alternative society: the groups have gone but the attraction remains.

The Project is a place to 'be' for people who are drifting. It is their place, they have chosen to come and they choose to keep on coming. It does not necessarily provide immediate treatment for a problem, in the way that a hospital is expected to do. Any behaviour is accepted, whether it is aggressive, depressive or sociable. There is a fair amount of self-help among the clients... (*People Adrift*, 1974)

Clients typically had backgrounds involving 'separation from parents by death or divorce, poor educational achievement, experience of children's homes, approved schools or prisons, miscarriages, drug taking, poor marriages, no prospects of work and no settled accommodation'. In other words, the classic syndrome of the unattached person, as presented to social work agencies. Additionally, this was the era of the alternative society, and the libertarian outlook of some of the clients was largely shared by the Blenheim/Notting Hill Social Council - 'the project (aims to play a) part in (clients') attempts to help themselves in spite of their own personal difficulties and the difficulties created by the attitudes of a society which treats them as failures'.

In appraising the early working methods of the Blenheim, it should be borne in mind that - unlike the CDP or Hungerford - the Blenheim did not specialise in 'drug cases'.

Some who come to the Project do not ask to speak to anyone. They come for a bath, to sit and read or to drink coffee and stare about. Most are eventually approached by a worker, but that need not result in any follow-up. Clients sometimes approach a worker weeks after they started coming to the Project. Some clients are picked up by a student and are taken on by the worker supervising that student. Someone who comes to the Project may, because of the pressure of work, be overlooked until the weekly staff meeting when a specific worker may agree to link with him, though only to make sure

that he has a worker to talk to if he wants to, not
because he has to explain his presence. (ibid)

This 'permissive' style of work was partly a function of the
work-setting; it did not originate exclusively in the perspectives of the staff (although of course that was important);
and it tended to draw criticism from a range of more
conventional agencies, as one observer's unfinished book on
the project suggests:

The small voluntary and unattached youth projects tend
to be more radical in outlook partly because of the more
exposed areas of their work. They are therefore more
likely to see when the policies carried out by social
security officials, the police or housing managers are
inhuman, and to say so.

A Catch 22 comes into operation then: the workers are
accused of being too identified with the people they are
trying to help, told that they have allowed emotion to
sway their judgement instead of remaining objective and
that this gullibility has made them 'anti-authority'.
(Winter, p.M8-9)

Such accusations continue to this day in the drug field, as
in other aspects of social welfare work. They probably had
more restraining influence on CDP (with its Institute of
Psychiatry base) than on the Blenheim (with its voluntary
social services background). This is not to imply that the
Blenheim was successful in its attempts to develop what later
came to be described as 'radical social work'; there were
constraints built into the situation, the clients and the
workers, and these tugged harder as the housing shortage
worsened and as barbiturate use became more common,
making any kind of social work increasingly difficult.

Winter notes that work seemed to go in phases, deluging
the project alternately with young girl absconders, heroin
addicts, pregnant women, job-seekers, Scottish migrants, and
barbiturate users. Up until 1974, the workload was sufficiently varied for staff to seek the key to the problem of
'drifters' not in any specific environmental or psychological
cause, but in the wrong expectations of society - in the
tendency to label those persons who don't seem to 'fit' the
available roles. The adoption of 'labelling theory' is reflected
in a section in the 1974 report entitled 'Towards a concept of
drifting':

Those who cannot find a role that satisfies themselves and the community are labelled to show how they fail to conform...

So begins the process of stereotyping in which a misfit's image of his deviance is reinforced by the behaviour of others, until he accepts their label as a correct description of himself. Some writers have called this process the beginning of a career of deviance, criminality, or mental illness.

It was around a perception of the importance of intervening in such already half-established careers (or at least not consolidating them) that the agency adopted short-term aims of providing practical help (somewhere to wash, to eat, to get advice), 'a place to be' (and an address which meant that the homeless could get social security benefits), and relationships with the workers, volunteers and other clients. Longer term aims were taken to be the education of society and of other agencies, and positive changes in the client (such that he or she is cleaner, pays rent, makes decisions etc.). Within this context, a psychiatrist came in once a week to see selected clients and to advise the workers.

The Blenheim never had a fixing room as such, since it dealt with a variety of groups (amongst whom drug injectors were but one) - but it did have a toilet, and fixing would occur in there. As barbiturate use became more widespread amongst those who could not find rented accommodation (owing to decreasing supply, and rising rents), this became the main problem area for the agency. An October 1974 report to SCODA (Standing Conference on Drug Abuse, the 'umbrella' organisation for voluntary agencies in the drugs field) records the staff's alarm about barbiturates/homelessness:

Death. In the last year there have been 15 deaths reported to the Blenheim Project; we have known most of these individuals over a period - some of them very well - and because of inadequate facilities outside and inside the Project there has been nothing we could do to prevent these deaths, despite the fact that in every case we have referred the individuals to hospitals, clinics, psychologists and psycho-analysts. We are just able to keep abreast of the problem

of the young person newly inducted to the use of
barbiturates, and this is the only role that we have
been able to fulfil successfully.   The hardened user
we are sad and anguished to say, we simply can
do nothing for.   As explained, we have no money
for facilities, no medical staff, and can only concentrate
as stated, on those who are not so far inducted as
to be considered hopeless cases.

The project would have liked to have been able to
adopt a dual approach, 'keeping open house as a means
of picking up clients and then arranging single appointments
for those with more motivation for getting out of the
drifting scene.   But our less than adequate resources
forced us to choose' (Open Door - or Appointments Only,
Blenheim 1974/5 Report, p.3).   The choice between open
door and appointments only was weighted in favour of
the latter, because the former:

> means that the drifter comes to see the project
> as his place.   This is good.   But the danger starts
> when it becomes more his place than the workers',
> when his culture starts to swamp that of the workers;
> and when the worker can no longer put across his
> alternative view of society. (Section on 'The Year
> of Change' in untitled project report).

Underpinning this problem, for Blenheim staff, was
the fact that their own 'alternative view of society' was
corresponding less and less to developments in the real
world, and would have been difficult to put across to
drug users, even had they been more attentive.   It had
become increasingly apparent that it was not just a question
of people's roles and of society's inability to allow flexibility
and experimentation with roles, but also of the material
situation of drifting.   The project had always operated
on the assumption that:

> the provision of temporary accommodation and comfort
> alleviates the anxiety of most youngsters and provides
> a situation in which it is possible to work out a more
> considered approach.   This 'breathing space' makes
> it possible for the youngster to contribute his own
> aspirations and ideas.   In this way the process of
> residential resettlement can become a more cooperative

venture. (1966 Annual Report)

This had been the practical basis of the project's work, on top of which sat the concern to overcome problems of labelling, etc. Problems in the housing market dealt the project a serious blow: 'Until 1967 it had been difficult but not impossible for the Blenheim project to help young people find somewhere to live - the situation is now out of control, however...' (Winter, p.EC1). The emergence of the chaotic, homeless 'multidrug user' - partly caused by the clinics' continuing retreat from heroin prescription, partly by an increase in the young homeless, and partly by a 'chaotic' style of use of drugs such as barbiturates in this context - thus affected Blenheim at the same time as it did CDP and the Hungerford. Blenheim, like them, abandoned its open door (and open toilet) policy, and instituted an appointment system in 1976.

Characteristically, the agency made the best of a bad job, and presented its action as path-breaking:

> It would appear from the innumerable enquiries regarding the project's work and experiential knowledge, that the project's change of emphasis away from an open day-centre to a more structured and controlled situation, has influenced a number of agencies throughout London who are now also changing their own policies. There has been a corresponding increase in respect for the project's work from both statutory and voluntary bodies; both the media and its representatives have been referred to us by outside agencies who consider our approach both progressive and positive. (Director's monthly internal report)

It may well have been the case that all three street agencies became perceived as more 'professional' by statutory agencies that had long been ambivalent about their previous, 'permissive' styles of work. But the results were mixed as regards work with clients. Many clients rejected the appointment system, and broke off contact with the agency - after a short period during which some picketed the building. Subsequent plans to refocus on off-premises fieldwork did not really come to fruition in the Blenheim (any more than they did in the other two agencies):

> At the second (weekend, review meeting) the factor
> which came to light most strongly was the difficulty
> of maintaining fieldwork on a regular basis in its
> existing form. Fieldwork days were missed altogether
> when the worker was either e.g. attending court,
> taking holiday leave, or was absent due to ill-health...
> (with a) consequent lack of continuity. (Fieldwork report,
> December 1975)

Fieldwork picked up gradually from 1975, the worker
quoted being described in reports from 1975-6 onwards
as having a 'role as a community worker', visiting squats,
cafes, pubs and street locations.

It also took time for the new appointments system
to work properly.

> There were three main reasons for this. Firstly,
> the new approach was something of a compromise
> between an open day-centre, and a centre functioning
> for four days a week in a more restricted fashion.
> Secondly, if one worker was absent, this put more
> pressure on the two that remained, making control
> of the door tenuous and thereby laying the appointments
> system open to abuse. Thirdly, many of the older,
> more dependent clients found loop-holes in the system,
> making up fictitious reasons for appointments, asking
> for baths, etc. Clearly, the perception of the Project
> as simply 'somewhere to be', was still prevalent.

What occurred in the Blenheim's history, then, was a
change in the working practices of the agency, and a
quite sharp resistance by clients to this change.

Historical convergence of the three street agencies

The crisis experienced by the Blenheim parallels, in some
respects, that undergone by CDP and the Hungerford.
Because the Blenheim had not been exclusively concerned
with injecting drugs users, however, and because it had
been rather more concerned with homelessness, the consequences of the 1976 barbiturates/homelessness crisis were
rather different for the Blenheim. The crisis made CDP and
the Hungerford less drug-centred, and perhaps more worried
about homelessness than hitherto (although CDP's dive into
individual psycho-analytic ideas served to delay this).

The Blenheim, on the other hand, became more drug-centred, since its clientele became less varied, and more 'druggy' (and they were already conscious of housing issues). All three agencies campaigned for restrictions on barbiturates (which were never incorporated into law, the medical profession managing to 'police' their membership in respect of barbiturate prescriptions), and also campaigned for a crisis unit (the SCODA Short Stay Unit, now called City Roads Crisis Intervention). In many ways, they emerged as more similar, at the end of the 1970s, than they had been at the start of the decade. They had all become drug-focussed (but not registered heroin addict-focussed) street agencies, with a drop-in and telephone advice system, appointment systems for counselling, variable amounts of fieldwork and detached work, and an increasing tendency to work together -around individual clients, within SCODA, and in campaign work. They formed (with Release) a Street Agencies Group. Each agency had modified its initial working practices - which had been articulated around ideas of rehabilitation (Hungerford), community psychiatry (CDP), and resettlement (Blenheim) - and had developed a shared 'street agency' identity (though with specific features reflecting specific origins, ways of weathering crises, and responses to late-1970s' conditions).

These 'careers' of the agencies are summarised in Diagram 2.2. In the following section we examine, rather more closely, the common problems facing the agencies, and come rather more up to date by asking what those problems are today.

THE CONTEXT OF DEVELOPMENTS IN THE DRUG CONTAINMENT SYSTEM AND DRUG CULTURES

The crisis experienced in the mid 1970s by each of the street agencies was, in many respects, a result of changes in the statutory drug care and control systems that had been in progress since the early 1960s - and a result of developments in patterns of drug use that are variously related to those changes, to broader changes in housing, employment and cultural trends, and to the responses of specific social groups to these changes and trends.

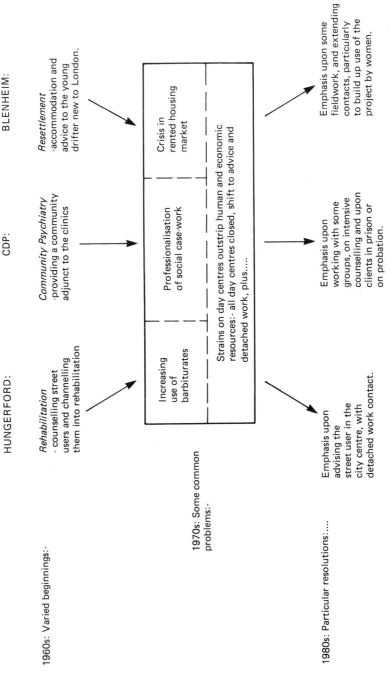

Diagram 2.2   Mapping the past: varied beginnings, common problems, and particular resolutions of the three street agencies

Historical development of the 'British system'

The current 'British system' of containment (a term that
encompasses elements of control and of care) of opiate
addictions originates, in a bureaucratic sense, with the
Rolleston Committee (1926), and developed through two
reports of the Brain Committee (the most important
of which reported in 1965, after an increase in the numbers
of registered addicts), and through the 1968 Advisory
Committee on Drug Dependence, to the recent Report
on Treatment and Rehabilitation of the Advisory Council
on Misuse of Drugs (1982). The ideas behind these policies
and practices are, however, considerably older, reflecting
their initial development within nineteenth century debates
on morality, public health and medicine which took as
one of their foci the then quite widespread patterns of
opiate drug use.*

Throughout the late nineteenth and early twentieth cent-
uries, medical debates about addiction and its management
revolved around the choice between a sudden cutting off of
supplies, and weaning the person off slowly with the aid of
alcohol and/or other drugs. Both of these presumed abstinence

---

*Up until the mid nineteenth century, extracts of the
opium poppy had been used in some parts of the country
in traditional folk medicines, and poppy heads were infused
to make a tea-like beverage. During the period of rapid
industrialisation and urbanisation, opium was marketed
in penny pills sold over the counter and included in a
vast range of heavily-promoted patent medicines. The
subsequent history of how the use of opiates became
defined or recognised as a 'problem' is a complex one
that has been only partially unravelled. A number of
nineteenth century campaigns, associated with rising
professional interests (pharmacy, medicine, etc.); temperance
movements (which, it will be remembered, had a feminist
aspect); complex alliances concerned with public health,
moral control, the family and the child; eugenics; and
international trade (the Opium Wars) were involved.
Drawing upon this rich mix, the ascendant definition
of problems associated with opiates such as morphine
(an injectable derivative of opium) had two main elements
- (Berridge & Edwards, 1981) - morphinomania, or hedonistic
and 'lunatic' use, a failure of morality (requiring control of
the person); and morphinism, a disease state recognised by

as the treatment goal and/or moral aim. The idea of 'stabilising' the opiate user by prescribing him or her sufficient quantities of the drug to prevent withdrawal dates from the inter-war period, the Rolleston Committee considering morphine and heroin addiction to be confined chiefly to those having professional access to drugs or becoming addicted during the course of medical treatment. These persons were deemed to be of 'good character' and the habit not a 'vicious indulgence'. It was in this context of largely middle class use that stabilisation of those unable or unwilling to withdraw became seen to be an appropriate policy.

This predominantly (but not totally) 'medical' (but not specifically psychiatric) definition remained in the forefront of UK domestic policy and practice until well after the Second World War, when it was slightly reformed to correspond more closely to the thinking of the times. In 1960 - following trends in the broader fields of health and social welfare, rather than any specific shift in circumstances in the drug field - the first Brain Committee shifted the perspective from the question of the physical illness that might inhabit the body of the person of good character, to the mental disorder that might underlie this illness.

---

the medical profession (requiring care of the person).

These two aspects continue to frame public and professional perceptions of opiate (and other illegal drugs) use today, and can also be found in concepts, policies and practices of alcohol problems and control. Additionally, in the case of smoked opium, there was an eugenic concern, triggered by the association of the practice with Chinese persons (and Berridge suggests, by guilt over Britain having forced the opium trade upon the Chinese during the nineteenth century). By the end of the nineteenth century, open sale of opium (e.g. in grocers' shops) had been stopped, and a series of controls applied to the sale of opium-containing products. From the late nineteenth century, working class opiate use fell (as did working class drinking, which reached a 'low' in the 1930s). Subsequent government concern in the first quarter of the twentieth century seems to have been motivated not so much by any widespread opiate use or associated social disorder, as by the passage of international drug control conventions (e.g. the Hague Convention of 1912), and by a resurgence of eugenic concerns around fitness of the armed forces (Defence of the Realm Regulations, 1916).

This shift (back towards a concern with moral/psychological aspects) occurred in the context of increasing recognition of working class drug use. As one early drug clinic psychiatrist observed of her East End patients, they were close to 'the stereotype of the kind that gets nothing from the school in the working-class area. Truancy, then petty stealing, a joy ride in a car, typically at least one appearance before the magistrate. Then drugs, any or all that were available, including heroin once it came on the street' (Tripp, quoted in Judson, *Drug Addiction in Britain*, p.47).

Then, following an unexpected surge in the statistics of addicts notified by GPs to the Home Office, the Brain Committee reconvened in 1964. The Committee stuck to its earlier definition of the problem - as essentially one of mental disorder (a composite of morphinism and morphino-mania) - and suggested that the problem could be ameliorated by the setting up of specialist, hospital-based treatment units and the withdrawal from GPs of the right to prescribe heroin as a treatment for addiction (though they could continue to prescribe substitutes such as methadone). Following this 1965 report the government acted to encourage teaching hospitals to set up Drug Dependency Units, headed by con-sultants in the 'relevant' specialism, i.e. psychiatry. (Given the perceived need for hospital control, the resort to a consultant was necessarily implied, and there seems to have been no specialist 'candidate' available other than psychiatry.) The initial setting up of the DDUs in 1967-8 saw a doubling of numbers of persons recorded as receiving a prescription for heroin from 1966-9 (see Table 2.1) as clinic staff worked to pull as many heroin addicts as possible into this new containment system.

There were, subsequently, some attempts to widen the newly-narrowed 'specialist' definition of the problem, the first of which brought in social work. In the midst of the setting up of the drug clinics, the Advisory Committee on Drug Dependence (forerunner of the Advisory Council on Misuse of Drugs) recognised broader 'social problems' - such as homelessness, and other social welfare problems - in addition to psychiatric problems in the narrow sense. The Committee recommended (1968) that social workers be appointed to the DDUs (as employees of the then Area Health Authorities, rather than of local borough social services

Table 2.1. Increasing methadone prescription to addicts in the 1970s

Dates	1945	1955	1965	1966	1967	1968	1969	1970	1971	1972
			2nd Brain Committee Reports		DDUs open: Advisory Committee report					
All known addicts*	367	335	927	1,349	1,729	2,782	2,881	2,661	2,769	2,994
Those receiving methadone only	–	–	61	74	102	196	1,063	1,319	1,417	1,745

*at any time during the year.

Source: Judson (1973), from a number of official sources.

departments). There is a sense, then, in which social work (and, in particular, social casework rather than a community-focussed approach) was 'tacked on' to the psychiatrically-run service. Later, in 1982, the Advisory Council on the Misuse of Drugs reworked the definition of the problem yet again - but did not recommend any very decisive break from past practice.

For our present purposes, it is useful to summarise the main trends in the policy and practices of management of drug use in Table 2.2. The following paragraphs then go on to place the street agencies in this history.

The 'British system' and the street agencies

It is in the latter stages of the history of drug containment policies described above - in the shift from 'good character' through 'mental disorder' to 'mental illness' and 'social work problem' - that the setting up and subsequent crises of the street agencies occurred.

The very existence of the DDUs, and the policies which they subsequently pursued, had consequences for drug users and for other statutory services (e.g. GPs) and non-statutory agencies (including the street agencies). At the same time it has to be borne in mind that these drug-specific medical/social containment measures evolved within a broader context of increasing concern with law and order issues in society (Auld, 1981; 11), a concern bolstered by the invention of new media-promulgated terms such as 'permissiveness', and by campaigns against the moral faults thus identified. Media-orchestrated reaction against youthful exuberance, fornication and violence framed the discussion of all issues touching upon young persons in this period (and later culminated, in the late 1970s, in concerns over mugging by presumably over-excited and under-socialised ethnic minorities). Anti-permissiveness and law and order concerns were represented within the drugs field by a further weakening of the Rolleston assumption of 'good character', as it became clear that 1970s addicts were not the professionals of the inter-war years, but were of increasingly 'mixed' social origins: increasingly young, working class as well as middle class in origin,* and often seemingly epitomising

---

*For discussion of some possible processes behind this shift, see our review of the work of Ditton and Speirits (Dorn and South, 1982).

Table 2.2: Summary of trends in containment in the twentieth century

Period/report	Definition of addict?	Opiate prescribing?
Pre-Rolleston	Morphinist (sick)/ morphinomaniac (hedonistic lunatic)	Not established as a treatment for addiction.
Rolleston (1920s)	'Good character' in most cases.	Yes: 'stabilisation' by opiate prescription through GPs and other doctors.
Brain (mid 1960s)	'Mental illness' - leads to setting up of DDUs, psychiatric leadership.	Yes, but only as an adjunct to specialist hospital psychiatric services. (Clinics set up: GPs can no longer prescribe heroin to addicts).
Advisory Committee (late 1960s)	Adds 'social problems' to 'mental illness' - recommends social workers.	Maybe: prescribing doesn't put a roof over your head, or solve personal/family problems. Shift to methadone.
ACMD (1980s)	Heterogeneous mix of above (including 'serious personality disorder' = code for	Unresolved questions (contradiction between competing definitions and practices). DHSS funding of 'drugs

the immoralities represented in the term 'permissiveness'.

The 'British system' of drug containment thus came into being, with social work in a subordinate role. This is a complex system in which, in order to be maintained, the addict has to negotiate with members of a mixed clinical team consisting of a psychiatrist, nurses, and (generally) a social worker(s), within the immediate setting of a specialist psychiatric unit, and within the general context of continuing criminalisation of possession of non-clinic-prescribed opiates. This system is sometimes, rather misleadingly, described (and decried) as a 'medical model'. But the 'British system' cannot be said to represent 'medicalisation' of the problem, or the imposition of a 'disease model' (cf. Smart, 1984a). Indeed the shift away from GPs, and to psychiatry/social work/legal containment, suggests a degree of de-medicalisation, if anything. And indeed lack of access on the part of 'heavy' drug users to basic medical care has been an oft-remarked and worrying aspect of the post-1960s drug containment system. What seems to have emerged is a new specialist element in the broader system of social care and control, conjoining concepts and practices of moral improvement, social casework, psychiatry, and legal controls.

It is in relation to this system of containment, and to shifts of emphasis within it, that the non-statutory agencies have struggled to find their feet and to develop a viable social work approach. Because the three agencies were started at different times (Blenheim in 1964, CDP in 1968, and Hungerford in 1970), and because they started from differing initial concerns, the agencies were differently affected by the birth of the clinics.

For the Blenheim, the impact of the clinics was initially slight, since the Blenheim already had a well-developed role of helping young 'drifters' with housing and other related matters, and most of these 'drifters' were not deeply involved in drug use. Blenheim was not initially a 'drug agency', and not decisively affected by the birth of the drug clinics.

For CDP it was a quite different story, since this agency was set up in the same year as many DDUs (1968), and as a supplement to them. Addiction specialists and researchers at the Institute of Psychiatry were foremost in initiating CDP as a 'community' resource - a day centre that could back up the fleeting clinic-client contact with a more extended relationship of surveillance and social care, and that would keep drug users off the streets.

The Hungerford Day Centre opened in 1970, i.e. three years after the first DDUs, by which time many of the latter had already changed their prescribing policies. These policies had some repercussions for all three street agencies, as we now describe.

Clinic policies and injection of non-opiates

Whilst the increase in barbiturate injecting cannot be attributed solely to the tendency for the DDUs to reduce prescriptions of injectable drugs (primarily heroin and ampoules of methadone) as a proportion of total opiate prescriptions from the late 1960s onwards, neither can this policy of (most of) the clinics be completely unrelated to subsequent patterns of drug use.

From the outset, the clinics were caught in a 'Catch 22' situation. If they prescribed heroin or other injectables reasonably freely, they would find themselves open to the accusation of 'irresponsible prescribing' which had previously been levelled at GPs - thus undermining the whole system of psychiatric specialist discretion so recently set up. If, on the other hand, they adopted a tighter prescription policy, then many would-be patients would foresake the clinics altogether, and partake in the illegal market. Faced with this dilemma, the clinics as a group took a middle course, 'borrowed' from the United States, of prescribing methadone (a synthetic opiate) in oral form. This was an attempt to maintain the clinical relationship with the client, whilst not 'condoning' pleasurable, injected drug use. (Oral methadone does not give a 'rush' in the way that many injected drugs do.) It must be borne in mind that there was considerable variation in policy from one clinic to another ('clinical freedom'), and that many of the established heroin users were allowed to continue to receive this drug: but aspiring and recently initiated users were increasingly likely to be denied any injectable drug, and to be given oral methadone (typically in a soft drink or orange juice, on the clinic premises) - or to be turned away.

Tables 2.1 and 2.3 illustrate these trends with reference to England and Wales. Overall numbers of persons attending clinics continued to grow, but the absolute amounts of heroin and of injectable methadone prescribed fell from 1975 onwards; heroin prescription fell especially sharply, such that by the end of the 1970s, it was only 60 per cent of the 1971 level, in spite of an overall increase of clinic attenders of one third. Amounts of oral methadone prescribed tripled in this same period. Around 1975 was the turning point of these changes, as Table 2.3 illustrates with reference to England and Wales, and as an unpublished set of tabulations compiled by Dr Martin Mitcheson (1979) confirmed for the fourteen NHS drug clinics in London.

Implications for social work practice

Now, had these restrictive policies vis-à-vis clinic injectables been put into operation in the absence of a supply of other substances that may be injected, or alongside a reduction of those wishing to inject, then the consequences might have been unequivocally beneficial. Neither of these conditions, however, obtained. One drug that was successfully brought under control in the 1970s was amphetamine - but sedatives, and particularly the widely-used barbiturates, were available from prescriptions (from GPs) and by way of illicitly diverted pharmaceutical supplies. Illegal heroin also continued in circulation. Of these, it was barbiturate injection that presented the drug agencies (including the three street agencies) with the biggest problems. Initially, perhaps, it was dissatisfied clinic attenders who turned to barbiturate injection; later, a wider group. As an Addiction Research Unit team put it:

> We do not suggest that the drug situation would be improved by making opiates and amphetamines more freely available, but we would emphasise that increasing control over any one group of drugs is likely to result in some increase in the abuse of other substances. Hence the present increase in sedative abuse is in line with American experience where opiate users turn to alternative drugs, including

Table 2.3 Heroin prescriptions hold steady, oral methadone triples in the 1970s

Dates:	1971	1972	1973	1974	1975	1976	1977	1978
All known addicts*	1,549	1,617	1,816	1,967	1,949	1,874	2,016	2,402
Those receiving methadone only*	916	1,054	1,201	1,299	1,313	1,290	1,360	1,693
Those receiving heroin alone	111	98	112	109	87	78	69	70
Index of amount of heroin prescribed**	100	101	101	108	109	93	77	60
Index of amount of injectable methadone**	100	23	165	186	181	150	127	121
Index of amount of oral methadone**	00	220	242	222	256	312	375	468

* at 31st December of the year. Source: Home Office, 1982, *Statistics of the Misuse of Drugs in the UK 1981*, London: Home Office (table 14). Applies to all recorded addicts, whether attending hospital clinics, GPs, or private doctors. Note that only DDUs, and not GPs, can prescribe heroin to addicts.

**during the year. Source: ISDD, 1980, *UK Official Statistics Relating to Drug Abuse.* Supplement to Druglink, No. 13, Spring. These indexes, taken from table 8, record the amounts of heroin, injectable methadone, and oral methadone prescribed to addicts attending NHS hospitals in England and Wales, with a 1971 'base of 100.

alcohol, when unable to obtain their drug of choice. (Mitcheson et al, 1970;1)

Consequences for the health of the users, and for the voluntary agencies that worked with the clinics' cast-offs, were severe - as noted in relation to the Blenheim, CDP and Hungerford, earlier in this chapter.

Furthermore, the operation of the 'British system' in the 1970s actually reinforced residual (pre-Rolleston) tendencies to shape the problem as one of 'vicious indulgence', involving chaotic styles of use of drugs that are largely obtained by fraud or crime:

> The practical implication of our research findings that 80% of these heroin addicts had injected barbiturates is that an increasing demand for sedatives can be expected in the illicit market. This illicit market is traditionally supplied directly or indirectly from medical prescription or thefts from wholesale and retail chemists. The figures quoted above minimise the extent to which medical prescriptions supply the illicit market; since, where an illicit source was given as the immediate source of the drug, the ultimate source was almost always a prescription or theft from a pharmacy. (ibid)

This 1970s report foresaw some of the problems that were later to throw the street agencies and other open-access helping agencies into crisis, as chaotic behaviour, poisonings and overdoses increased. The non-statutory agencies were much concerned with these trends and SCODA, an umbrella organisation to which street agencies and other non-statutory drug agencies belong, said:

> Some workers recall observing the beginning of this trend as early as 1968 and feel that the implementation of the 1967 Dangerous Drugs Act and the intervention of the statutory drug treatment clinics into what was until then, a relatively free market in opiate drugs, had a major part in this process. The treatment policies of most London clinics had been towards more restrictive prescribing of opiates and an emphasis upon weaning the user to physeptone (not initially a drug of preference to the addict). While many drug dependents have been helped to achieve a greater

degree of social stability through this approach and others encouraged to detoxify and enter rehabilitation programmes, a significant number of more poorly motivated drug users sought other drugs from illicit or quasi-legal sources to supplement their prescribed amounts. (SCODA, 1973; p.3)

Whilst this is a reasonable perception of the chain of events as seen from within the drug field, other factors were also in play. In the remaining parts of this chapter, we relate these problems not simply to the statutory drug containment systems (the clinics and the problems that they experienced in displacing the GPs), but also to housing and other circumstances of the 1970s 'chaotic' user, and to the latter's responses to these drug-specific and general circumstances.

The main point to observe in relation to social work in these circumstances is quite simple, and salutary. It is that, in the circumstances described in this chapter, social work styles that emphasise decision-sharing and genuine power-sharing with 'customers' (as street agency workers sometimes prefer to call their clients) became quite impossible. As the drug containment system came to be seen by a proportion of drug users as acting against them, rather than negotiating with them and meeting their felt needs, so the relationship between users and day centre staff became described by the latter as 'struggle', as a conflict over who was to define the purpose of the few physical spaces and facilities to which drug users had access.

A degree of conflict with the client is not incompatible with some approaches to social work, but severe conflict and struggle - when neither side has much more room to manoeuvre - is certainly incompatible with the good-humoured, democratic style of social work attempted in the early days of the street agencies. With the closure of their day centres, these agencies closed down a libertarian social work style that no longer fitted the circumstances. Only a social work approach that was less closely identified with the client - a more 'professional' approach, as some street agency staff somewhat uneasily describe their practice - could withstand these turbulent times.

THE HOUSING PROBLEM AS A CONTEXT OF DAY
CENTRE CONFLICTS

Conditions in the housing market were of particular relevance
for the street agencies in the 1960s and 1970s. Increasingly,
as the market deteriorated (as seen from the perspective
of unhoused persons), a greater proportion of street agency
clients found housing a major and long-term difficulty.
The interaction of homelessness and drug/alcohol use
can have especially deleterious consequences for health,
and poses intractable problems for social and advice-
workers. Homelessness may also, for a proportion of
those affected who form themselves into certain kinds
of subcultures, provide the conditions in which involvement
in a street drug or alcohol scene can be more socially
(and sometimes economically) rewarding than the search for
low-paid jobs at the bottom of a deteriorating inner city
labour market. Other persons may find themselves trapped
in intolerable domestic circumstances, yet unable to
move because of the housing shortage and begin to rely
upon alcohol, tranquillisers or other drugs.
     In several respects, then, changes in the housing market
in the 1970s are relevant for understanding changes in
non-statutory agency social work in that period.
     There are a number of recent reports into homelessness
by the Department of the Environment (1981), the Greater
London Council and London Boroughs Association (1981),
the Office of Population Censuses and Surveys (1976),
a DHSS/LBA Joint Working Party (1972), the Housing
Advice Switchboard (1981)*, and two London School of
Economics researchers (Austerberry and Watson, 1983).
Some of these reports look especially at the position
of young, single women, and one-parent families. The
main backcloth of trends in housing provision against
which the position of all such groups can be understood
is described by the General Household Survey of 1978
in the following terms:

     The 1978 results confirm the main trends observed over
     the seventies in particular: the decline of the private

---

*Each of the preceding sources is abstracted in Austerberry
and Watson, 1983.

rented sector (from 20% of households in 1971 to 14% in 1978) and the improvement in basic amenities and living space (ie. for the majority who are housed). (O.P.C.S., 1980;22)

Thus, for those who constituted households in the 1970s, access to amenities such as sole use of bath or shower, sole use of WC inside the building, central heating etc. improved.   The total number of households, however, fell during the 1970s, rather than increasing. The contribution of an ageing public housing stock primarily orientated to two-headed family units, a decrease in privately-rented accommodation, and an increase in rents relative to incomes, caused particular difficulties for would-be single-person households.   During the 1970s, the number of single-person households increased by over one million (*Social Trends*, 1982), but this increase did not absorb all those single people seeking accommodation; young people found it increasingly difficult to settle, especially in large metropolitan areas such as London.

The single homeless and the drug agencies

Within the GLC area, 56% of housing stock is owner-occupied, 20% privately rented and 31% Local Authority (1981 figures).   Buying a flat or house is not a viable possibility for most young single people, the 1981 average selling price being in excess of £24,000 (Dept. of Environment figures).   That there was a problem of (particularly single) homelessness became evident to many agencies in the mid-1970s, and there was an attempt to clarify Local Authority responsibilities in this area.   A combination of recognition of limited LA stock, reluctance to cater for single people rather than for families (except, in some cases, in relation to 'hard to let' accommodation), and an increasingly restrictive fiscal policy, formed the background to the passage of the 1977 Housing (Homeless Persons) Act, which laid quite limited obligations on Local Authorities.   From 1977 onwards, Local Authorities had a duty to house only those who were homeless by virtue of natural disaster (e.g. flooding); and those who were 'unintentionally homeless' through old age, mental illness, violence in the home, or coming out of LA care (in the case of young persons); and pregnant women.   Most

single young people who move in order to find work, or to
make room for younger siblings in the family home, or to
attempt to live an independent life, do not fall into these
categories.

Indeed, as Austerberry and Watson (1983) have pointed
out, the workings of the housing/welfare system are
such that you have to become ill, incapable or otherwise
vulnerable in order to qualify for Local Authority housing
in the immediate future. It is worth noting that, up until
1983 (the coming into force of the Mental Health Amendment
Act), drug (or alcohol) dependence was categorised as
a mental illness. Those who could get themselves accepted
as such by a Drug Dependency Unit, therefore, qualified
(in theory, at least) for Local Authority housing (if homeless).
In this sense, then, the DDUs could be regarded as part
of the housing/welfare system - and the street agencies,
insofar as they had referral relations with the DDUs
(as well as with more orthodox channels of housing provision),
were also part of this system.

*Compression of housing and drug needs and conflicts
into the day centres*

As the numbers of migrant and locally-originating single
homeless in inner London rose during the 1970s, so these
housing-related issues pressed more closely upon the
drug containment system as a whole, and upon the street-
access, day centre-based street agencies in particular.
Those drug users who did not manage to find accommodation
other than short-term hostels (from which they were
often excluded, in common with alcohol-users) would
especially value the shelter, food, and other material
resources available in the day centres in the early mid-
1970s. It is not surprising that these attenders at day
centres sought to make those still-available spaces 'theirs'
as far as possible. Thus the general housing crisis in
the 1970s, together with intermittent police action to
clear the streets (noted, for example, in Hungerford
reports), led to a compression of drug users and their
needs into the limited physical and social spaces of the
day centres. As the clinics' developing policy of restricting
prescription of injectable methadone and heroin led many
users to seek out other available injectables - such as

barbiturates, which supplied the 'bottle' needed for dealing with social workers and other 'authorities' - so a series of sharp territorial conflicts developed within the day centres.

Finding themselves at the pressure point of a broader set of problems originating in drug containment, housing and other social welfare systems, the street agencies simply could not withstand the pressure. This is the housing-related background to the closure of the day centres in the mid-1970s, and to the subsequent development of a social work approach that drew rather less from libertarian and community work approaches, and rather more upon 'professional', individual casework by appointment.

The street agencies and residential work

It is clear from the preceding sections of this chapter, that the street agencies were in a position to observe the inter-connectedness of drug-related and housing problems as these manifested themselves among day attenders. Each of the three agencies attempted, in their various ways, to address problems of homelessness amongst a proportion of their clients. Two of the agencies experimented with setting up residential services associated with their day centres. As might be expected, from our account of difficulties experienced by the day centres, these residential houses suffered problems which were no less intractable.

CDP, for example, ran a short-life house for two years, from 1974-76, and tried to run it upon lines that assumed a degree of co-operation and common cause between the project staff and the clients.

> There were no staff on the premises and the residents were expected to take responsibility for using their rooms, the house and the facilities provided, and to pay their rent weekly to the Community Drug Project ... For a period of twenty-eight months we were able to offer cheap, rented accommodation, a temporary 'home', and a period of comparative stability for a number of the (day centre) attenders who might otherwise have been drifting aimlessly from one unsatisfactory situation to another, moving between squats, cheap hotels, Reception Centres

and the odd night with friends. (CDP report covering 1975-6)

In September 1976 (ie. two months before the project staff decided that they had to close the day centre) the house reverted to the GLC for purposes of renovation, and:

> It was decided that in spite of the desperate shortage of accommodation available for rent, combined with the difficulties peculiar to the drug addict in finding accommodation, we could not realistically consider taking on another property at this time. We had experienced problems arising out of our conflicting roles with those addicts who were both regular attenders at the day centre and were living in the house. (ibid)

Similarly, the Blenheim - which had always made its housing work a priority, and had been able to utilise a network of supportive agencies, private households and even squats in the 1960s - attempted, in the light of the deteriorating 1970s housing situation, to run a hostel. In this case there was a staff member on the premises and, for some time, a cook was employed. The hostel was seen as a valuable extension to the work of the project, but was especially vulnerable to the pressures and contradictions that were later to contribute to the closure of the day centre:

> It seems that the hostel provided a safety net for some, gave some space to decide what to do and where to go, helped others to take steps away from drifting and gave them a place of security where they could work out their behaviour problems on each other and the staff. Others apparently gained little.
>
> The hostel's main weaknesses were its financial difficulties and the problems that arose from the proximity to the project. The combination of these difficulties put an increasing strain on the hostel staff and added to the day-to-day stress which is an inevitable part of residential work. (Blenheim's *People Adrift*, p.59)

Although 'the decision to close the hostel was difficult and painful to take', that decision seems to have been overdetermined by the same mix of circumstances that later closed the project's day centre, i.e. over-extension of financial and human resources in the face of severe need. Whilst the house was open, 35 people in their late teens and early twenties stayed there for periods between a week and a year, and, at the end of this period, about half were 'relatively stable'.

In the case of the Hungerford, in its day centre days, the pressure seems to have been too great to contemplate running a residential house, since the 'Centre works mainly with clients who are on the lower end of the motivation scale, and have been addicted for many years ... Referrals are often reached when a person has reached a crisis peak ...' (1972 report, p.7). In this context:

> A seven hour day is long enough for the staff to be exposed to the demanding clients the centre deals with. We have also deviated from the original idea of trying to provide overnight accommodation for using addicts. There are several reasons for this, the over-riding one being that very often the accommodation crisis is one that pushes people towards deciding to withdraw. To provide accommodation confirms the addiction and dependence on others. (ibid, pp.7-8)

In this statement we see how a crisis of staff exhaustion and financial inability to expand a project's facilities can operate in tandem with an ideology of self-help, to rationalise a social work practice that is both feasible, and professionally defensible. It is not clear to us that the street/squat/hostel circuit is, on balance, a reinforcer of abstinence. On the other hand, it has indeed to be recognised that the provision of accommodation does not automatically reduce drug use (though it may reduce associated health and other problems). In any event, the determining factor in the street agencies' various involvements in residential work seems to have been as much practical (e.g. availability of money, extendability of staff, relationship with day centres), as it was derived from any commitment to a particular view of 'the problem' or to ways of responding. In circumstances in which many related problems were compressed into day centres (see preceding sections of this chapter), leading to the eventual disruption of those day centres, any further compression into 24 hour residential houses was obviously even more tenuous.

CONCLUSION: THE LIMITS OF THE POSSIBLE

It is not easy to sum up, in retrospect, on the utility of three agencies each of which tried, in its particular way, to cope with people whose presenting problems - in relation to drug use, homelessness, and general problems within an economically and socially crumbling urban environment - deteriorated throughout the 1970s. Each reader must make his or her assessment of the work of the agencies, which we have tried to present as clearly as possible in the context of wider developments going on at the time.

Looking at it negatively, we could say that each of the three projects failed to develop a coherent social work practice, and achieved little else of substance: it is doubtful if drug use *per se* was reduced or slowed by the agencies; their day centres were closed as untenable as were their residential houses; detached street work, meant to compensate for the restrictions on immediate street access to the agencies, remains patchy to this day; and the agencies did not succeed in making any decisive intervention into the broader drug containment, social welfare or housing systems. The agencies remained low-status social work 'dustbins' (as one project report suggests) within which fermented some unwanted consequences of social and health policies.

More positively, we want to suggest - albeit without convincing evidence - that things would have been worse for the client groups had the day centres/street agencies not existed. In providing the services (shelter, food, companionship, advice, criticism) that they did, the agencies gave drug users and other troubled persons in the late 1960s and 1970s opportunities and resources that they would otherwise surely have lacked. The received image of street-level drug-related cultures is that they are wholly bad, 'chaotic', and offer inducements to further drug abuse. Yet every culture has its norms and regulations, and these generally have some health-positive aspects, as well as a health-negative side. Drug users do sometimes - given the resources - look after others (especially younger and more naive drug users), giving practical advice and material assistance, and aiming to reduce problems such as overdoses, infection, freak-outs, etc. We think it reasonable to suggest that the 1970s day centres offered physical space in which, with the encouragement of centre staff, some health-positive aspects of drug-related cultures may have been reinforced.

On a broader front, the street agencies put into circulation to other agencies and to government a body of useful experience that may be drawn upon today. This is probably the most useful legacy of 1970s street agency work -three important perspectives upon social work around drug-related problems, showing the limits of what is possible in given circumstances.

Finally, there is one aspect of the work of the day centres, in the years before they closed, that is particularly difficult to evaluate. These centres provided a 'contestable space' at a time when changes in drug policy and housing markets were squeezing many users out of other arenas - a breathing space and a focus for reorganisation for a cluster of deviant sub-cultures that might otherwise have been completely fragmented into more isolated and more vulnerable individuals. The struggle of day centre attenders against the social work staff, and against the closure of the centres, belies the image of the drug user as incapable of directed social action. The sub-cultural resources generated in this struggle between drug users and social workers were then, with the eventual closure of the day centres, directed onto the streets, and form an element in today's street drug scenes. What was learnt in these confrontations, what was lost, and what was gained (by drug users and by staff) is being reworked today, in the context of the 1980s drug scene. This is the subject of the following three chapters on the work of the street agencies today.

3 The Hungerford Drug Project in the early 1980s

LOCATION AND PREMISES

The Hungerford Drug Project is situated on the first floor of a building occupied principally by commercial offices. The building is owned by British Rail and stands in the shadow of Charing Cross station, a short walk up Craven Street from the Hungerford Bridge (the site of the original premises of the project - hence the name) and the Embankment. Craven Street itself runs from the Embankment up to the Strand, at which point the entire West End fans out before it, placing the Hungerford Project in the unique position that it occupies with regard to the drug using population of central London.

The building itself seems well kept, entry through the front door being controlled by an entryphone system. Nevertheless, as several stories of clients slipping in unannounced (using toilets to fix, wandering into the wrong office, and so on) would suggest, the Project has clearly been fortunate (and presumably diplomatic) in its relations with its landlords and fellow tenants.

It seems universally agreed upon by all who know the agency that it is small and cramped in its premises.

Concern has been expressed about the effect of its small
size on morale of staff, on first impressions of clients
and of professional visitors, and of course (perhaps most
importantly), on the very ability of the staff to provide
the service they see the demand for. As one staff member
of the London crisis intervention centre City Roads told
us, the Hungerford are 'at times almost under siege and
this is bound to affect the quality of their work'. As
she put it, 'the workers don't have enough head space
to get into their work as effectively as they might, because
of the chaos that is going on all around them'.

The front office is the funnel into and out of the project
- it is the reception area, the first physical point of contact
with the project for people coming in off the street.
First impressions and the subsequent social work relationship
between agency and client can both be determined by
how a client with problems is received when entering.
The chances are that, whether the client is new or old,
entering the reception area will not guarantee the immediate
personal attention that he or she might seek, because
the front office also deals with the administration of
the project, handles all telephone enquiries (many of
which can be long and sensitive sessions of advice-giving
or sympathetic listening), and may also already be host
to between one and four other visitors, all crowded together
on plastic chairs in the small shabbily carpeted square
between the 'gate-keeping' front desk and the doorway
of the project.

Even without the regular flow of visitors into and out
of the project the front office would appear crowded.
It is actually well organised in terms of the space available,
but the festooned walls, the front desk barrier, the piled-
up box files and the movement of people all inevitably
create an impression of managed chaos. The room's
green and cream paintwork matches the old green carpet.
Its walls are decorated with large tube and bus route
maps, a large A-Z street map, photos, postcards and
poems from clients; a year-planner noting important
meetings, annual leave and staff birthdays, a large tell-
at-a-glance list of telephone numbers for other advice
agencies, rehabilitation agencies (henceforth referred
to as rehabs), drug dependency units (DDU's), switchboards,
detoxification facilities (detox) and general agencies,

(e.g. SCODA, ROMA, Centrepoint); a Degas print, a space of wall above the administrator's desk covered with various memos, important phone numbers, postcards and so on. There are stacks of box files behind the administrator, a small card table against the wall for the day book and for writing up contact sheets, a counter at right angles for coffee and tea, the fridge by its side; and beyond the counter, by the door, three or four plastic chairs for visitors.

This front desk point is staffed by Linda, the administrator, and also, nowadays, by a social work staff member (either full time or working 'cover') who is supposed to handle most of the phone calls and reception work.   As Linda put it when talking of the design of the office: '...we have to accept the layout of the office because we don't actually own the property and can't change it, but we are limited by the structure of the place'.   Both the placing of the reception office - the front room over-looks the street whilst the back room does not - and the need to have two staff tied up at the reception point, followed from the spatial limitations of their premises.

The middle room of the project tends to be the one most used for confidential client counselling.   It is also the office in which Benn and Chrissie have their desks and, at the start of our study, it also housed a number of filing cabinets containing the agency's material on other agencies and its client files.   During the period of fieldwork the cabinets were moved, because their location in the room where most counselling sessions took place led to a lot of unwelcome interruptions when another member of staff had to get some information on another client or agency. (The files could not be situated in their logical location, with the administrator, simply because there was no space for them there.)   The middle room is the largest in the project, again with shabby green carpet and fading paint-work, though the room is brightened up by plants and posters, and has the advantage of two large windows facing out onto the street letting in light, air and a sense of the street for those clients who may feel slightly claustrophobic.

Finally, the back room is generally reached through the middle room, though in truth it could as easily be called a front room as it also has a door leading out onto the stair landing. This door may be used by staff to get from the reception to the back office which is used by the senior worker, Jane, and which now also houses the client and other agency files (i.e. pertaining both to Jane's job and to Linda's job as administrator). It may seem trivial but the work of the agency has probably been helped quite a bit just through the rethinking of where the filing cabinets should be placed. Information is now easily accessible for staff moving between the front desk and the senior's office, without disturbing counselling of clients. The workload of the senior does not allow as much social work counselling as the two basic grade social work staff, but she does nonetheless have her 'own' clients, and in addition handles staff supervision in her office (which is the only one which would routinely afford any privacy and quiet). It should be noted that towards the end of the fieldwork the Hungerford were planning a move into two additional floors of the same building, considerably expanding their office space, allowing them to keep all their information files together in one place instead of the present situation of files being spread across three offices. Such a move and expansion of space will undoubtedly also have profound implications for the actual social work practice of the agency (presumably for the good).

We have already discussed (in chapter 2) part of the history of the Hungerford agency and its physical siting. The history has a legacy for present workers in that, in making sense of their own practice and feelings about what the agency does, they have (albeit to varying degrees) sought to understand where the agency came from and how it has developed.

It should be remembered that the oft-cited incidence of staff burn-out in the non-statutory drugs sector tends to be around three or four years, and many workers in a whole range of agencies throughout this sector will have little direct experience of their agencies' past development. As chapter 2 indicates, the street agencies in particular have had an erratic and sometimes stormy lineage. Their courses have been changed and their own histories virtually re-written, (witness the lack of reference to the early Hungerford project in post-1976 reports). Before moving on to discuss the backgrounds and orientations

of present staff members we shall just briefly note some
of their perceptions of their agency's past.

It was generally agreed that the siting of the project
made sense in terms of the kind of area that the Hungerford
Bridge vicinity had always been:

> In some ways it was the day centre in the West End
> ... And the area around here has always been an
> area where the homeless have tended to congregate
> regardless of what other, if any, problems they may
> have had - drinkers and drugtakers and everybody,
> and I think that made it more straightforward (when
> it was set up). (Jane)

Benn, the Hungerford's detached worker, agrees that
the location would have been 'an obvious choice', but
thinks it equally possible that 'the reason it ended up
there was that it was the only place available. Just like
any project starting off, you go for what you can get
...'. Despite changes in staff, philosophy, premises and
the nature of its services, the Hungerford has remained
locked into its West End setting, despite the temptations
that there might have been to move away from the difficult
clients which the West End drug scene brought them.

> I suspect there may have been more difficulties
> when the scene began to change which actually led
> to the change from day centre to an advice centre.
> People were using (drugs) more chaotically, more
> noticeably, more anti-socially in some ways. (Jane)

The Hungerford remains however, the West End drugs
street agency. As Benn observes:

> I suppose the reason we stayed here is because Piccadilly,
> up till recently, has always been the main, one of
> the main drug areas in London, with Soho and the
> red light district as well. The reason we ended up
> with all the local services we have, I suppose, is
> because of Piccadilly attracting all these homeless
> kids, that a lot of other West End agencies set themselves
> up, so I suppose we stayed here because everybody
> else stayed here like Piccadilly Advice Centre (PAC)
> and Soho Project and Centrepoint and what have
> you. We just stayed about because it was the most
> obvious place to be, and still is I suppose; although

the drug scene has diversified itself all over London it's still quite a good central place to be. It's quite easy to get to as well.

THE STAFF: QUALIFICATIONS, EXPERIENCE, WORKING PHILOSOPHIES, AND DIVISION OF LABOUR

Qualifications and experience

The Hungerford Project has four workers and is currently seeking a fifth worker who will be employed as a fourth social worker. Its staff is augmented by back-up workers hired to fill in when they are particularly pressurised. Usually these back-up workers will have some close familiarity with the project itself (e.g. an ex-worker in the drugs field). The project also gains additional staff through taking social work student placements - an arrangement which is obviously of benefit to the student, the social work educational system and the agency itself. Taking placement students also has a financial pay-off for the agencies; the agencies receive £8 per day from the DHSS for any student on placement and receiving a grant for a CQSW course (which over a long placement can produce a welcome amount for an agency concerned about its cash-flow problems).

The senior worker, Jane, joined the Hungerford staff as a basic grade social worker in 1981. She had previously worked at the ROMA (Rehabilitation of Metropolitan Addicts) hostel, another Turning Point project, for two years. Jane had moved into the social work field, as she put it, 'by accident'. She had not taken a social work course at college but does have a degree in Social Policy which she feels indicates some early interest, however vague, in social work. Her initial interests in this direction lay in medical social work, but she expressed a feeling of dissatisfaction with the way that 'hospitals and statutory provision seem to be about a lot of restrictions and a lot of very false limits, and a lack of feeling in the way that you work or choose to work'. Her accidental move into social work (as a real job as opposed to an 'interest') came through knowing someone who knew of a job vacancy at ROMA. Her acceptance for the job led her directly into social work with

drug using clients - not a form of social work which traditional social work training would have well prepared her for. (We
shall have more to say about the absence of such preparation
in traditional social work education later.) Hence Jane has a
rather pragmatic view of her own socialisation into drug-
related social work:

> I just sort of accepted it and learnt as I went along
> - which is perhaps not the ideal way for the clients
> in that particular set-up, but on the other hand I
> was always working with someone who'd been around
> for a while. So I don't think I did anything drastically
> awful, I think social work is an awful lot of common
> sense. I mean if you walk in with a whole load of
> theories and preconceptions, I think increasingly
> that you're likely to make more errors than if you
> go in with an open mind and learn. I mean maybe
> there's a balance there. You've got to do some learning
> and then get some theory, and then go back into
> the practice situation.

It is worth noting that all experienced workers in the
drug field expressed concern to us during the course
of the project about the (presumably related) absence
of information and training concerning working with
drug users given in social work courses, and the widespread belief among practising, generic social workers
that drug users are somehow a 'special' case, requiring
highly specific and specialised social work skills which
they themselves, unfortunately, do not have. The implication
of much of what we have been told by the supposedly
specialist professionals in the drugs field is that, in general,
with few difficult exceptions, the skills of social work
with drug users could be learned and built up by anyone
with an interest or background in social work, with some
common sense, sound information and, initially, the guidance
of somebody who can help demystify the strangeness,
horror, fear and so on which surrounds the subject of
drug use. Having done her learning, Jane feels she may
go back to theory and take a social work qualification
'at some point - but I don't see any great urgency about
it, that's purely an insurance; if I want to leave the field
and come back then having my bit of paper is going to

be useful'.

Benn joined the Hungerford at the same time as Jane in 1981, and is the social work team member who has taken up the detached work side of the project. After originally starting to train as a solicitor he decided that he would be interested in taking some time to do voluntary work in Dublin, and having made the move into the voluntary sector, he stayed there for four years working as a social worker. With an increasing drug problem in Dublin, Benn came to England to take a CQSW course at Portsmouth and to learn more about drug-related social work. This latter interest brought him on his final student placement to the Hungerford project. Shortly after his course had finished a key Hungerford worker, with whom Benn had worked during his placement (particularly on detached work) left the project. Benn applied for the job and started in the September following his CQSW course.

At the time that our fieldwork began Chrissie, the other basic grade social worker, had just joined the team. Like Jane she came into the drugs field accidentally, and to the Hungerford via ROMA. The experiences of both Jane and Chrissie emphasise the point that social work with drug users is not something that has to be approached by very special people with very specialised training, but is a skill or professional aptitude that can be learned by any social worker or lay-person with an interest.

> I had no idea about working in the drugs field or social work until I went to ROMA, where I... worked until last summer. In fact I've never stopped working because I continued doing relief work after I resigned. I wasn't sure what I wanted to do next but I did a bit of relief work at the Hungerford -really liked it and thought I'd apply for the job. So, I did. And I got that last October (1982).

Clearly, Chrissie's approach is not based on formal social work training, in respect of its theoretical prescriptions or its practice guidelines. So how does her approach, deriving from an eclectic, non-'professional' background, fit into the agency?

> What people tell me is that I am an empathiser. I've always felt quite natural with the client group,

quite easy to relate to them. So, perhaps because initially I was an over-empathiser, I had to learn balance. I think I invest my job with quite a lot of my own personality ... nevertheless, I've actually got parameters and boundaries ... Sometimes its non-directive, at other times - and that's partly through training at ROMA because we used to take various groups - I find I can be very directive as well.

Chrissie's account is worth quoting here because it highlights the social work resolution of working with a 'difficult' client group who often need to be directed or pushed in some way, but whose reactions (and over-reactions) to being pushed too much can be dramatic, disastrous, or tragic. The aim, it seems, is 'to learn balance' and we shall return to the importance of such principles shortly in discussing practice in the agencies.

The fourth member of the Hungerford staff is Linda, the Administrator. Linda has been with the project since 1978, starting as a part-time worker, becoming full time as the agency and need for the post expanded: 'I wanted some kind of administrative work and it seemed more practical for me to work in a voluntary agency: I mean, yes, I wanted to work in a social work field but didn't actually want to become a social worker.' Linda was the first to occupy the administrator's post at the Hungerford, so she has created the role that she fills within the project, starting and developing the filing and recording systems with the help of the rest of the staff. The job in general, and the information recording component of it in particular, have changed over time, most obviously as the project has become more busy generating more statistics, requiring more reports and so on.

Working philosophies: responding to immediate needs

As the discussion and Diagram 2.1 (p.12) in chapter 2 indicate, the development of the street agencies has been conditioned by a number of factors. They find themselves in a tri-partite working relationship with the rehabilitation houses and with the clinics. Additionally, each street agency presents itself in a particular way in its relationships with the other street agencies - who must nevertheless, as a group, present a united front. Hence how and where

the street agencies perceive themselves in the drugs
field is a matter of considerable interest.   Speaking of
all street agencies, Benn of the Hungerford offered the
analogy of a step-ladder system:

> If you think of a ladder, we're at the bottom of a ladder
> to do with drugs ... For the sort of client group we see
> normally every day, we would be at the bottom of a
> ladder and catching them when they fall off the ladder.
> We give them the options and if they don't want to move
> on, that's fine, but if they do, they move up the ladder to
> whatever, City Roads, clinics, or just coming here for
> support which could be going up the ladder. On the other
> hand they don't have to go through all the agencies and
> we're quite happy to be a sort of base for them to move
> from and ... be a net for them when they fall down.
> That's the way a lot of street agencies work because of
> the way rehabs are done - like a Concept House has a
> high turnover rate...

The consequence of this is that many of these 'splittees'
from the rehabs are thrown or drift back in to the street
drug scene and face a very definite likelihood of losing
all contact with those agencies, quite apart from the
rehab, with which they have previously had some sort
of constructive relationship.   They may do this feeling
that either they have lost respect for the rehabilitation
network (including the street agencies), or fearing that
the rehab network has lost respect for and faith in them.
In such circumstances the persistence of an open-door
policy by the street agencies, as well as the avowed intention
of detached work (which we shall discuss below), has
been seen as 'a sort of catch-net for these people, ...
then maybe passing them back up to a rehab or sending
them into a different sort of avenue and getting them
somewhere else.   That's why I think the street agencies
are at the bottom of the ladder.' (Benn)
    In general, the safety-net metaphor is a popular one.
We shall explore other perceptions of the place of the
street agencies in the field of provision for drug-related
problems when we come to consider the three street
agencies together and their relationships with the statutory
and non-statutory sector agencies.

More clearly than either CDP (which has a coordinator and management committee) or the Blenheim (which is a collective with a management committee), the Hungerford fits into a hierarchical structure. This is partly dictated by the fact that it is part of the Turning Point organisation, which thereby imposes a weight of organisational accountability upon the project. As the senior worker Jane put it, this structure:

> to some degree defines our jobs (but) there are other sorts of definitions which happened by accident ... all the jobs in the agency are different, sort of defined by head office and by circumstances. And there's a lot of respect within the team for individual ways of working - we all have different styles.

Clearly the agency workers share a sense of difference in their approaches and styles of working with clients, so it can only be in a shared sense of complementarity that they perceive themselves as a closely co-ordinated team. In exploring this kind of working concept with the three agencies we found that all of them had some difficulty in explaining in any precise sense the nature of their working philosophy or internal interaction as individuals and as team or agency. The difficulties in 'thinking through' this latter relationship are well illustrated in the following excerpt from an interview with the senior worker at the Hungerford:

> I'm not very sure what it means actually, because we say we're a team .. in so far as we respect each other and respect our individual ways of working, and there is mutual care as well in the team, but beyond that I'm not sure to what extent it is a team. It's a kind of team held together by a tolerance of individual people going off and doing all different things; and not a team in a conventional sense of talking about, discussing and allocating and doing everything together at some level, because there are lots of things we just go off and do and report back, or find out by accident that someone's been doing something very interesting. (Interviewer: complementary rather than being co-ordinated?)

There is co-ordination because a lot of time is spent
in the staff meeting, talking about who's doing what,
who wants to do what and who's got work that they need
time to do. That sort of thing is co-ordinated but I mean
the whole thing about a team, I quite genuinely don't know
what that means. I think we ought to go back and define
what's meant by a team. I don't think that we are one, this
is a concept that I have, I don't think that we are but we
work well together - which is the same thing but different.

If the actual nature of the team's operation has not
been the subject of much reflection, this at least is not
the case with the priorities of the project which are
not simply the results of inheritance and evolution but
have undergone serious review and re-orientation at
several points in the history of the agency. The use of
a consultant to the project as well as guidance from
the advisory committee all feed into a sustained examination
of whether the project is doing what it says it wants
to do. Before moving on to consider the realities of
day-to-day practice within the Hungerford, it is worth
noting one expression of its (perhaps idealised) priorities
offered by Benn:

> ...most of the theory written on drug addiction clearly
> says that if you catch somebody at the one minute
> in their life when they say I'm fed up, I want to do
> something, you have more success than, we'll say,
> telling them to come back in six weeks like a drug
> clinic would. So I see a lot of what we .. do .. is
> getting to know people, getting people very friendly
> with us and breaking the ice for maybe months,
> so that when that time comes, when this unmotivated
> person, maybe for a split second in their life, maybe
> about half a day, but they all of a sudden become
> motivated, then we already know them anyway,
> so it's quite easy for us to get the wheels ... of rehabilitation
> moving. An awful lot of what the street agencies
> are doing is getting to know the drug users, very
> unmotivated people. I think we have a priority to
> them as much as to the motivated people, so when
> the unmotivated people become motivated, then
> we move in.

We now turn to some observations of how these ideas relate to the day-to-day practice of the staff of the Hungerford.

Division of labour

Unlike much practice in the statutory social services, the clients of the Hungerford do not find themselves 'allocated' to a particular worker's case-load by bureaucratic and numerical formulae. Rather, the social work relationship with a particular worker seems much more likely to build up on the basis of chance or choice; initial contact in the reception area, whoever is around with some free time, perhaps the expressed preference of the client to talk to a man or woman, or about a certain subject which one worker is knowledgeable on, or to a worker whose name has been mentioned by someone else. Once the contact is established between one client and a worker, it is obviously seen as a positive development if that relationship can be nurtured to encourage the trust of the client in the worker, and also to allow the worker to assess the degree of faith that they feel they can have in the client. Unrealistic expectations on either side are not helpful. The openness of the initial contact between client and agency always remains, however, as agency workers seek to ensure that a client has the option to talk to any staff member:

> People seem to gravitate towards the worker they feel they can relate to best because we all get to meet people at some point and if you get talking informally, people will often say 'Can I see you properly sometime?' We're not precious about keeping our own case-load. As far as possible, I think it's more productive for the client to say 'I don't want to talk to you any more, I want to talk to her or him.' (Jane)

Despite such a policy of openness it is, of course, inevitable that, owing to the particular responsibilities which devolve on workers as part of the overall division of labour, a certain pattern in the distribution of clients should emerge. The senior worker obviously has her own case-load capacity reduced by the onerous tasks of administration, staff supervision and inter-agency liaison. Of the two basic grade social workers, Benn explained how their own division of the clientele had tended to emerge - in large part determined by Benn's involvement in detached work out of the office.

> Chrissie tends to see more of the long-term clients than I see. Because I'm out on educational work or on detached work, I do the straightforward client group, the sort of guy who comes in, I'll maybe see him for a month, he wants something, I'll arrange it with a drug clinic, and we get that done and then he wants to talk about rehab, we get that done, I refer him to rehab, and I don't see him in the office again. Hopefully, if there's a rehab nearby I'll be up to see him; that's as far as the social work input's done. That's the type of work I do mainly. But with Chrissie, because she's in the office longer, she has the tendency to take on the sort of guy who comes in every week for two years.

We shall have more to say about the division of labour between staff members as it operates in practice later in this chapter. First, however, we discuss one particular job-role - working on the reception desk - and its relation to the important question of record-keeping, which occupies a key place in staff information-sharing and self-management. This description acts as a bridge to discussion of the range of demands made on the agency, and description of a quite 'typical' day.

ORGANISATION OF THE WORK IN THE OFFICE

Reception desk and record-keeping

Working on the reception front desk also involves filling in the day book, which is kept there. All staff fill in all the appropriate contacts that they have had and the day book therefore constitutes an important data base and review resource for the work of the project, as well as being a simple daily record to keep everybody in touch with what is going on. Briefly, it records which staff members made the entry, whether it refers to a phone call or visit, who was calling or visiting for whom, and if it was the person concerned personally or someone acting on behalf of another (this information being coded S for self, P for professional and O for other, eg. parents, family, friends). The book also records entries in an 'information wanted' column, a column for new referrals and a file column denoting whether the client already has a file at the agency (if not they are entered in the 'New' column and an initial contact sheet is filled out which may in the future become the start of a file). Finally an 'Appointment' column notes the date and times of any appointment made for future contact at the agency. The day book of the Hungerford is the most comprehensive and detailed daily recording system of the three agencies - recording everything from minor telephone enquiries to lengthy, crisis point counselling sessions. Coupled with the other record sheets that the agency keeps, valuable informa- tion is available to staff for internal purposes and for purposes of presentation to its parent organisation, Turning Point, and other external audiences such as potential funders. This value is well understood by all in the agency, especially the administrator:

> At the end of every month I have to go through the record sheets and make up information sheets on every single phone call that we get and on everyone that comes in. I then make up cards and use an index system for easy recording. So it's very important for me that the others do fill in the diary. I use all this information to do the statistics ... and a monthly report, so a lot of my work is determined by how well the social workers actually do their work.(Linda)

The range of demand upon the agency

All three street agencies sometimes have periods when things seem remarkably quiet. At other times, the depth and variety of demands made upon the staff seem quite over- powering. In what follows we describe how the staff at the Hungerford organise their work so as partially to even out the demands, and how they gear their styles of work around their daily routines and client's demands. The Monthly Report of the Hungerford Project for February 1983 starts:

> February was a difficult month for the project. The inevitable strain caused by staff using up their leave entitlement was exacerbated by sickness, exhaustion (due to the high levels of demand from clients) and the considerable distress caused by the murder of a client.

Late afternoon, 14th February 1983, an appointment had been arranged by the fieldworker for 4.30 p.m. to interview one of the social work staff. The front office seemed crowded, even with just four people occupying it; one woman visitor was just leaving. Linda, the administrator literally seemed to be trying to do several things at the same time, talking on the phone, moving a box file, writing something down. Hilary, their student placement, was clearly more subdued than usual. In one of the chairs by the door Jim, a street survivor and regular Hungerford visitor, was still sitting, though being amicably dismissed, having been reminded of the project rule that the 'allowed time' for hanging around was a quarter of an hour and he had already been there for three-quarters of an hour or more. The punk-style woman visitor left with supportive words from Linda and Hilary that she should drop into the project again for another chat.

Benn did not emerge from the middle room of the project for the arranged appointment. He was tied up with a woman visitor who had said that her niece (who lived with her) had problems that she wanted to talk about. In the reception area an extra cover-worker, previously a worker at Phoenix House, had appeared to take the desk. Jane was out at a meeting for the day and Chrissie was on holiday. Around five p.m. Linda interrupted Benn to offer him the opportunity to break off his now lengthy session with the visitor with the problem niece, announcing that his 'important earlier meeting was still waiting'. Benn emerged looking harassed and showing signs of obviously having worked hard with his visitor who, in his opinion, was the person with the problems, not the niece. Against the advice of Linda who felt that Benn had put quite enough into this particular session, it was agreed to re-schedule the interview and Benn returned to his client whom he had left with Hildy, a second student on placement, who was sitting in on the session. Whilst waiting for Benn the conversation had turned to what Hilary referred to as the 'events of Friday', when it had been realised that a body found murdered in a West London house was that of a client of the Hungerford. He had been a client of Chrissie's and was the first that Hilary had met when coming to the project. Through Turning Point the Hungerford, after considering issues of principle, had passed on information to the police which may have been of some use in reconstructing his last known movements. That afternoon had clearly been a difficult one for the staff, and discussing the matter again was still depressing. Such events are of course rare, though (for all the street agencies) hearing of the death of a client is not an unfamiliar experience by any means.

Perhaps a more typically mundane day is described by Linda:

> ...the phone rings ... it could be a mother who is worried about her son who is using drugs; he has said he is using drugs and she does not know what they are, and he has said that he does not want to stop using them and she is distraught. What we would do in that situation is give her support and try to find out a bit more about what he might be using and counsel her and say to her that it's up to him and if he wants to contact us, fair enough. Then, say a couple of people could come in who had been living homeless, and we know them quite well, off the street, and maybe one of them is slightly stoned and we would suggest that they come back later and they may or may not want referral to emergency accommodation or whatever. But we do have quite a large group of young people who are not particularly at the moment wanting to stop using drugs, needing some kind of local support and a bit of advice now and again, maybe getting into trouble with the police and needing a bit of advice about that. Sometimes when we get very busy, we get a very wide range of people who come wandering in. Basically, we sort of advertise ourselves as seeing anybody about anything to do with drugs. It could be the person

themselves, or a relative or friend or whatever. It's very broad.

We turn now to describe one such (quite 'typical') day as observed (amongst others) by the fieldworker.

A DAY OBSERVED

The agency officially opens at 10 a.m. At 10.05 on a hot summer morning Chrissie is already using both telephones on behalf of a client already there. He stays until about 10.15 by which time Chrissie has sorted something out for him. By now both Jane and Benn are also in. Benn has cleared his desk from things left over from the day before, checks a file in the cabinet and is soon on the phone enquiring about a client who hasn't kept appointments for two weeks. Chrissie goes off to wash up cups and fetch water in a bucket from the bathroom at the top of the stairs for the endless cups of coffee and tea consumed by visitors and staff. Meanwhile Jane is also on the phone engaged in some kind of negotiation. During the course of our study, the fieldworker took the opportunity to work in each agency for a week as a substitute staff member. By 10.45 the researcher was working on the front desk, at the agency's point of reception, filling in the day book, making appointments for clients to see staff, taking general calls of enquiry and so on.

Working at the front desk requires a skilled mixture of discretion and consistency. Both qualities are particularly necessary for workers when imposing their agency sanction of banning a client from the project. They have to be clear about who is banned and why, and enforce the measure with firmness but sensitivity, allowing a measure of discretion (for example, banning from the premises but keeping in phone contact) when the circumstances of the client seem to need it. At the same time, in order to present the rules of the project seriously to the client population so that they are not treated lightly, there has to be consistency in the imposing and policing of bans and evictions from the office. On some occasions, for example, the workers note with some irony, they have had to call in the police to assist them or witness them remove troublesome clients.

In these circumstances it has been the agency staff taking the policing role, 'moving people on', whilst the police have taken the conciliatory advisor role - 'come along now, let's avoid any trouble and have a walk down to the park ...'.

On this particular day there is only one person banned from the project, a woman who had been throwing furniture around in the project, and causing trouble in the street until she got 'nicked'. However, because she is in a particularly vulnerable state, she has not been banned from telephone counselling and staff make an effort to keep in touch with her (lest she finds herself unable to cope or perhaps loses contact with them).

At 11.30 Sandra comes into the project. She has an appointment for 4.30 the following day but wants to talk to somebody today. Sandra is known to be nice, but she wanders a bit in her conversation, going round in circles and inducing a degree of frustration. She sits down with the inevitable Hungerford cup of coffee and Linda and I talk to her for a while about her new-found commitment to God. Benn has now finished his phone calls and comes into the reception area and talks to Sandra for half an hour about how she can start to sort out her difficulties with her DHSS claim. Sandra keeps returning to the subject of a Christian community and of other hostels she has heard of, while Benn tries to keep her focussed on getting emergency payment from the DHSS for a one night stay - as she has no money and nowhere to go this seems the immediate priority. Eventually, she leaves intent on sorting out the DHSS money. It should be noted, especially with regard to the idea of accounting for agency wokers' time through recording systems, that, at least at present, the project has no way of recording such time spent with clients (outside appointments in the afternoons). Hence half-hour sessions like that with Sandra which occur in the morning when clients are supposed to be restricted to a fifteen minute chat or thereabouts, are 'lost', as far as the records are concerned.

Throughout the morning there is a regular flow of visitors, some stopping briefly, accepting their cup of tea or coffee and the familiar five or six spoonfuls of sugar, and then leaving. Others want more than brief contact, settling into their chairs as if for the morning, engaging in conversation with the initially receptive staff, then provoking further conversation as the talk flags, and finally being encouraged to leave after their time has been well extended. At 1.00 p.m. the project closes for lunch for an hour, windows and doors are locked and it is now standard practice that everyone leaves the office. This practice is emphasised to clients who are discouraged from hanging around outside during the lunch break.

Sometimes a client calls and wishes to speak to a particular worker on occasions when that worker is, for a variety of reasons, unavailable. Whoever takes the call has to handle it in such a way as to assure the caller that they can safely and confidently talk to another worker either at that time or perhaps on some other occasion. In one case, Ian called the project wanting to talk to Anne who had been working in a cover role the previous week. When he was told that she wasn't with the project that week and asked if he would like to talk to anybody else about anything, he said he would call back at 3 p.m. as it was 'all a bit complicated'. In fact he called back less than half an hour later. He was trying to come off tranquillizers and had already phoned up an agency with an interest in tranquillizer problems. Apparently, however, they would not help him unless he gave his name and address and that of his G.P., because they wanted to make sure he didn't need them for serious medical reasons. Ian refused to give his own name or that of the G.P. precisely because he did not want his doctor to know of what he was trying to do. He now wanted to know if there were any other agencies that could help him although, as regards the Hungerford, he could not come into the project or talk to a worker because he was at work himself during the day. Ian was asked to 'hang on for a minute' and put on 'hold' on the phone whilst a brief consultation among available staff members sought suggestions for further referral agencies. The best next step seemed to be that he should call Release who have a lot of experience and ideas about working with 'tranx' problems. Even if Ian had been free during the day, it would not have automatically been assumed that he should make an appointment at the Hungerford. The agencies are well aware that the Piccadilly street clientele that the Hungerford serves can be disturbing to some more con·

tional clients; furthermore the relationship between the street agencies is sufficiently close to ensure that they can confidently suggest a client uses the agency nearest to their home or place of work. So, depending on where he was, Ian could have been referred to either CDP or the Blenheim. Ian was able to hold on while the workers consulted over the most appropriate agency to suggest next. It must be easy, however, in any conversation with a rushed or panicked client, for a flustered worker, or one with a lot on their mind, to forget about a useful service or contact until after the phone has been put down. The problem then, given the anonymity of many clients, is that it is impossible to call them back to pass on the additional information.

The office closes its doors gratefully at 5.30, though it aims to have no clients around after 5 p.m. This, of course, is wishful thinking. Nonetheless, 5.30 is a closing time which is treated with respect. It is not, however, the end of the day for the agency workers themselves, who now congregate in the middle-room, pulling chairs into a circle for their recently-initiated handover session. This involves going over the day's business, going through the day's diary with each worker explaining for the benefit of the other workers what each phone call, new referral, old contact and so on was about. Such updates can be matters of trivia and swiftly covered, or matters of seriousness with regard to the agency's relationship with a client, in which case they will be dealt with at some length.

A long day at the Hungerford may be coming to an end around 6 p.m. - that is unless someone has to go to a meeting, visit a client at City Roads, do some voluntary work at ROMA, or spend the evening on detached work in Earls Court.

CONTACTS WITH GENERIC AND WITH SPECIALIST DRUG AGENCIES

The Hungerford is very much a part of a network in which the maintenance of contacts and the negotiation of the referral process are central. Being aware of available resources is seen as being an integral part of good social work:

> An awful lot of our work is actually referral, just
> passing people on, and to do that you have to keep
> in touch with all the rehabs, and that's also good
> social work.   To me, being a good social worker
> is knowing where you can send somebody, so there
> is an awful lot of getting to know people on the
> other end of the phone ... so that you actually know
> who you are talking to, you know what the house
> looks like, so you can describe it and give that information
> to your clients, which is good social work practice
> as I see it. (Benn)

Such knowledge of the field is also an important resource
for the liaison process with other professionals in the
statutory or non-statutory sectors - especially where
it may not be particularly appropriate for the client
to actually come to and use a drugs agency like the Hungerford:

> Or you can give that information to a youth leader
> or probation officer ... so the person on probation
> doesn't have to be sent to a drugs agency like us
> to be referred on ... (or we can help) the probation
> officer feel confident enough for him to pick up
> a phone and phone Phoenix and say, 'I think this
> is an appropriate referral'. (Benn)

Whilst the Hungerford workers feel that it is useful
for generic professionals to have sufficient confidence
to deal with 'drug work' without the constant support
of the street agencies, they also sometimes feel that
certain professions may not keep sufficiently in touch
with them to be knowledgeable about the range of referral
possibilities for their clients.   Without the maintenance
of liaison between different agencies, the particular
expertise and knowledge which is the street agencies'
stock-in-trade is wasted:

> So (probation officers, for example, can) actually
> bypass us, which I think is quite good at some times.
> On the other hand, it's quite bad.   It's quite good
> in the sense that it doesn't give the person (client)
> the name of being your street agency junkie - he
> doesn't come from the Hungerford project or the
> Community Drug Project.   It removes that sort of

drug stigma from it. But then the bad part is you get probation officers doing things like - they think the only concept house in England is Alpha, so somebody gets sent from London to Alpha, when it would have been quite easy for him to go to Phoenix. So there's two sides to that story, I think.

In a sense the Hungerford faces similar problems about being sure it is making appropriate referrals. These relate to distinguishing the actual nature of the problem that their clients are presenting. The Hungerford sees clients with a wide variety of problems some of which they do not feel equipped to deal with in terms of time, expertise, and the fact that they may be doing work which another agency ought to be doing.

That's another frustration, where somebody goes into a G.P. saying I'm using (drugs), gets landed down here, and the person turns out to be psychiatrically disturbed and the G.P. hasn't taken the time or patience to sus that out. So we end up getting somebody who's very disturbed, and we've got to deal with it because nobody else will. Sometimes we end up doing things that other agencies should be doing, or statutory bodies should be doing, which is very time-consuming. And I suppose, because of the way we work, we have a tendency to take them on. If somebody comes down here, and after two weeks we realise that they're mentally disturbed, you can't actually just turn around and throw them out. All this is very time-consuming. One guy took months and months to sort out and we were getting into a whole realm of things we didn't want to. We were getting into the MIND, the mental health rights people, and then getting into social services and stuff like that. That's very time-consuming, we shouldn't have to do that, so that gets very frustrating when we get a bum referral, which has happened more and more often because as soon as you say 'drugs' people panic. (Benn)

Thus the Hungerford may have some clients who have psychiatric problems and who use drugs but for whom

they cannot provide an adequate service - while more properly falling into their net would be non-psychiatric cases who
use drugs even though their drug use may not be their only or
main problem (for example, problems with housing, social
security, etc.) In between such clients there may be border-
line cases, such as amphetamine users, whose 'paranoia' may
be related to their use of drugs. Appropriate onward referral
may be sought for many such clients but staff still try to
work with them, 'talking to them in an ordinary way'.
Hungerford workers now feel the need for more training in
being able to make effective distinctions between the type of
clients that they are getting. The ability to operate with an
effective working distinction between types of cases has
important consequences in terms of the appropriateness of
referrals.

Finally, here, we attempt to give the reader some sense of
the breadth of contact with the other agencies that Hungerford
has. Because it makes a particular priority of young people
and the wide range of problems that they face, especially
being young, unemployed drug users in the inner city, the
agency seeks contact with other agencies beyond the narrow
focus of 'professionals dealing with a drugs problem' and
along the lines of tapping community resources. Youth-
orientated professional contacts include ILEA youth workers,
a wide range of welfare sector workers and those involved in
health and drug education in schools. More regular contacts
are spread across and divided between members of staff.
These contacts include involvement in a managerial or advisory capacity with other agencies, involvement with other
agencies which arises out of being part of the Turning Point
organisation, contacts with the rehabilitation houses (especially Phoenix House), weekly contact with City Roads,
detached work contact with central London agencies like
Piccadilly Advice Centre, and contact with hostels like
Centrepoint and Riverpoint - and, of course, with the other
street agencies. the project takes an interest in trying to
help find a client some employment if the person seems
interested rather than deal with the Jobcentres, it will
probably refer them to the Piccadilly Advice Centre who may
know of something or suggest a list of hotels in the area who
may have some casual work. Another option is to encourage
the interested and the capable in education, and to this end

they maintain good contact with a Fresh Horizons course at the City Literary Institute in Covent Garden.

DETACHED WORK: REASONS FOR IT, AND AN EXAMPLE

Having given some feeling of the day to day practice within the project's premises we now describe the role and form which detached work takes in the Hungerford. This is particularly important as the Hungerford is the only street agency (and one of the few of any type of social work agency) that still retains a firm commitment to some sort of detached work. Finally, in this brief discussion of the Hungerford and its daily practice, we shall examine the sources of referrals that they receive.

Reasons for detached work

The project has been practising some type of detached work since at least the mid-1970s, its development coinciding with the abandoning of the Day Centre system (see chapter 2). Initially, it focussed on following up day centre attenders outside, on the street, checking that they were alright; but the project workers soon found that this was largely unnecessary with what was, at that time, a very 'streetwise' set of clients.

As detached work is represented now by project staff, it seems to have lost any early ambitions actually to provide a service on the street, and is aimed more at publicising to street users the existence of the Hungerford's service in the office. As one staff member describes:

> So we had a look around at who was there on the streets and using whom we weren't actually seeing, or who wasn't represented in any proportional way in the client group, and there was at the time (1981) a very big group of young people who had started off maybe sniffing glue butwere starting to take pills and inject other drugs. It seemed important to try and catch them fairly early, using detached work maybe as the primary tool, not saying, 'you have got a drug problem, come to the office and we'll make you better', but just getting to know

> them and passing on information, really, sort of
> replacing the bit of the grapevine that seems to
> have gone. (Jane)

Similarly, for another Hungerford worker:

> The aim of detached work is not to go out of the
> office to meet people to bring them back here.
> It's to go out on the street to let people be aware
> of the agency should they need it.   There's a lot
> of support and advice you can give that you don't
> actually need a phone for, and for a lot of our older
> clients that we've known for a long time they're
> quite happy just knowing we're there walking around
> a certain area, and if they do have problems they
> drop into the office. And it is good, certainly recently
> with the large number of young people on the streets,
> it is useful, if you know a face, and go up and talk
> to them, they introduce you to somebody else, and
> maybe one out of three or four people introduced
> might want 'to come to the office'. (Linda)

There may be other reasons that we can tentatively
identify as encouraging some form of detached work.
With many clients it is difficult to work in depth (i.e.
psycho-therapeutically) since it would be an irresponsible
practice to stir up painful feelings inside people and
then send them back out onto the streets feeling raw
inside and vulnerable to drug use.   Detached work is
defined here partly by what cannot be done in the office.
Some kinds of opening up by clients may occur more
comfortably on the familiar streets.

At the same time detached work allows the Hungerford
to indicate to clients who have had social work sessions
in the project that its concern for them does not end
as they pass out beyond the project door - they are also
concerned about how people are feeling outside on the
cold, wet streets. One of the most common retorts from
drug users to social workers is 'you don't know what it's
like', referring both to their use of drugs and their circumstances
and life-style. The presence of the agency workers on
the streets can indicate that at least they know what
it's like to be cold and wet.

The pressure on working space in the project itself
also makes detached work seem a logical idea.   Some

clients can be met and worked with as effectively on the street as in the office, at least for the short, chatty type of session. There seems at times to have been a strong continuity between in-office and out-of-office work with young people, as, for example, with a group of young women who were writing essays about what they wanted to do with their lives. This little project started in the office but continued outside, in the park, in the summer. In fact, as we found when we were looking at how other agencies appraise the work of the Hungerford, their work out of the office cannot be seen as detached work in its strict sense (as developed in youth work), and the general style of the project might be characterised as something in between the usual practices of detached work (outside) and project work (ping-pong, motorbike maintenance, health discussions, etc., inside). They seem to do a detached style of work in the office, i.e. the street is contacted and encouraged to come in.

Having said all that, we must still describe the actual practice of the Hungerford's detached work. Apart from the assistance of the occasionally interested placement student and the equally occasional accompaniment of one of the women social workers, most of the detached work is done by one worker (Benn). Fortunately for the project Benn had arrived on student placement in time to work with the previous detached worker and so, when he joined the project full-time, replacing the detached worker, he was able to move into the role with some degree of continuity.

> When I started ... a predecessor had done an awful lot of detached work. The main type of group is 25 year old plus people who had been ... the old Hungerford Day Centre type of person, whom (my predecessor) used to know either as a social worker or in some cases as a user, because he's an ex-user. They centred mainly on the pubs around Shaftesbury Avenue, Soho, around there. So when I was a student that's mainly where the patch work was done; and just when I started work.

> Then in early 1981, with the increase of young people on the streets, and the awareness amongst most SCODA membership agencies that there was little done for women, the type of group focussed on was

changed to young people and women. (Actually) women have still been left out, but the young people - that's our kind of group, they don't go into pubs, they stay in the streets, so an awful lot of detached work in the last two years would have been on the street, walking about the street. Especially in the summer.

That's now changed ... there's been a move to Earls Court, so I'm down the Earls Court Road now, and it's funny that in Earls Court they stay in pubs, whereas up here they don't, so it changes no matter what area you go into ... The plan for the detached work (with women) ... is to get women detached workers to try and contact women, that's the plan if we ever get a fourth social worker, who hopefully will be a woman.

The movements of potential clients on the streets - and of the detached worker, as he follows them - are not entirely random, nor aspects of 'fashion', but are largely influenced by the movements of dealers. Both dealers and users are influenced in their choice of location by the actions of other agencies, notably the police.

At the moment, with police activity, everybody's static because we had the SPG in at the end of last year, so that leaves the West End - staying in a certain cafe and just getting used to people coming in there; it's the main cafe that the dealers use and that's where I'm actually situated myself. But that'll last for two months until the police scare people off, and then I'll have to move off again. And then at night ... down the Earls Court Road, we do a joint youth project (with the Basement Project) on a Thursday night ...

In these descriptions, we see that the type of detached work that evolves depends partly upon the agencies, partly upon the movement of people on the streets, and partly upon the ways in which the agency identified particular problems and priorities (e.g. women) in this shifting collage. Within this context, each detached worker brings his or her own particular preferences and skills into play:

My way of working is different from that of our
current student. I would use people I know from
the office to introduce me to people I met on the
street. I would go out of my way to talk to somebody
whom I already knew. Say I knew a guy named Geoff
who was with a group of guys, I would talk to Geoff,
knowing that he would introduce me to some of
the people. A lot of guys who come down here know
what I'm doing, so they're quite happy to say, 'Oh,
he's o.k., Benn's alright, Benn's from the Hungerford',
and very slowly get into that. Now, there the guys
mightn't talk to you, but ... six months later one
of them might trust you enough to walk up and say
'I got busted last night, can you get me a good solicitor?'
That was my predecessor's sort of view, which I
agree with because he planned it as a very long-
term thing, like over years.

Benn does detached work for most of the afternoon on
most Mondays, Wednesdays and Fridays, generally covering a
by now well established route around the West End. Getting
to know this kind of area, the hang-outs and the people, takes
time and unless care is taken to pass this knowledge on to
other workers in the agency then effective detached work
will be ruined by the departure of the only worker who knows
the scene, and has become accepted on it. As a previous
worker had said to Benn when he first started taking him
round the scene, he would expect to take up to a year before
he would really get to know the key places and the key faces
and be accepted by them.

An example of detached work

When the fieldworker accompanied Benn on his detached
work round one of the first things that Benn had said was that
he really didn't expect anyone at all to come and talk to us
and that although he might say 'hello' to a few people they
were not likely to hang around because of the fieldworker's
presence. A fairly regular route for the detached worker
would start off walking around Piccadilly Circus, searching
through the mass of faces for people that the Hungerford
knows or people that look like they are strung out and need

help, as well as for strange faces on the scene who don't quite look like they 'fit'. Such strange faces will often turn out to be undercover police officers looking out for drug transactions or any unfamiliar and suspicious-looking persons.

On this particular warm, summer day the walk around the semi-circle of Piccadilly underground station was unusually quiet, with most of its regulars probably sitting in local parks or hanging around in the Haymarket. The underground Dilly scene does get slightly confusing sometimes with regard to who is into what. It is used by both the hard drug users and the 'Rent Boys', with some overlap between them in that a lot of rent boys use all types of drugs, though in their use of uppers and downers they don't really see any problem, use the drugs as a way of keeping going and, of course, pay for their habit in their own particular way, which the other users do not. Subway four of the underground station retains its status as the legendary site of the late 1960s and 1970s drug scoring scene, but today sees few who would hang around as they did then. Subway four now plays host to the walk-in kiosk of the Piccadilly Advice Centre and Benn will often stop in there if it is not too busy, have a cup of coffee, sit by the window and wait for a familar face to drop in or pass by.

Out of the subway and into the sunlight, the detached worker may walk down part of Regent Street, cutting through an alley-way into the Haymarket, and back up towards Leicester Square. In the summer the Haymarket attracts a lot of people hanging around and scoring. Throughout this area, approaching Leicester Square, old meeting places, familiar cafes and the likes have been pushed aside to make way for unfriendly and unwelcoming hamburger chain restaurants, etc. In the summer, the Square itself nowadays attracts many skin-heads, unemployed, whiling away their time, sniffing glue. Despite their generally uncommunicative manner Benn eventually got to know a number of the regulars after finding out that a lot of them used the New Horizon Day Centre in its old days. Through visiting the centre on Tuesday mornings, chatting with attenders, buying cups of coffee and occasionally helping with any groups going on, he eventually became recognised outside of New Horizon.

From Leicester Square the detached worker's route could then cut through Chinatown, through the alleys where the Soho street walkers hang around and into the seeming insularity of the Chinatown community. The Hungerford has virtually no contact with drug problems from the Chinese community, and has not encountered either any association or conflict between Chinese youth and the youth that hang around Leicester Square and Piccadilly. The Chinese community keeps to itself. Others, more vocal, such as the Soho rates association, concern themselves with the problem of vice, the pornography shops and streetwalkers, and also ignore the West End drug scene.

From Chinatown and up Charing Cross Road brings you to Cambridge Circus, where Benn had recently discovered that there was a pub which was attracting users because it had good toilets, with locks, which were accessible from the door without being seen by the pub staff. Hence people could slip into the toilets and have a fix without being seen.

Down Compton Street and back into Shaftesbury Avenue takes you past Halls Chemist. Halls is now the major central London dispensing chemist for maintenance scripts as well as stocking syringes which can be obtained across the counter. They have a good reputation for helpful, sympathetic staff and, for a while, were enclosing copies of the Blenheim project's leaflet on 'How to Stop' in the bags in which the filled prescriptions were wrapped. Halls is now a regular meeting point for users wishing to kill time or to score from somebody who has just had their prescription filled and for whatever reason can afford to sell some of their drugs (cf. Burr, 1983). Hence, standing by a bus-stop which adds apparent legitimacy to the congregation of people, the detached worker can try to strike up conversation with new, as well as old, faces. In the many old and dingy cafes dotted throughout Soho and the West End, users congregate for the same reasons - to chat (usually about drugs) and to score. More of the detached work that Benn does may be aimed at surveying such cafes and discovering which of them is currently a good scene to meet old and new contacts in. Again, having identified such a scene, it has to be carefully broken into; it requires patience to become a familiar face. Such work is easily negated, however, by a police raid, the moods of cafe proprietors, the movements of dealers, and so on.

By its very nature the drug scene is always shifting, and as the detached social worker can never be a real part of it, the charting of where people are hanging out and what they are into will always be difficult. The attempt to fulfil such a task remains an important part of detached work, however, and it is difficult to see how, without this particular social work out-reach strategy, any agency in the field could have a much clearer grasp of the transient nature and diverse composition of the drug scene. It is because of such detached work that the Hungerford remains one of the best-informed drug agencies in the non-statutory sector (and much more up-to-date on trends than statutory drug agencies).

Contacts made by detached workers out of the office are not included in the Hungerford's client count, nor is much real information actually kept on those that are talked to on the streets (unless, of course, they become Hungerford clients). Instead a diary is kept for street work, using code-names descriptive of contacts whose real names are often unknown anyway. The information that can be drawn from office records on detached work can thus be said to be sketchy and impressionistic; nonetheless, it does give a valuable, sensitising idea of what is happening on the streets, and provides information about trends in drug use. Perhaps most importantly, as the Hungerford workers themselves stress, it takes out into the street culture the message that part of the 'straight' social work culture offers at least an open door, a cup of coffee and an experienced ear.

WORK WITH CLIENTS

The Hungerford sees more men clients than women in a ratio of approximately two to one according to their own estimate, and these break down into two (approximate) age groupings - from around 17 to 21 years, and an older group in their late 20s and early 30s. According to Jane, the senior worker, 'the youngest person we have had was twelve and a half and the oldest has been sixty'. The Hungerford does not operate any age limits or catchment area policy and welcomes all potential clients. That said, it is necessary to note one restriction on clientele that has developed without intention on the part of the agency staff.

Lack of contact with ethnic minorities

It is a matter of concern to some people in the drugs agency field that the drug advice and rehabilitation agencies seem to have a poor record of making connections with non-white groups and clients. Most of the clients that the Hungerford receives are Caucasian:

> In the last year - and the only reason I remember it is because it was so unusual - we have had one man who was Chinese, and that was unusual because the Chinese usually look after their own but he had worked in Soho and for some reason that community hasn't provided the support that it normally would do. And it's either two or three people of West Indian/African origin.(Jane)

Observations on the kind of supportive networks that blacks may be using instead of agencies like the Hungerford and so on, were taken further by Chrissie:

> The unrepresented are women, and racial minorities certainly. I've been working the last month with a young black woman ... I wish there was a way to actually develop through her, some way of bringing more people into the project. But in fact the only reason why she is here is that her whole cultural set-up has been based among whites ... I personally don't think we are ever going to make great inroads into racial minorities. I think they've got quite good support systems themselves. They've got some pretty healthy extended family networks that a lot of whites don't have and ... it's just the obvious mistrust and I don't see us overcoming that.

Jane agrees about the existence and efficacy of a separate system of support for ethnic minorities and links it to reservations about the extent of hard drug abuse among them anyway:

> Well, I don't think there is that much heavy drug use among the black community. I think it's more gana and that sort of level of drug use, which is

not to say there isn't any at all because people say
there is quite a heavy scene going on around Finsbury
Park which is predominantly black, but ... I'd just
feel very uncomfortable about walking into a black
agency and being a white middle-class do-gooder
and I imagine the same works both ways, and that
they use their own neighbourhood structure, and black
advice agencies are doing a fair bit and that's where the
people from these communities prefer to go.

'Survivors' and Young 'Chaotic' Clients

Of their more regular and familiar clientele two groups
stand out as part of the West End scene. These are the
long term survivors - the legacy of the early history
of the clinics and of the day centres described in chapter
2 - and the new, young, 'chaotic' drug users.   Chrissie
offered a composite career of a long term survivor which
ran along the following lines: 'He'd be registered sometimes
with various clinics, he'd be getting methadone, perhaps
lose out on that when he got sent to prison, then coming
out he'd get involved in the black market, doing a certain
amount of illegal stuff,' and, in Chrissie's opinion, 'there's
nothing you're going to tell him that he doesn't already
know'.
     The younger 'chaotic' users are heavily dependent on
the street agencies, partly to fill their time. Such users
are not out trying to get a fix all day and they are not
necessarily addicted; hence they demand of the agency
a different kind of approach.   These clients are likely
to receive quite a lot of input from workers because
they frequently turn up at the agency nearly every day
on a drop-in basis, as well as attending perhaps twice
a week for counselling sessions arranged by appointment.
     These two groups have a high profile among the Hungerford
clientele:

> Those two groups, specifically the chaotic group,
> can be the most frustrating, because they are notorious
> for getting to the brink of wonderful things; or the
> other thing they do is to walk out sometimes and
> not come back, then you have to be quite frantic,
> phoning around, trying to find them, and obviously
> they could be dead.(Chrissie)

Workers in street agencies like the Hungerford have to be particularly sensitive to the circumstances and problems of such vulnerable clients. This sensitivity can result in deep frustration for workers when they have achieved a break-through with a client which is then rejected:

> Sometimes you feel that you haven't been able to do very much for somebody and you have to pace yourself and not believe that there has to be a right answer all the time for everybody ... (Then) sometimes you feel that you've done a really good piece of social work when somebody comes in and says I haven't got a problem, I just need some help with accommodation or advice', or 'I haven't got a real problem, I've just got an abcess', and then you make an appointment to sit down and talk to them and you really break through and people start talking about what's really going wrong for them. And if you feel good about what happens there and you make a link and then they break contact and don't come back, then that is frustrating.(Chrissie)

A constant sensitivity and awareness is also required about the counselling sessions, setting limits on how far a client's 'opening up' can be taken:

> Being a street agency you've got to remember that whatever comes out in a counselling session, those people have to take it back out onto the streets with them afterwards and, for some people, the way that they cope with whatever has come out, is maybe to go out and get stoned. So you've got to be aware of the consequences of the counselling work that gets done and how much you can actually do with that person. You've always got to be aware of the vulnerability of people. So it's frustrating because you feel like you want to go on sometimes but, again, you've got to pace yourself because of what a client can take and can't.(Chrissie)

Women's needs

Despite the commitment of the Hungerford to working

with women clients, they still see relatively few compared to male clients, although after efforts to change this there are some signs that the male:female ratio is being slightly re-balanced. Previously, as Jane observes:

> We weren't even seeing that many women on the street - we just knew they were around. They'd just sort of zoom into Piccadilly and score or do a bit of business, or whatever, and then go away again - very isolated. And talking to the women who did come here, they felt that that was an area where we should be concentrating because they themselves, when they were on the streets, had felt very isolated and cut off for all kinds of reasons. Their only contact with other people was usually through men, either being part of a couple or just being around with a gang occasionally just to find out where the man was, and that sort of thing ....

Women who are dependent on men in the West End scene will often be 'runners' for the man's drug dealing activities, with the men typically congregating and moving in packs and women attaching themselves to one particular man among them. There is evidence of some prostitution related to the West End drug scene (cf. Burr, 1983), but this does not seem to be a major aspect of the sub-culture. Far more striking in fact is the relative absence of women from visible involve-ment in regular illicit activity in the scene. Women are in fact marginalised and isolated in this sub-culture just as in the dominant culture. Their isolation and difficulties can be very seriously compounded if they also have children. In particular, women with children may be reluctant to ap-proach any helping agencies, confusing them with statutory services and fearing that the social work staff would remove their children. Even where the barrier is broken and women do make contact with an agency like the Hungerford, the problems of women with children make the next step to rehabilitation another major difficulty, because there are so few places where women can take children. This state of affairs has recently brought about the mobilisation of several groups of women workers in the drugs and alcohol field aiming to organise around the issue of provision for women with children. Involvement in such campaigns is intrinsic to the work of the street agencies. Of necessity they must keep their finger on the pulse of available provision and resources and where such resources are lacking they feel the gap as acutely as the clients they are trying to help.

The variety of needs presented by clients

> '...people who happen to be using drugs ... come here because other people sent them ... because they mentioned a drug ...'

Many such clients however will also be having other immediate problems which prevent the Hungerford from dealing directly with the drug problem, and lead the agency to work within a broader system of provision and resources. Such accompanying problems

> might be accommodation or supplementary benefit or medical things, practical things ... well over half the client group are homeless, that's where we start in a lot of cases. We're doing a lot of very basic work, practical stuff which overlaps into the single homeless bit, access to primary medical care, access to housing, access to money, all those things. Often that's where we start before actually looking at changing somebody's whole life style, getting them off drugs, etc. It's pretty hard to think about stopping taking drugs, having withdrawals and going into Phoenix House and everything else when the primary thought in your mind is where the hell are you going to sleep and you're awfully hungry. I mean that seems like a good place to start - that's what I see the agency doing ... it's kind of taking people where they are at that moment and moving on from there.(Jane)

It is in this respect - taking people where they are at that moment - that the Hungerford, together with the other street agencies, has developed a truly generic, highly responsible social work style that cuts across all the categories of work to be found in other, more professionalised or specialist social work drug agencies. This explains why they may sometimes, to outsiders, seem to lack professionalism or a theory to their practice: the range and depth of client problems hits these agencies too squarely upon the jaw for them to articulate very polished accounts of their practice.

TWO BRIEF CLIENT CASE STUDIES

John - and the importance of truth

John first started using the Hungerford project in December
1979, hearing of it through his probation officer'. He was, as
he puts it, 'in a right mess at the time'. John's girlfriend had
died just a few days before he came to the Hungerford and,
not surprisingly, he says that he 'just didn't want to talk about
that to anyone. So I never did ... I was in a right ruck, I was
just nowhere ... I just needed help. I came here and saw one
of the male social workers and two days later I was in City
Roads.'
    John was grateful and impressed: 'I was really glad they
could do that for me'. John spent three weeks in City Roads,
but didn't settle in: 'I just left. Split ... After three weeks,
yeah. About a week after that I was back in there.' John
himself felt that this failure to settle into the City Roads
environment was less a reflection on them or the Hungerford
and more on himself:

> I was just how it was. Just about me ... (Hungerford had
> told me what it was about in detail ... They said what
> would happen after I left City Roads if I was interested.
> But I was so muddled up with my girlfriend dying that I
> just didn't want to know.

After John's second return to City Roads, he managed to
stay the course; however, on leaving, he went back on the
street. Unlike some clients who use a range of agencies,
John just uses the Hungerford:

> I didn't know London very well. I'd been there two years
> before, but I didn't know it at all ... I was in a right mess.
> Just sort of a chaotic user, just take anything and
> everything, you know?... This is the one - I'm quite
> attached to this place, you know. Because, I dunno, it's
> just really friendly here. If you come here and you're a
> right arseehole, they'll tell you where to go. You know,
> tell you to go. A couple of times I've been barred from
> here. My own fault. I mean, they're only trying to
> protect the other people who use the place ... I used to
> come up here. But I used to sit down and lie to myself ...
> It's not so very long ago that I started being truthful with
> Chrissie ... It's only this last year that I've really used

this place for what it's supposed to be used for ... Every time I used to come up here, for a time like, they used to say things to me, and I used to think they was alright, but as soon as I got back out on the street I'd fuck up again.

John's pattern of attendance at the Hungerford during this period was fairly irregular:

It went in sort of bounds and leaps, you know, I used to come in, and go. And come and go and come and go. ... I've been coming here for a long time. I've never wanted to do anything up until about the last three weeks ... It's the only time I think I've come up here and been really truthful ...

As was noted in Benn's description of the work of the Hungerford, a lot of the agency's work cna be very simply directed towards building up a relationship and trust with a client so that when and if that client decides that they do have the desire to start getting off drugs, then the Hungerford can put things in motion as soon as possible. As John put it:

Well I was in City Roads in April, no, March, this year. I was in a pretty bad way and the staff at City Roads wanted me to go to some sort of rehab. And I didn't want to go to anything too heavy ... When the day came for me to go there, I just went to see a doctor and got a script. Mucked up. That was in June ... I went to the Stonehenge Festival and came back to London .. and I came down here ... While I was at Stonehenge I come up to see Chrissie 'cos I thought I had to tell her I'd blown it. But I told her a load of lies and I went away again and come back and she said to me, 'If you want me to continue working with you then you've got to sit down and tell me the truth'. Cos the times I come up here from Stonehenge - I come up a couple of times, up to here and back down to there - I told her two different stories. So she sussed me. Well, I was in a mess anyway. And a couple of weeks ago I come here and sat down in this room with her and told her what was going on and everything. And she listened. And she was really good about it. She was hard and firm but she just told me straight that if I don't be truthful about it then she can't

do nothing for me. So I went away and I come back here
last week, and I wrote, we talked about different rehabs,
Phoenix, Cokehole, Cranstoun, and she said she'd phone
up Paul at Phoenix. She got me an interview to see him
up there last Friday and I went away with the Cokehole
address and the Cranstoun address and wrote them
letters and Benn read them ... and he said they was good
letters, straight to the point, and he wouldn't bullshit you
know, which is good because you've got to be truthful
about it. If you want to get into these places you've got
to be truthful. It took me four years to realise that, but
I've realised it now ...

Keith - the discovery of 'motivation to come off'

Keith is now 22, has a history of opiate use and still uses
amphetamines, occasionally quite heavily. Like many amphetamine users he has a tired appearance making him look
older than his years. Keith 'never actually thought' that he
would 'need a place like the Hungerford', but started using it
in 1981. 'I got introduced to Benn (on the street) and started
coming down to see Benn quite regularly.' His initial
impressions of what the Hungerford actually did were vague
but clarified over time: 'Well, really it just says it's a place
where if you want to come off you can come down and talk to
them about it, and we never went into detail about it. Benn
explained it a bit better saying they would try and help me if
I helped myself'.
    Keith had 'been an opiate user for nearly six years, diconal,
amps', but had recently decided to try to come off all drugs.

> It took a long time, it actually took me two years for me
> to actually really want to come off. Up until this
> Christmas I never really wanted to come off. I just used
> the place and Christmas just gone I'd made up my mind
> that I *was* going to come off ... And I went into City
> Roads and went to Phoenix, had a few setbacks, still
> using but still wanting to come off...

As with John, the Hungerford developed a relationship with
Keith slowly until he himself decided that he would work on
the motivation to come off.

> It took a long time for that motivation to, you know
> what I mean, to go out to town, make appointments and

not turning up ... I did that for about a year, just make appointments and didn't bother coming, and make up some story why I never come. But when I make appointments now I just keep it regular because it helps ... .

Keith appreciated the way that staff had been tolerant of his use of the agency over time:

I think it was quite good really because I think they really understood that I didn't really want to come off at that time. But up at Christmas like they started to believe me. I started to do things for myself. Started to say that I wanted to come off and actually keep my appointments ... and it's difficult actually keeping appointments, doing things regularly on a time basis. I got into a routine and I like coming here. I do like coming here ...

Once Keith's new degree of motivation was evident to the Hungerford they could begin to put more work into supporting him.

...they put a hell of a lot more time into me. I get two or three appointments a week because they believe in me. They believe that I want to do something which means a lot to me, you know. It means I can't afford to waste their time because they could do other things ... But they have put a hell of a lot of energy into me. ...We talk about me, and why I take drugs, and what to do and what I want out of the rest of my life. Because I'm only 22, so I've got a few years left, apart from the health problems I've got through drugs.

The concentrated time and interest now directed towards Keith mean a lot to him: 'if I didn't think they were interested, I wouldn't bother coming down'. Keith knows of other agencies but only uses the Hungerford:

Oh, I've been told to go to other places. But, I mean, I'm attached to this place so that does me, if I've got any problems I come here. A few mates used to come down here. But, like one of them has been using for 15 years and he's got to the stage - he did want to come off for a while - he's got to the stage now that I don't think he cares if anybody does want to get him off so he hasn't been down for months now. Which is a pity really, because he's a nice geezer. I see him on the street, I always mention, 'when are you going down to the Hungerford?' and he says 'aw, I'll have to pop in' but he never bothers. That's his choice ... I don't know how many people know about the Hungerford. But some people I know have been on the drug scene for a long time and they don't know about the Hungerford. But I think you've got to be interested to come off to want to come here, you can't come and waste time. And anyway, you can think, o.k. you can come in for a cup of tea, a chat, or whatever, but basically this is a place to help you get somewhere else, to go from here, you know, even still using, but actually get you to go somewhere, if you want to go somewhere. Like I hope ... go back to Phoenix ...

Keith had first heard of the Hungerford through meeting its detached worker, Benn:

I've met him a few times on the street. I think that's how I first got to know (about the Hungerford) ... I seen him when the Haymarket scene was going. I seen him a bit like, I thought he was a cop or something like that ... I'd always talked to him if I saw him on the street, do you know what I mean? I think it's a very hard thing to do, well, what he does, to go out into the street and actually try and get to know people, it's really hard. I don't think he gets much success but he sort of sticks out, you know what I mean? We're talking about numbers, so ... It is hard but I don't think they make any contact whatsoever really because people are just not interested. They are just, like Shaftesbury Avenue is full of junkies, you know? ... most junkies I know are all doing alright for themselves, they've all got council houses or are living with their parents and they are quite happy.

Clearly, however, detached work does make contact with some people, as it did with Keith himself; and people who have not been interested in coming off before may change their minds in the future. At that point the help and influence of the Hungerford can be decisive:

Well for me personally, they've done a hell of a lot. I've had a hell of a lot of support from Chrissie. And I think that they've actually believed in me, they believe in me that I can actually do something. They can actually put time into me. Yeah, I think it's a good place.

These, of course, are the accounts of enthusiasts for the project. For most clients the contact is far more fleeting and carries less significance.

OTHER DIRECTIONS: INTER-AGENCY LIAISON; MONITORING THE PROBLEM; EDUCATION AND TRAINING; WOMEN-ONLY PROVISION

In their monthly reports the Hungerford Project lists its range of commitments and involvements. As with other projects, such lists illustrate (among other things) that no matter how client-orientated a project is, a surprisingly small amount of time is actually spent working with clients - after all the other meetings, report writing, administration and so on are taken into account. A typical list could include sickness and leave time; staff training (first aid, supplementary benefits, counselling); visits to rehabilitation houses, City Roads, etc.; periods of detached work; dealing with professional and lay visitors to the Project; attending meetings (e.g. SCODA, street agencies group, women drug workers group, Administrator's support groups, etc.); one-off talks (e.g. in prisons, schools, etc.); the supervision of student placements and so on.

In addition the Hungerford contributes to SCODA's compilation of alternative drug returns, and has been engaged in its own project - monitoring what the clinics actually do for the Hungerford as an agency. The drug return to SCODA is compiled every two months (though it tends to fall behind schedule), and aims to provide an alternative to the Home Office figures. The returns are derived from the drug histories of clients that the Hungerford takes:

At the bottom of our info sheets it says, 'Drugs being used, please notify principal drug e.g. Heroin, other drugs, where they get it from', stuff like that ... Everybody that comes in here is given an information sheet (and) ... is given a number and I keep a card on them here, and at the end of eveyr two months I get the card and write up the drug use of those two months ... so

(SCODA) ends up with a lot of numbers, male or female and their drug history for that two months. (They've) got that number in a record book so (they) can see that 402 clients used heroin in June/July, whilst two years ago so many used barbiturates, and they can actually trace the increase of opiates and stuff like that.(Benn)

As with the other street agencies, the Hungerford sees itself as making an important contribution to education and training about drugs, offering a point of view which aims to de-mystify and which supposedly has some street-level credibility:

I think it's people who are very close to the street user or day-to-day users who should be the people who actually come out in conferences and say, 'that's not true, what actually happens with glue is a,b,c,d, ... I think we should be the ones to do that as part of our job.(Benn)

On a more ad-hoc basis they are engaged in training by virtue of explaining their work and their perceptions of drug-related problems to professional visitors such as nursing staff, health educators, other professionals and lay visitors who may be involved in local youth and social work projects.

The project is trying to develop its own drug education and presentation to improve on their current style which probably incorporates 'too much information for the kids to take in, with not enough for them to actually do'. In this respect they perhaps reflect a fairly typical, and now outdated, style of drugs education, favoured by many drugs workers. Staff see liaison with other agencies involved in education and training (such as Lifeline) as a direction to pursue in improving their approach.

One of the project workers is seeking to 'create a package relating to various areas that are about workshops and training schemes', literally a listing of available resources for their clients seeking some form of employment or structure of opportunity into training, education and the like.

Proposals for the development of women-only facilities, with creche space and staff, have been worked through with staff members of other agencies, while intervention into general debates and responses to policy statements are increasingly being coordinated between the three street agencies at their own level (apart from their submissions to

SCODA).

In detailing the work of the Hungerford at such length we have obviously made a number of observations which apply to all three of the agencies with wich we are concerned and we shall not repeat such points in the following discussions of the Community Drug Project and the Blenheim Project. We shall, however, draw together impressions and observations about all three agencies later in the report.

4 The Community Drug Project in the early 1980s

LOCATION AND PREMISES

The Community Drug Project was located (during the period of fieldwork of this project) in a minor road, New Church Road, running off Camberwell Road, in south-east London. The area is marked out by large post-war housing estates of tower blocks. It is a working class district that visibly suffers from the grey drabness of urban blight - lack of resources, indifferent past planning, deteriorating amenities and ruptured communities. This is an area with neither the bright lights and energy of the Hungerford's Central London nor the old bohemianism and new gentrification of the Blenheim's West London. the nature of its clients and their problems, of its contacts and referral work, and of the way it actually works, is then, obviously different.

There is a popularly used term to describe social work agencies that operate at street level: 'shop front'. Very few agencies, however, remotely resemble a shop-front: they are hidden away down alleys, perched in the corners of buildings above two or three flights of stairs or they have found it necessary to barricade themselves behind boarded up windows and electronically controlled doors. But the Community Drug Project does look exactly like a shop-front, with a small side-

door beside a large display window presenting its face to the
street. The agency is in fact easy to miss for the casual
passer-by, whilst for others more purposeful, the potted
plants in the window create the illusion of it being a florist's
shop, and the occasional confused customer walks absently
into the agency in search of a swiss-cheese plant. Physically,
despite its cramped quarters, the agency - both inside and
outside - has a welcoming disposition, its threshold is not that
of the daunting institutions with which some of its intended
clients may be more familiar. with a large front office, neat
kitchen, counselling/meeting room and administration office,
then, certainly at the start of our project, the CDP seemed
to inhabit premises enviable by the standards of the crumbling building which the Blenheim project shared prior to its
move.

Nevertheless, despite the potted plants, the hissing gas fire
turned up high in winter and bright paint, CDP's premises are
in bad structural condition and need of repair. Throughout
our fieldwork, the agency had disagreements with its landlord
about repsonsibility for certain repairs and this had caused
some degree of anxiety among agency staff about tenure (as
well as about the suitability) of their premises. Towards the
end of the year these feelings were resolved to some extent
by the agency actively seeking new premises.

THE STAFF

Qualifications and experience

The Community Drug Project has four workers as its
basic team, occasionally augmented by student placements.
The coordinator of the project is Ronno, supported by
two other social work staff, Lena and Paul, and an administrative
worker, Stuart.

Rono moved into social work through an interest in
community work, however ill-defined that idea was at the
time, and took a four year social work degree at Hatfield
Polytechnic.

> I learnt then that social work wasn't really what I wanted
> to do, by which time it was too late. And then, in my
> final placement, I went to the Hungerford, and it was a
> prolonged placement ... and I stayed on as a locum, and

> by that time I was quite certain that I didn't want to be a 'social worker in quotes, given that I'd been taught that when you had to go and do house visits you were supposed to go and look in people's toilets, and if they were clean they were alright, and if they were dirty they had psychological problems, which I didn't really agree with. All the questions I'd been asking about the world in general were still there, and hadn't been answered by the course, and that area of discussion wasn't really catered for in social work teaching either in theoretical concepts or in being taught and how to apply those concepts in practice.(Ronno)

It was with the development of an interest in the sociology of deviance and criminology that Ronno felt she had found an area of social work where she could begin to relate theory and practice.

> I chose deviance because that seemed to raise a lot more of the questions that were around then, and ... in then going to the Hungerford, that allowed a place to start relating the theories of deviance and criminology ... with actual social work practice ... Because of that I felt easier about a certain area of social work ... it seemed sensible to stay in that area because I could look at it through a criminologist's or a sociologist's spectacles rather than from a social worker's. And that stays with me.

Ronno sees her move to the CDP as a natural progression, having met many people in the field whilst at the Hungerford, and citing the well-known 'incestuous' character of the drugs abuse 'industry'.

Lena had previously been a nurse and moved into social work when she tired of the approach to drug-related problems that her nursing training dictated:

> When I was a student nurse in psychiatry ... I went to see people that had drug problems and all that happened was that they were in for three weeks detox and then back out again. So that's when I decided that I wanted to do something more about the drugs issue because it just seemed crazy doing what we were doing.

Lena hasn't taken any specialised social work training, feeling that personal experience is just as important and that she can draw on elements of her work in nursing, such as two years'

work in intensive psychotherapy whilst a staff nurse in
Scotland. On leaving nursing, she first moved to a crisis and
support centre in Hampshire seeking to work outside the
channels and constraints of the statutory sector and then
moved to CDP, attracted by the idea of drug-focussed work
in the non-statutory sector.

Paul moved towards working at CDP through an early
interest in many of the problems with which the agency now
deals. At school he had had an interest in the single homeless
and then, after taking a degree, he moved into the probation
service, which he sees as a step in his career towards more
mainstream social work, whilst at the same time reflecting
his continuing interests in criminology and working with
offenders. Feeling that perhaps the probation service was
not exactly what he wanted and that it did not necessarily
offer a 'wealth of opportunities', Paul was attracted to the
description of the job at CDP when it came up, and joined the
agency in 1981.

Stuart is the full-time administrator of the Project. He
joined CDP in 1981 after 'generally looking around for
administrative-type jobs in the voluntary sector ... So I
wasn't in the social work field so much as the voluntary
sector generally.' For Stuart then, part of the attraction of
working at CDP lay in its character as an agency in the non-
statutory sector with a relatively non-hierarchial structure.

*Working philosophies: discovering 'hidden' aspects of the
problem*

A lay perception of agencies working in the drug field might
frequently be that their raison d'etre is to 'cure' people of
their drug taking. The people that are thought of as needing
such a cure are to be found dishevelled on the streets, or
sleeping and fixing alternately in dirty basements or attics,
or slumped in the corner of a public toilet, hiding from the
glare of the bright lights of Piccadilly Circus.

The Clients of the street agencies certainly include people
with drug and drug-related problems who closely fit the
latter stereotype. But their clientele and the problems that
they deal with encompass a much broader range of the social
spectrum. 'All human life is here' as the Sunday papers might
say - from the socially deviant to the very ordinary. From
the old to the young; middle aged, middle class housewives;

working class and upper class young wives and single mothers; working class traditional labouring males and upper class aspirant professional males; a few white professional women. It is essential to understand that the work of the street agencies is not confined to 'helping sick street deviants'. Nor, with any of their clients, is it necessarily orientated toward getting that person to 'come off' immediately or totally or withdraw from their drug use. Drug use and its related problems cut across all social boundaries, classes and situations; a social work adequate to working in this area has had to recognise this. It has also had to learn to respond with an understanding that there is no simple 'cure', and that removal of the drug or withdrawal from it (not necessarily the same thing) does not solve all the problems. It may solve a key problem or it may solve a peripheral, tangential one.

More than anything else social work practice in the street agencies has grasped and responded (however imperfectly) to the fact that their services are needed by 'invisible' populations of people with drug-related problems (in the domestic home, in the 9 to 5 routine of occupational life, in the prison and probation system and so on). Agency staff also feel that, at least initially, what is needed is not a 'cure', or withdrawal, or coming off, but stability - the founding of a base of trust, calmness and confidence on which to build short- and long-term plans towards drug-free (or at very least) manageable independence.

At CDP, Ronno recognises that the development of this approach has been fairly recent:

> We are coming across more and more people who want support, counselling, help, whatever, to maintain some kind of stability. Whether or not that is drug free I don't suppose is particularly important but if they want some kind of stability but don't want to go to rehabs or whatever, then they can now do that through work here. I think that is new to CDP in a lot of ways, I mean we certainly weren't doing that four or five years ago. I think that's how we see we are now, that somebody can come here and use *us*, in such a way as to attempt to achieve various long-term and short-term goals rather than coming in, sitting down and having a cup of coffee or wanting to come in out of the rain until they go off and get their next fix or coming in in a crisis. That's an important use of CDP and one that we steer ourselves to

respond to.

While the street agencies may have developed their practice in this fashion, popular and lay opinion as well as much
other professional practice remains geared to belief in the
attainment of the specialist solution or cure for drug problems. Not surprisingly, where such convictions do not accord
with the beliefs, hopes and, importantly, fears, of drug users
then the way forward is difficult, not least because they may
not come forward but also because when they do the understandings, expectations and rules that they confront can so
easily be seen as a game that has to be played, with obstacles
to negotiate and an unreal (and ultimately often unhelpful)
conclusion at the end. For the street agencies a significant
part of their practice is aimed at breaking through those
'game-playing' skills which are so easily learned and reinforced in the 'treatment and rehabilitation' and 'public opinion'
mingle uneasily but powerfully.

> You've just got to try and break down the fears that
> people have. It is basically fear ... (you) just have to try
> and make people aware that they don't have to play the
> games that they have to play in other places, so if a
> problem should come in you can spend two weeks getting
> to it, but hopefully it can be earlier because you don't
> have to play silly games, or come out with glib things
> they expect are actually acceptable to hear. There are
> other ways of looking at what's going on.(Paul)

Street agency social work may be geared to encouraging
confidence and some optimism about short and long term
plans for individuals, but it also has to be fundamentally
realistic. It has to be straightforward about what clients can
expect of it, and it also has to be clear about what it thinks
of its clients. For example, it is obvious that one should have
no illusions about the motivation of some clients who are in
prison and who suddenly express a desire to join a rehabilitation programme. On the other hand, the development of an
attitude of cynicism on the part of workers is not helpful
either:

> I think our role is to describe what rehabs are around,
> because some people just haven't heard of what's on
> offer for them, and also to be honest about whether we

think they would actually manage to handle them - some people there's no point in them going on to anywhere, they'd be much better doing their prison sentence and coming back out again, but at least there they'd get support from us. So it's (a) to suss out with them what they want to do, (b) to give them addresses 'cos they've got to contact the rehabs themselves, (c) if we both decide that there's just no way are they ever going to get out this time, that they've squeezed through the old system several times before and this time there's just a definite sentence, then to try and be positive about that, even though you can't really be positive about a prison sentence. Well, you *can*, actually, because there's a couple I know that at least they're not being crazy on the streets, I suppose that's a positive move. So, after the rehab issues and perhaps doing a court report, the next part of it is to carry on seeing that individual and writing to that individual while they're inside. Maintaining some kind of contact with them. (Lena)

CDP's clients in prison, on remand, serving sentences and seeking parole, are part of the generally invisible population of people with drug related problems that it works with.

The other major group that it has identified as an important group for the extension of its work is women, although such work has long been a priority at CDP. Women seem to have a low profile in their take-up of drug related services despite the informed opinions of so many in the field that their incidence of drug related problems at least equals that of men. Most services however have a male character and are orientated towards men. For some time CDP workers have been seeking to collaborate with members of other agencies, including the Hungerford and the Blenheim, to establish new facilities and, within existing projects, women-only spaces and times - to be able to accommodate to the special needs of women with drug related problems (for example - space and staff to help with child-care, an atmosphere free of potential violence from males and so on).

Obviously each client group, and each individual within it, will tend to have specific types of problems demanding specific responses. Nonetheless, CDP workers can offer a surprisingly low-key and modest assessment of what they can actually do for and with their clients:

I don't think we change many people's lives ... I mean I
think we do quite a lot of good work, and even on a
middling day, like today, I think we do do something , if
only the fact that we are around and people can come
and go ... But what do we give people? Not a lot! I think
we are a very useful place for people to come to to
actually start working out where they want to go. I don't
think that we could be or should be in a position of
telling people what to do but I think that we have a very
useful function in giving space, and allowing people to
look at the various alternatives open to them.   And
trying to get them to look at the implications of those
choices.   I mean it's one thing to make a choice, it's
another to understand where the choice will lead you. I
think we have an important part to play there. I think
we have an important part in terms of the fact that we
are a stable point, we are always here ... That is,
somebody leaves prison, leaves a rehab, they can always
come back, and we can try and put a spoke in that wheel
of total reinforcement of their own failure, and given
that a lot of the people that we meet are sort of weighed
down with lack of self-respect, very poor self-esteem,
especially if they get picked up by the police or they feel
they have failed because they haven't gone through a
rehab programme, we are in the business of saying, 'no,
you are alright, you're not a total failure. Look, you're
here, let's get back on the road again', and actually
helping people back at that point... (Ronno)

One problem that arises in trying to discharge such a role
over a wide geographical area is that of being stretched too
far. But this can lead to constructive attempts to liaise with
and use other community resources:

I think that we also fill a lot of gaps, which is why I think
we tend to get stretched in too many directions ... I
mean, I don't think that we can possibly do it all
ourselves but I think that we can try to co-ordinate other
community facilities, try and get in unemployment resource centres ... groups, adult literacy schemes, to go
to college, and the whole area around that.

This is a philosophy that requires time, energy and resources
to implement - CDP is at present some way down the road,
but has not fully and consistently put the philosophy into

practice.

Division of labour

CDP is not part of a larger organisation which requires a visible structure of accountability (as in the case of the Hungerford), but nor is it a collective project based on joint-decision making (as is the case with the Blenheim project). Ronno describes the agency's attempts to negotiate a system of decision-making and responsibility that lies between the two models:

> I think it's sort of everybody's responsibility when anything goes wrong. And similarly, I think it's everyone's responsibility when everything goes right, and when things are going well I think that we have the benefit of collective decision making, but somebody to see that the decisions go through. And like, more of the responsibility rests with me. And I think that's fine, I mean that's why I get paid more money ... So, when it's going well, it's going very, very well, but when it's going bad, it's horrid. And that isn't altogether unconnected with how different workers fit into this agency.

With a concern to give individual workers a measure of autonomy to develop and exploit their own skills and approaches, the agency must necessarily emphasise the positive aspects of differences between them, whilst retaining a conception of the agency as a cohesive unit:

> Now we've got to a position where there are four very individual people in the agency with very different ideas and very different styles of working which are often complementary and, I think, probably very healthy for the project, and make a lot of sense ... what I can see happening now is that there is room for my approach and there are clients whom I could no more work with than fly out of the window. I can't work in prisons, I mean, it is a mystery to me how the other two enjoy it. I just can't do it. but that's OK because there are other people who can and enjoy it so that's what's important about CDP ... in what it can offer people because we do come from different points, I mean, there is something to that, if we were all poles apart, we wouldn't be able to function, but within the agency there are so many

> different styles of operation and flexibility. I think
> that's quite important - that balance between what we
> can offer as individual workers to various clients.(Ronno)

Ronno's role, like that of Jane at the Hungerford, has had to
accommodate to the responsibilities and administration, liaison, meetings and reports; and with a serious interest in
education and training about drug use and related problems,
her involvement in the actual social work activities of the
project has declined. She retains a number of clients with
whom she has counselling sessions but the bulk of social work
within the project is carried out by Lena and Paul.

Lena has developed interests in long-term counselling,
building upon skills learned during her nursing career and
taking advantage of the relatively low key and less pressured
atmosphere which CDP enjoys (if compared, for example, to
the Hungerford). Relationships can be built up over time in
such sessions and the value of long-term, in-depth counselling
of this type is recognised by other agencies unable to provide
it themselves and who instead refer clients to CDP. Paul has
retained an interest in the probation and prison services, as
well as an interest in housing issues, representing CDP on the
management committee of South-East London Consortium
Housing Association. Lena also works with clients who are
involved with the probation or prison service in some way and
it should be noted of CDP that as an agency they seem to
have developed their services in the direction of offenders
with drug-related problems as a major rather than incidental
initiative, a point we take up in more detail later.

Stuart is, as he says himself, 'largely cut off from the day
to day work of the agency'. His own tasks he describes as
routine accounts work, servicing the management committee,
the drafting of funding applications, and liaison with Ronno
over them.   There may also be a common role which
administrative staff play in such agencies, that of 'keeping
our feet on the ground a bit more' as a member of the social
work staff described Stuart's role, echoing an observation
made of Linda at the Hungerford. Stuart's points of integration into the rest of the staff team illustrate the ways in
which it tries to achieve its sense of cohesion.

> Being a fairly small staff team, and given the way in
> which we work, I tend to be reasonably involved in at
> least knowing what's going on in the agency. And the

> policy within CDP of having regular staff meetings and
> also the policy of having all the staff attending manage-
> ment committee meetings means that we are all fairly
> involved in what's going on. (Stuart)

There is a sense in which an interest in the division of
labour that exists within an agency like CDP does not give an
adequate picture of the way it works until it is extended to
include that division which exists between the agency workers and their management committee.

It was made evident in interviews with workers from a
wide variety of agencies that relations between staff and
management committees can frequently be strained. Perhaps
this is almost inevitable and certainly not wholly surprising,
yet if points over which difficulties arise can be identified
then some improvement of management-staff relations should be possible with benefits all round. What seems particularly prevalent is the feeling among staff members of various
agencies that their management do not really understand
what the agency does, what goes on 'on the job', and what it
is like to do it. Staff from various non-statutory agencies
who sit on each other's management committees suggest that
they see the same lack of understanding from management
committee colleagues as they feel they receive as staff
members from their own management committees. Ronno,
who sits on the Hungerford's advisory committee feels that
she detects a degree of worry on the part of Turning Point
representatives over any attempts by the Hungerford to
assert a sense of relative autonomy from the parent organisation. There is also the feeling that management committees
generally may misunderstand (or even resent) the way that
the three street agencies have begun to work together.
Oddly, however, the strongest source of unease with management, at least from the point of view of CDP, is not that
they have dictated and confined but rather that they have
done the opposite. They have not managed effectively, but
instead have let CDP staff shape, change and direct agency
policy - at least at the day to day level. Not unnaturally the
coordinator has strong thoughts about the staff-management
relationship:

> I think that one of the main problems that we've got with
> our management committee is that they quite genuinely
> don't understand what's going on. They don't actually

come in and say, 'hello, how's it going?' or 'what's it all about?, and they don't pick up points in social work reports ... I don't think that they really realise how it feels when clients die. Things like that. They just don't understand. I've given this some considerable thought and it's occurred to me that no matter how much they say to us 'what do you want us to give you in terms of support', we're not going to be able to get a satisfactory solution because we don't know what we are asking for. We're not asking for anything tangible, we can't say we want you to help us out and buy a new set of mugs because that's not what it's all about ... They can't understand what we are about - and how can you explain it?

We should stress that such feelings are by no means unique to CDP staff. As our project drew to a close, management and staff at CDP were initiating an internal assessment of their relationships, of the aims, philosophy and priorities of the agency, as well as trying to restructure the way the management committee operates (so as to facilitate more direct, personalised and informed communication). Our own - admittedly speculative - feeling about this issue is that the somewhat 'disengaged' inter-relations between CDP staff and the management committee may have historical roots. As we noted in chapter 2 of this report, the transition from mid-1970s local day centre (a kind of day asylum for the injecting clients of local treatment clinics and for other drug users who subsequently moved onto barbiturates and multi-drug use), to a 1980s advice and counselling service (that made up for a decline in local clientele by broadening its services on an almost regional basis), was particularly difficult for CDP. The original 1970s management seems largely to have abandoned the agency as the original concept became unworkable, and the present loose and uncertain staff-management relations may simply be a reflection of the difficulty of simultaneously defining and consolidating a workable practice consisting of several disparate (though linked) elements, and reconstructing a management system that encourages and supports such diversity whilst fostering some sense of an overall coherence, purpose and identity for the agency.

This difficulty (for the agency) in turn presents further difficulty to us, the authors, in summarising the work of the agency. CDP's work is much more disparate and exploratory than that (to take one example) of the Hungerford; although this does not make it less valuable, it makes it more difficult to capture in print.

A DAY OBSERVED

In this section, we describe a day in the working life of CDP staff, insofar as 'the action' takes place within the premises of the project. The account seems more fragmentary than that of the Hungerford, not only because of the greater diversity of tasks making up the work of CDP (in contrast to Hungerford's staple fare of walk-in clients), but also because observation of CDP's premises fails to capture the reciprocal nature of telephone conversations with other agencies seeking advice or referral for their clients, and completely misses out the agency's work in education and training on other premises and its visits to clients in prison. These considerations, plus an understanding that the CDP works at a less 'frantic' level with clients than does the Hungerford (having a generally less precariously-balanced clientele) and can hence develop a more relaxed or conventional (and often lengthy) style of counselling some of those clients that do visit, should help the reader to absorb the following description.

On a typical day on which the agency was observed by the fieldworker, the day started with a joke - an aspect of CDP which recurred. The agency opens at 10 a.m. This morning, Ronno has arrived at 9.45 to clean and tidy up the agency before visiting American participants in the UK/USA Institute on Drugs and Crime arrive at 11 a.m. Whilst she is still rushing about attending to various bits and pieces some of the visitors arrive early and have to be directed to the Antique Market on the corner of the street for 15 minutes. 'A good start', she mutters ... With staff working overtime in the evenings to see clients or attend weekend meetings or conferences lieu time accrues: today Stuart has the morning off and Lena has taken the morning to see off friends at the airport. When the visitors return at 11 a.m. Paul takes care of the phone calls and day book. He is expecting a client in half an hour or so, but the phone does not ring continuously, and he assures us that as long as there aren't too many calls he can handle the phones while Ronno and the now participating observer talk to the visitors upstairs. Ronno launches into

a survey of drug use problems and policy in the UK, emphasising the perspective of the street agencies and where they
fit into this system. By the time that the visitors leave, Lena
has arrived back from the airport. She has come into the
agency early and could have taken the rest of the morning
off. Calls come through regarding training resources and
speakers, the phone is passed to Ronno. During the rest of the
morning, the phone rings about every five minutes with
enquiries and requests from existing and prospective clients,
worried friends and family and the queries of other social
workers.

Ronno is out most of the afternoon at a management
committee meeting of Consortium, a south London agency
coordinating contacts between various groups and organisations in the non-statutory sector. Lena is seeing a client in
the meeting rooms of a feminist bookstore in Islington, a
venue that is both more convenient and more comfortable for
the woman client. Stuart came into the office and left again
to attend a union meeting and Paul is giving a description of
CDP's services and ideas to two visitors, both student placements, one from a local probation hostel and the other from a
concept house. Despite the larger number of calls, the desk is
manageable even with everyone else occupied or absent. The
day book and appointments book are less detailed than at the
Hungerford and the recording procedure takes up less time.

The general pattern of work at CDP is to concentrate on
working together on the premises in the morning, and to work
more independently in the afternoons (some counselling of
clients on the premises and some clients elsewhere).

One exception to this occurs on Wednesdays, the mornings
of which are designated as a regular visiting time for clients
who want to attend a clinic; there is now a new scheme
worked out between CDP and the consultant at the St. Giles
Clinic, whereby, in order to cut down on the waiting lists at
the clinics, St. Giles will call CDP and let them know if
someone has not turned up for their appointment. CDP can
then send any waiting client along. (The idea might be
popular and useful so long as St. Giles finds it can fit in more
clients. If it can't then some clients will find themselves
travelling long distances for little purpose.) On Wednesday
afternoons the agency closes for a staff meeting, but on
other afternoons regular commitments take certain workers
out of the agency, to help run a drugs and alcohol group

session for the probation service at their local Day Training
Centre and to help run a counselling and discussion group for
women at the premises of another agency - the Blenheim.
Client sessions are held during the afternoon if possible,
although they will be fitted in at almost any time if necessary.

As in most social work agencies, the amount of time
actually spent working with clients seems to suffer as administrative and clerical tasks accumulate and proliferate.
Social workers commonly complain of their backlog of case
reports, personal administrative responsibilities, unanswered
correspondence, etc., and CDP workers are no exception.
For this agency, as well as for others, there is certainly a
case to be made that the overall efficiency of the agency
could be improved if the social work staff had clerical
support that would allow them to spend as much time as
possible working as social workers with clients. As a serious
caveat to this, however, it should be noted that although
clerical and administrative tasks are not necessarily what
social workers should be doing, were they not doing such
things then they might reasonably and constructively seek
some other task to do other than full-time work with clients.
For the fact is, of course, that their work with clients can be
very demanding and the interruption of it by other tasks can
constitute welcome 'natural breaks' in the day to day routine
of the agency. No tool is more useful in creating breaks than
humour. And (as has been noted in a variety of studies of
pressured occupations), humour can play a significant part in
the transmission of information, as well as taking some of the
grimness out of what workers see and experience - as the
following extract from our field work notes suggests:

> The other striking thing about this 'catching up on things'
> period was the joking going on between Ronno and Paul
> for much of the time. Whilst this may cover a whole
> range of things - like who has pinched the paper/City
> Limits - it could also swing into semi-serious enquiry
> about clients or, remaining at the level of humour,
> describe people in really bad states giving sympathetic
> horror descriptions of users ... (participant observation
> fieldwork notes)

Humour, then, is an essential working tool for the staff of
some 'front line' agencies, and carries a variety of functions

ranging from the exploration of complex casework situations, to coping with the feelings that such situations generate.

This afternoon, some of the clients expected do not turn up but others drop by on the off-chance of being able to see somebody without making an appointment.

Some court reports are written and the irony emerges that in preparing them it is those clients who are best known and liked by the agency who seem to come off with the least positive sounding report. The better-known clients receive a fuller report which tends to balance negative points with the positive ones, whereas less well-known clients are more likely to receive the more positive support of a suggestion that they 'deserve a second chance'.

The phones are officially closed at 5.30 and the ansaphone switched on. The detritus of the day is cleared up, files replaced, cups carefully washed up. The health risks of this particular social work job are not mentioned in conventional social work training courses. Workers in the drug field stand a higher chance than most of contracting hepatitis from their clients and there is no programme of immunisation for which the street agency workers are eligible. (There has been dismay and anger over the action of the DHSS on this subject, considering specialist medical staff for immunisation but not workers in the non-statutory sector.) The condition of ill-health in which many of their clients are to be found makes the health risks of the job something which the workers try not to treat lightly, being careful about aspects of hygiene in the agency whilst trying not to offend clients - which can be especially difficult in cases like deciding what to do about dubious gifts of food, etc.

The jokes are fewer by now; sometimes people drift off singly or everyone sits around and discusses anything significant that has come up that day. Sometimes, there may be the occasional client with an evening appointment, or there may be another meeting to go on to or a talk to prepare for the next day (and somehow it's going to have to be finished at home), but generally it's the end of the day some time after 6 p.m. at CDP.

In the next section we turn to more focussed discussions of the three main aspects of CDP's work - working with other agencies and professionals; education and training; and work with clients.

ORGANISATION OF WORK FROM THE OFFICE

Whereas most of the Hungerford's workload walks through the front door, most of CDP's comes to it initially by way of the telephone. Whilst much of this telephone contact is direct client contact, a great deal of it is made up of enquiries from professional and informal carers, and involves the agency in an education and training role (by telephone and/or letter or, in some cases, by out-of-office consultancy and training). Hence the title above - organisation of work *from* the office - is apposite. CDP organises its work in such a way as many users of its services do not attend at its premises.

This being the case, the question of the character of CDP's referral system must be addressed before we can begin to understand its day-to-day practice.

The referral system (as seen by the agency)

All street agencies depend upon and find themselves utilised by networks. Such networks stretch well beyond the locality or even London. As Ronno suggests:

> If somebody 'phoned up from Reigate and said 'you're our nearest street agency', which we are, it's a bit silly for them to be carting people up, so we'll build up some kind of relationship with agencies down there and sort of make suggestions as to how they could be dealing with it.

So it would be wrong to see the street agencies as providing only a local service. Their networks stretch not only geographically but also across the statutory/non-statutory divide, passing clients along in an occasionally direct, sometimes convoluted, chain of referral. Most contacts and referrals probably come from other agencies in the London-wide non-statutory sector, most obviously those others dealing with drug-related problems and those which are involved with alcohol-related problems or housing or health advice. Agencies like Narcotics Anonymous, City Roads and Phoenix House might be the most obvious links in such a referral chain, but through joint work for the Day Training Centre with the Alcohol Counselling Service, and similar joint ventures, the scope for referral sources and resources is increased. Coordinating agencies like the South London Consortium of non-statutory agencies and SCODA also direct attention to

CDP.

In the statutory sector, CDP has surprisingly less to do with their local social services than it does with the probation service. Social services do call CDP for help and advice about solvents and they do make client referrals to the agency, but despite the presence of a representative of Social Services on their management committee the relationship between the two does not seem as close as might be expected. Within the local Housing Department contacts have been made with community housing officers, and the local solvent sniffing problem is at least partly approached by CDP and the housing officers as an issue within the context of wider housing problems. Local schools ask for CDP to give presentations and the local youth service has built up an understanding of what the agency does and how it can be used appropriately, which introduces the agency to a range of young people.

The Home Office Drugs Inspectorate maintains good contact with CDP and an observer attends management committee meetings while relations with several officers in the DHSS are described as good.

The agency seems to have little contact with GPs, finding them generally unhelpful and suspecting that they are wary of CDP because it threatens their professional mystique by their non-medical approach to drugs. But lack of positive contacts does not mean that they view all GPs negatively but, rather, they suggest that a good, interested GP will probably not refer enquiries to another agency but will instead deal with the client themselves, especially if there is social work support attached to the practice.

CDP themselves feel that they have odd relations with the clinics. For a start, they have relatively few clients who are attending the clinics. This is largely because what the clinics prescribe is not what the client wants, or else the clinics do not prescribe the demanded amount. Hence there is little regular working contact between CDP and the clinics and few referrals seem to be made in either direction, although there are of course exceptions. Contact has not always been at such a low ebb. At one time the Maudsley had a social work staff member who joined the CDP management committee. However when she left the post was frozen and this regular point of contact was lost.

Health Education Officers approach CDP for assistance with their training courses and health visitors know of CDP as a resource that they can use when they encounter drug-related problems. These have principally been to do with the use of tranquillizers, though at one time CDP were referred clients when they discovered cases of white working class males smoking heroin (with the common belief that so long as heroin was not injected then it was not addictive). Working with the health visitors, CDP discovered a chain of connections between the men.

Rarely is there any serious contact between the agency and the police but occasional contact with community policing representatives is maintained and CDP clearly finds some favour in their eyes - the agency had received a donation from the Police Box Fund just the previous year.

CDP are involved in some court attendance but their involvement here is principally at the level of writing court reports or letters of recommendation for clients, suggesting for example referral to a DDU. Such letters have no legal standing but are seen as welcome by the courts and are usually used, which of course is a source of pride to CDP. This welcome in court may have to do, they suggest, with the fact that they don't provide social enquiry reports, assuming that social workers otherwise assigned to the case will provide background profiles. Hence their reports are short, and this tends to find some favour with the bench. Their general line of recommendation is usually to suggest some sort of drug-free rehabilitation house as an alternative to prison. Many such clients going before the courts will have had experience of the law before, so CDP does not try to develop services related to legal advice or the provision of legal aid, etc. Where such advice is sought they themselves will turn to the local law centre.

For CDP the probation service is a particularly important area of work. About four years ago, at a time when CDP's resources were not fully committed, the agency was consciously if not programmatically seeking new avenues of work to explore. At the same time, their then limited contact with clients in prison indicated to others that CDP was interested in the drug related problems of offenders. CDP were themselves considering expanding this area of work:

> We put a lot of effort into contacting the prisons and saying 'look, we are willing to come along and see people or to talk to you about any druggies that you might have, and that kind of took off and so other agencies now know that we do that, and the rehabs know it as well.   (For example), if Alpha House went along to visit somebody who had contacted them initially, then they would possibly say, 'look, you're not appropriate for us, maybe you'd like to talk about the different options available', and it actually saves more time if we go in first rather than Alpha go, then Phoenix go, then Suffolk go, then we go because we can actually explore the options.(Ronno)

The interconnecting of agencies which is described here is significant.   Not simply because it demonstrates how agencies in the non-statutory and statutory sectors can, and should, use each other.   It also indicates a maturing of those involved in such relationships and the development of a basis for such cooperation.   In a sense some of the old artificial and unhelpful boundaries are being blurred. It is essential, of course, that given the different roles and aims of different agencies, they should retain their probity and autonomy.   There is some danger in the blurring of boundaries between agencies which must always be borne in mind (Cohen, 1979).   However, if the construction of an inter-linked 'social control continuum' can be avoided, then there is much that is positive about such developments. For example, within the non-statutory sector, it is only in recent years that appreciation of each other's philosophies and a measure of mutual tolerance have permitted the concept houses, non-therapeutic environments and the street agencies to engage in such close and confident cooperative work. With regard to the non-statutory/statutory divide there is much value to be found in the example to other agencies offered by the relationship which has built up between CDP and the probation service and prison authorities.

CDP staff themselves suggest that this might once have been an odd, uncomfortable relationship and one that clients might view sceptically - a point echoed by a probation officer contact of the Hungerford's. However, there are now softer edges to the old 'street versus state' dichotomy. The experience of CDP staff in teaching on in-service training courses, and their interests in provision for offenders and in criminological matters generally, mean that they are by no means blasé about the implications of such developments for the practice of social work with a commitment to the client. However, as with much street agency work, theory is tempered by pragmatism. The present levels of cooperation have developed as a system (however ad hoc) that has a pay-off for the client. And that is the underlying objective. CDP has a commitment to emphasising the preferability of alternatives to custodial, prison sentences, where that is a possibility. In this regard they are also enthusiastic about their training work with Intermediate Treatment workers. In a less than ideal world however, it must be stressed that the apparently exemplary relationship with the probation service is not always wholly amicable. Tensions can arise and compromises have to be made:

> I think you have to be very careful about how you work with probation, because I don't think you can afford to be seen as an arm of the probation service or part of the judicial system. I don't think that's fair on the clients because one of the reasons why they come to us is because we are not part of that system. And it's a matter of a balancing act. Obviously we have to give a certain amount, and then it's down to negotiation and compromises with the probation service, but we tend not to pass on information unless we've got the go-ahead of the client or unless it is very obviously in the best interests of the client. I think for the most part, probation officers, especially if they work with us quite regularly, are aware of that dilemma, and they won't ask us to compromise ourselves over areas of confidentiality.

Nonetheless, any success that the relationship has is based on some certain degree of trust and confidence in the honesty of each agency with regard to the client, even if the understandings of the relationship are sometimes slightly stretched.

They quite often phone up and ask if you've been

seeing somebody because they want to put it in the
report and are actually fighting for the client, but
then sometimes things still get a bit confused because
we say no we haven't or whatever. We won't take
people on any kind of court order because we want
people to come here because they do want to come
here. But what might happen is that we'll make
a recommendation to the court that if they are on
a probation order then we would see them if the
client wanted to ... So I think the relations with
the probation service tend to be very good. I think
they could be better at times but again I think that
comes down to a lack of basic training of the professionals
in the field anyway.

The ways in which CDP works with individual clients
referred informally from the legal system and probation
service, and with clients whose referrals or self-referrals
to CDP come about in other ways, are described (with
examples) at the end of this chapter. Before moving
on to that, however, we pick up the thread of training,
mentioned above. Training may be regarded as a routinised
and more intense form of giving practical advice to professionals
and agencies, and it grew out of the sort of contacts
that we have described above.

The development of the agency's training role

It seems a common criticism in the social work field
that social work education neglects a wide range of issues
and problems that manifest themselves with unanticipated
frequency in the case-loads of practising social workers.
Among such problems are the use and abuse of glue,
tranquillisers, hard drugs, alcohol and so on. The marginalisation
of such problems in much social work training is seen
as a serious problem by street agency staff. Indeed,
at CDP, Ronno suggested that social work students may
feel deviant themselves if they take up non-statutory
placements with agencies working with such problems,
'despite the fact that the work is just as central to social
work and is occasionally a more relevant source of experience'.

Within CDP the educational component of their work is
something that has evolved over several years. Many
agencies in the non-statutory sector have a fairly high

turnover of staff and so the experience and expertise of a worker who has been in the field for some time is an especially valuable resource to be tapped. Most education and training work that CDP is involved in is undertaken by Ronno, partly because of this length of experience and partly because of her own interest in it. This is not something that was ever originally conceived of as part of the service CDP should provide. However its development has been based primarily upon demand and, as Stuart suggested, its importance as part of Ronno's job and CDP's function is now such that were the staff actually to have to outline where CDP's services now take them, then 'training would be regarded as an integral part of the job'.

Like many others in the drug advice field, Ronno is sceptical about primary prevention and feels that there should be more emphasis placed upon secondary prevention. She sees a need for more support and materials for workers who encounter drug users 'off the streets', who see 'signs' of somebody showing a moderate or bad problem and who need an approach which is realistic for secondary prevention. Realism requires a stress on the diversity of drug-using groups and sub-cultures, and the variety of drugs (including alcohol) used in different ways which make up the 'so-called drug problem'. Education and training should, CDP believe, de-mystify both the shock-horror images of drugs and the feelings held by other social workers that they cannot deal with such problems - that it is a job for 'the experts'.

CDP lays at least part of the blame for the persistence of misinformation about drug use and users at the door of the popular media:

> I think the media are responsible for an awful lot. Often negatively. I mean, OK, they can argue that they've got to sell newspapers ... But more responsible reporting would make a lot of sense. And I think things like women's magazines could be used to more effect. Was it *Woman's Realm* that did 'What every caring parent should know?' Things like that make a lot of sense. And that's all to do with attitudes, especially among professionals. I mean, if they could be changed it would alleviate a lot of frustrations in individual clients ... (Ronno)

Lena agrees (though perhaps with rather more optimism):

> I'd like to see a wider ... education of a decent sort,
> none of this 'shock horror' and all that kind of routine
> for people, but reasonable teaching that means that
> you're not cutting off a whole slice of society because
> they're somehow bad and disgusting people. Somehow
> educate your average person to see that; which is
> easier done than we think it is, because you just
> have to re-educate the media a bit more, because
> they're appalling in their attitudes to drug use.
> And for professional workers not to be so hide-bound
> by stereotypes, because they're forgetting that people
> aren't stereotypes. (Lena)

Clearly, CDP staff see adequate and enlightened education
and training about drugs and drug use as confronting
a formidable range of obstacles: from personal prejudices,
through professional structures, to mass-cultural sources
of stereotype reinforcement.

In the following extracts from our interviews, Ronno's
description of CDP's approach to these various issues
is not only an account of how the agency has developed
a flexibility which can discriminate between the needs
of different audiences, but is also illuminating about
the limitations which such education and training must
face. Finally, to take us back into the flow of our survey of
the three street agencies, it illustrates one further aspect of
the complementarity of their services.

> In terms of training and going out and taking part
> in a session on solvents, you are then labelled by
> your audience as being 'the experts'.

> Given that one of our philosophies in life is to demystify
> substance abuse of any kind, it seems a bit silly to
> further mythologise what we're doing simply because
> we're going out and tutoring it, so I think that's what we
> have to be a bit careful about ... We could do a lot more
> if we had more staff in that we can't always do the
> things that we are asked to do, we quite often have to
> turn people away or put them in touch with other people
> or whatever. If somebody phoned up and said 'can you
> advise me how to deal with the client?' or 'I want to
> refer this client to you', we would deal with that, but

offer as an optional extra coming along and giving them (the staff) a session on it. Or people might phone up and simply say 'will you come and tell us what to do over solvent users?' or 'on drug use,' or 'how to cope with drug takers in our youth club' or whatever. Or it could be taking part in a more specific course which would be arranged and advertised, which I think is a very different thing. The kind of work that you would do (there) would be very different.

On methods and content of in-service training sessions:

We try and get people to challenge their own attitudes and the attitudes of society which give rise to all the myths and misinformation that is around and put in their place actual factual information. And then away from that, move on to actually working with drug users; I mean how to plan work and break it up into facets. And then to actually look at what skills they've got and work with that; so it's an enabling process. I mean, I can't see the point of just going out and saying, 'This is heroin, this is what heroin does', etc., because I don't think that that in the end is particularly helpful. I think we should be in the business of getting them to see their drug users as people with a series of problems and also to see the fact that they have got the tools to cope with the problem, more often than not, (although) there are some cases where they obviously can't cope with it.

CDP tries to introduce an affective dimension to in-service training, acknowledging staff members' anxieties about their clients' drug use, and relating these feelings back to existing understandings about more familiar forms of recreational drug use:

I try not to just go and talk about solvent abuse, because I think it has to be seen in context. Just the fact that a lot of kids who sniff solvents feel a bit like the worker does when they've had a drink is quite an important thing to acknowledge ... and to look at why these workers are horrified and terrified and frightened and full of the hopelessness, helplessness syndrome because they've got a using group among their youth club members or whatever, and to actually identify their fears and where the problem actually lies I think is quite important and that is immediately moving away from the specific substance oriented approach ...

Finally, in a move that other 'specialist' drug and alcohol agencies with some involvement in training would do well to emulate, CDP seem to have broken with self-centredness:

> We don't think that there is a lot to be gained from going out and talking about the work of CDP. I mean there might be an element of that, in that people need to know what other facilities are around, but the difficulties you experience as a worker working in a youth club, or residential home, or social services or probation would be very, very different from the difficulties experienced among the CDP staff, even if you were dealing with the same client, because you've got different pressures, different responsibilities, a different function. And I think that that has to be clearly understood when you enter into the training relationship. I mean, obviously, there are similarities, and it is useful to share the experience we might have here, but I think just to go out and say, 'This is what CDP does', isn't necessarily helpful for someone ...

In the long term, the contribution to training of generic agencies, professionals and volunteers, and the demystification of the role of 'specialist', may be the most enduring contribution that can be made by the street agencies.

Meanwhile, however, whilst some training is being done, referrals are still coming in, and clients are seeking help.

WORK WITH CLIENTS

Acknowledgement of the individual

The street agencies always emphasise that they have no typical client, rather that they have a wide-ranging client group with a wide range of problems, which, they suggest, have to be responded to in particular and individualised ways:

> I think perhaps confusions come along because it

is such a wide-ranging client group and, although you might have a particular interest with working with one of those groups, you've got to be able to swiftly change your way of looking at the world to cope with another group or another client. I think that's something that's sometimes forgotten, that we haven't got just one or two client groups but a great range of them and you have to go from one to another. (Ronno)

Lena's intense and highly empathetic approach to counselling work with clients most clearly illustrates the nature of the level at which she, and to some extent, all CDP workers, see each client case as different and individual:

A lot of the time we're talking about reasons why you take drugs rather than the drugs themselves, obviously. It's so varied isn't it? Each one's an individual, so you can't really generalise about it, obviously you have to at times. So many people are just lonely. They just want the things that we all have. You know what I mean, they want a 'normal' life which is having somewhere nice to live that they want to live, some kind of self-respect, some kind of relationship with people that is not geared round either the whole drug circuit, or the worker relationship - just ordinary reasonable things like friends and lovers that they can trust and be with. And the trouble being that I never know whether they'll ever find that, because they've been through so much before and they'll never be able to trust people really, and no wonder. (Lena)

'Categories' of problems related to individuals' circumstances

The quite individualistic orientation that characterises much of CDP's approach to understanding and responding to drug-related problems stems in part (we suggest) from the earlier history of the agency (described in chapter 2). But it is also clear that, currently, the agency approaches its clients as individuals falling into broad categories of problems. The most frequently recurring 'working' categories would seem to be: housing; employment; relations between the sexes (power, violence); and legal/police

difficulties. As we have observed earlier, the actual
problem of drug use may accompany these related problems
as a causal factor or as a tangential and peripheral issue.
But, most significantly, what is happening in terms of
the work of CDP is that such problems are being presented
to the agency as and through 'drug problems'. The appended
label of 'drugs' gives clients a legitimate 'ticket' to use
the agency as a place to talk about drugs *and about other
things*. It is unlikely that CDP could actually be a solely
'drugs problem' focussed agency, even if it wanted to
be.

The nature and range of presenting problems coming
to the notice of CDP staff members prompts them to
develop ad hoc theories attempting to link their repeated
emphasis on the unique and generalised working concepts of
'types' of problems and of the cultures surrounding drug use.
Stuart, for example, suggests that the problems which CDP's
clients face have a complex relationship with wider developments in society.

> Well, I think it's very significant that drug use has
> risen a lot in recent years at the same time that
> unemployment has risen drastically, and I think,
> certainly as far as a lot of our clients go, we look
> upon it as a very serious problem. I mean we've
> got a lot of clients who are unemployed, and whilst
> it is obviously a very complex issue to ascertain the
> relationship between drug use and unemployment,
> I think a lot of informed opinion would confirm that
> rising drug use is a result of underlying problems
> of society that are on the increase, and as well as
> unemployment, I think bad housing or lack of any
> sort of housing is also a major problem for our clients
> and for drug users generally.

As in the nineteenth century trinity of idle hands,
drink and crime, so in the twentieth century unemployment,
drugs and crime are linked in the minds of philanthropic
and helping agencies:

> We are certainly aware that a lot of our clients
> are involved in crime. A lot of them have got criminal
> records, mainly for petty crime offences and as
> you know we have a lot of drug-dependent offenders

... either in prison or who have been in prison at some stage in the past. I don't think we've actually got any figures that give a correlation between rising drug use and rising crime statistics, but I think (some research) organisations would say that a lot of the recent increase in crime is being associated with the rise in unemployment and if our clients are anything to go by the issues of drug use, petty crime, unemployment and bad housing are all things that many people are involved in at the same time. (Stuart)

CDP staff share the more general impression that there is probably some correlation to be found between crime and long-term unemployment, particularly at a point of intersection between the quasi-legal forms of dealing (in stolen goods, offering various services 'off the books' etc) that characterise the informal economy in which the unemployed may become involved, and more clearly recognisable criminal activities. They further suggest that such shifting boundaries are also reflected in changes in style of drug use.

I think gut reaction tells most people that there has to be some kind of correlation (between crime and) long-term unemployment ... the level of black economy (involvement is) increasing through to other kinds of crime.

What I think is disturbing is the lack of a culture around drug use ... Whereas in the '60s there was a stability in use, it grew out of a fairly stable population, gradually grew, and then exploded into the cultural thing - but there were boundaries, parameters, they sort of put their own boundaries on it. Drug use now seems to be carrying on in a fairly vacuum-like way. Various groups identify with certain drugs, but it seems very much that people are trying because it's available and the whole thing is (based on) whatever is available. Quite a few people phone up here and say 'I've been taking these black pills, what are they?' That sort of lack of information, lack of knowledge of what people are doing to themselves.(Paul)

The 'chaotic' poly-drug patterns of drug use (if that is the right description) of many users that CDP comes across make it difficult to categorise clients by drug used. The principal discriminating feature, especially given the predominance of white, male clients, is age.

> We are now seeing a younger age group. They come, I think, in a category of people who are young in age and also reasonably young in their drug use who are slotted quite quickly into heroin and things. Now it strikes me that a lot of the older people we see were also using these substances when they were 15 or 16 but they didn't seem to be coming forward, or so it would seem. (Ronno)

One disturbing trend which CDP workers observe is that the same young age range of between 15 to 19 includes both solvent sniffers and heroin users:

> There is a lot of solvent abuse over the road in that estate there but we still haven't formed a coherent picture, but it's beginning to form, and I think it's beginning because they are finding out who we are and if we are OK and I think we're going to lose that a bit when we move. (They are in their) mid teens. It's quite unusual for us, I mean it's only in the past six months that we've been getting that age group in. I mean obviously we'd have the occasional solvent user of that age, but now you get more heroin use, fifteen to nineteen year olds. Which is really unusual for us ... (Ronno)

Ronno relates the use of solvents by young people to wider social considerations such as the boredom of school or unemployment, and the simple fact that for young people with few resources it is a cheap form of intoxication:

> A lot of kids are getting involved in solvent abuse or whatever, because they are bored. I mean they are just *bored*. And that's quite reasonable ... I suppose where we see it most, it's in terms of solvents, because that's cheapest ... it seems that in some areas some kids don't make such an early transition from solvents to alcohol because they haven't got any money coming in. So there's that, I mean, sheer boredom. I think

a lot of commentators assume that because kids, young people, and older people are involved in that kind of thing, it's because they're using a drug to cope with some deep emotional, domestic, whatever, underlying problem - but it's to cope with the fact that you've got nothing to do. (Ronno)

The next age group which CDP identifies is distinguishable partly by virtue of being over their teens and partly because they are distinct from the older 'ageing hippy' clients with which CDP has generally been familiar.

Then we have the next age group which I suppose is the 20s, who are not the 'ageing hippy' group or not the people that have been around for years, but they've still gone through the various chaotic forms of behaviour. And for whom Crisis Intervention is often the order of the day. When I say Crisis Intervention, I don't mean that social work technique that gets hold of people in a crisis and uses it as a turning point in their lives. I mean that they are going through just plain and simple crisis ... In fact, we don't have that many of those, I think that the Hungerford certainly, and the Blenheim probably, have more of that group than we do and that's a lot to do with the fact that people don't come down to the bright lights of Camberwell. (Ronno)

Unpredictability of patterns of drug use among clients is compounded by the likelihood that for some groups poly-drug use may become a matter of preference posited upon, and reinforcing, a 'chaotic' life-style. For other groups, however, across age ranges, particular drugs of choice are evident. Among the age groups around the late teens and early twenties that CDP is now seeing, the principal drugs of choice seem to be opioids.

One of the interesting things, certainly 18 months ago - it was unusual to get more than half a dozen cases of opioid dependence, and it used to be more poly-based or getting-hold-of-whatever-they-could-based. But that's definitely changed, head over heels, a lot more heroin, diconal, mainly those two, of varying quality. (Ronno)

Occasionally the agency comes across a particularly unexpected and unusual group of serious drug users.   Ronno
describes an example:

> There was quite an outbreak of heroin smoking amongst
> white,   alcohol-orientated   or   unemployed   working
> class men,   which is   quite   an   unusual   group   to be
> using heroin.   They usually sort of have twenty pints
> down the pub.   And within a few weeks we had quite
> a number, I mean about half a dozen, which is quite
> a lot from one small area, from Peckham, who were
> different from the old-time users in Peckham who
> we would know, they've always been there, a very
> very different group, very different ethos and attitude
> towards the drug-taking.

> And that sort of thing has happened quite a few
> times ... We suspected that there were pockets of
> drugs users here and there and all over around the
> Camberwell area, and some of them we could pinpoint
> given that our old-time clients are there but there
> are others now who are coming in who have perhaps
> only been using for a year, 18 months, two years,
> and a lot of smoking and snorting of heroin and a
> much younger age group on the estates.   Camberwell,
> as you've probably noticed by now, is one great morass
> of estates and it's a horrible place - and we are beginning
> to build up a better picture (about the new patterns
> of drug use there).

Once again the visibility of old and new drug using
groups tends to be restricted predominantly to males.
Among the CDP client group of offenders with drug-related
problems, this relative invisibility of female drug problems
is even more pronounced; referrals from Holloway Prison,
with whom there have been hopes of a close relationship,
have been infrequent.

Overall,   then,   CDP's   direct   work   with   drug-using
clients   includes   telephone   advice   work   with   people   in
a   wide   variety   of   situations,   people   whose   drug use   is
related to (but may be secondary to) problems with money,
housing, loneliness, relationships, violence, the law, unpleasant
consequences of living as a drug user, the legal system,
and   simple   boredom.   The   two   case   studies   that   now

follow can, obviously, illustrate only some of these aspects of the agency's work with such a diversity of clients and problems.

TWO CLIENT CASE STUDIES (AS SEEN BY THE CLIENTS)

Peter - an example of long-term but episodic contact

Peter is a young man in his late twenties. He had come to hear of CDP through another friend with a drug problem.

> At the time, as well as all the problems I have with the drug thing, it was a particular chronic health problem, you know, liver, lung infections and things that I got, and I was absolutely washed out, and wanted to talk specifically about the drug and the health problem and as well as, you know, what could I do, 'cost I didn't really know what to do. So I heard of them through a friend, another drug dependent junkie ...

> It was someone who lived in the same area, you know, a drug connection, people you visit to get drugs and get stoned with and all that type of thing, living in a community, living in Brixton at the time, where I've always lived, the usual thing, you get talking to them and they'd tell me about their difficulties, and about having been along to see somebody (at CDP) - I can't remember his name - it was a guy that was there before Ronno - tall, I think he had an American accent, a bit of a stutter: Ira! That would be about 1980.

Peter felt that CDP had not been particularly well-known in the late 1970s because, certainly among people that he had known, drug use had not really been problematic for them.

> I had been strung out I suppose since '75, '76. I was flirting with junk or opiates for about a year, 18 months, and just getting stoned, and, you know, it was fun, enjoyable and all that sort of thing. And then I got very strung out. It started to get very serious (and then), as they came - different problems that arise from having a drug problem - then the conversation turned to, you know, someone

that may have been of assistance or helped and thus
CDP came up in conversation. So I only began to
find out about an agency existing when, I suppose,
the going began to get very rough with the problem
itself. And that's when they looked familiar to me
and I heard a bit more from people in conversation,
about the problems they had, the help they'd got.

Peter approached CDP through this informal chain
of referral then, rather than through a GP, social services
or a clinic.

My first dealings with CDP, was the whole thing
overwhelmed me, very poor health, couldn't bear
any more, and I wanted very much to do something
about it, and we discussed many different possibilities,
and tried to attempt to see which one suited me
best, which was most appropriate to my needs, coming
off completely, and removing myself from my drugs
social circle, and environment .... an 18 month commitment
thing, one of the houses up at Lewisham or somewhere
- Phoenix House, yes, it was Phoenix House ... At
the time, my utter sort of hate of the whole thing
and not (being) able to help myself was very extreme
... I thought, because of my extreme circumstances,
that I was experiencing, I thought an extreme measure
was needed, and so, working with them ... (we chose)
Phoenix, and then I went along to Phoenix, and that
didn't work. Well, the first day I left.

Peter's reaction to his split from Phoenix House followed
a familiar pattern which the street agencies explicitly
try to break through. He felt that he had let himself
down and also the agency and hence lost contact with
CDP for some time.

I was completely disillusioned with everything; myself,
what I'd got myself into, the drug experience, and
trying to sort ways out, and I felt completely incapable
of helping myself. I felt that somehow the agencies,
the people that were trying to help me, existed for
other people, not me. People that were stronger
than me. People that were more capable than me.
And that wasn't because they'd given me that impression,

that was more my own inability to feel I could do anything about this massive problem and the massive effect it had in all the different areas of my life. (After Phoenix House) I stayed away from (CDP), I didn't try to help myself. I thought this is it, I'm stuck with this problem. I can't do anything about it. I won't go back. So I never came back again and I carried on and I got even more strung out and then I added barbs to that, and then coke, and ... the opiate problem, so I went away again and completely left the counselling with CDP.

Despite the failure of the referral to Phoenix House and Peter's feeling that he could not return to the project afterwards, he had benefited from and taken seriously the agency's advice about how to check up on his health problems. He was particularly worried about hepatitis, having already had it three times in 18 months and knowing several people who had contracted it recently. CDP encouraged him to have a liver function test at St. Thomas's hospital, which overcame the immediate worry in Peter's mind. He re-established contact with CDP in the same way as before, through the same friend.

A long period passed before returning to CDP and in that time when I hadn't been with them, I had attempted to come off hundreds of times on my own, and every time I'd do it, it's *next* time I'll manage it - I'll go to the country and that didn't work - I'll go to my parents' house and that doesn't work, changing residence, circumstances, degrees of drugs, how much, and all these different techniques that would this time work somehow, and never got to grips with it. The same person who was still a junkie and I, we were keeping company, as per normal, and the continual recurrent problems hadn't been dealt with and, as per normal, they had been brushed aside for a short period until they'd overwhelm again. Until they couldn't be ignored any longer. Then they would return, and again through my friend, these problems again got overwhelming, and tied in sort of my own personal ones, which were again out of control ... And again in talking, CDP had come up, and I was very bad, desperate, was very unwell, and needed, I couldn't see anything clearly, desperately needed to talk to people, away from my family and my immediate friends ... (because) one of the major reasons I had to begin to do something about it was that they could no longer take it, and all my friends, my parents, had collapsed, and everyone around me, and people didn't begin to care any more, because they'd heard it all before and then I realised the effect I was having on them was dramatic, and I needed to talk to people outside of that immediate friends circle, relationships and family.

This time Peter felt that the time to get something useful out of CDP was right. He felt himself to have changed, with a 'transformation of attitudes about drugs, life, everything'. As he puts it, he felt it was a 'make or break time'. He appreciated their approach which enabled him to decide on first steps and then encouraged him to take his thinking a little further along to the next step.

It was like they were in the sideline, prepared to then back me up, say, 'let's look a little bit further and see where that will take you' ... And if what I was saying was a load of rubbish and wasn't really going to lead to very much, then they would say (so) ... and would weigh up the different pros and cons of different ways and methods of overcoming the massive drug problem.

Peter suggests that there were then two stages leading him from how he felt at this point to how he feels now. The first stage began with CDP encouraging him to register with the Drug Dependency Unit at St. Thomas's hospital 'as a way of stabilising my life and the problem', and coming into CDP for sessions every two weeks. The visits to CDP could be more frequent whenever Peter felt himself 'emotionally or physically disturbed'. Peter had a painful time coming off, reacting unpleasantly to the withdrawal of the various drugs he had been using and to his maintenance on methadone linctus. The fortnightly, or more frequent, visits to CDP provided him with a timetable by which he could measure out his progress in sympathetic discussion, without the fear of the recrimination he had previously experienced with family and friends. However, despite coping with the lengthy withdrawal and finding support from CDP, Peter had not realised how difficult he would find it to cope with being permanently drug-free. For Peter there were more problems than those solved simply by the clinics' goal of withdrawing him from drugs.

> I really came off everything. It was all a very very painful year ... It was really about 18 months ... and after a certain period I went and started again because nobody ... I didn't know just how long it would take, of continued effort on one's own part to put the whole experience behind you. I thought that somehow you'd go three months and then you'd arrive at three months, and the physical dependency would have passed, and obviously, you would be detoxified and all the different drugs you'd been dependent on would no longer be necessary physically. I didn't realise the dramatic effect it had on my personality and all other aspects of my life. The fact that I couldn't appear to do the simplest thing like go to a telephone box on my own. I didn't know how to function in the world anymore. On my own, I couldn't do things, get tickets, ask people the way, the simplest of things I couldn't do. Apart from having no confidence, I felt like a baby, I did not know how to function in the normal world. It might sound crazy ... I suppose I've found it takes years, two years, and more, I'd say. Two years you can begin to feel a little bit back to what people think as normal ordinary self. (Anyway, I) started up in a minor way again, utterly desperate, very very disappointed in myself and immediately came back to CDP and (was) directed back to the drug dependency unit at St. Thomas's and then back in the process of weaning myself down off of methadone to the very minimum amount which is very very different - I feel as if I don't take any drugs now. You know, it's a private thing.

Peter now feels that his minimal methadone dose helps him stabilise his life, put his drug-use into perspective and enable him to get on with doing ordinary things in

life like making sure he cooks meals at regular intervals,
gets up in the morning to get to appointments and so
on.   Importantly he feels that he has re-orientated his
personal and social life. He tells nobody about his maintenance
prescription, has two or three close friends and nothing
to do with anyone in his old drug world:

> My entire attitude, life, dramatically changed regarding
> drugs ... it's nothing compared to what it was before.
> I lived and breathed it.   It was a philosophy, put
> into practice like a religion, and it is a religion,
> addiction, you know, is a religion.   A way of life
> that needs a sort of change, have your philosophy
> changed, from within you again, in as dramatic manner
> as you were converted, so to speak, to the drug way.

Armed with this new philosophy, Peter is now weaning
himself down again according to a timetable worked
out with the help of CDP.   Within this stage of minimal
use he hopes to be able to find some kind of employment
before moving onto total withdrawl.   Peter has found
that CDP's approach to him and his problems suited the
difficulties that he was having in trying to order his life
and priorities:

> The one thing that immediately struck me that I
> liked, was that they allowed me to find what my
> ultimate objective is, and then work with me, as
> encouraging as possible, and that's great. Particularly,
> that's one of the things that I liked very much and
> I've not found there's been anything I've disliked.

Peter doesn't feel that CDP would be able to help
everybody get to the point of withdrawal.   As he says,
he knows how hard it can be, and some people just don't
want to come off.   But even they get to a point where
their health or financial problems mean that the availability
of assistance and support can make a great deal of difference
in how they cope with those problems.
Peter is clear and unequivocal about the help that
he has had from CDP and the clinic and, perceptively,
he sees that there are understandable reasons for the
differences in approach:

> The help I've gained has been a hundred times better
> than the drug dependent unit who are, I've found

in my experience, more interested in maintaining the practical side of your drug problem and can only give you two minutes for two one-liners regarding the state of your life. And they have no time, and they are more interested in just, well, you're on 50 mls or you're on 7 amps and we'll leave it at that, and that's it. Because they have their very real reasons why they are like that. Probably it's because there are 25 people outside the door who are very very anxious to get in and have the same five minutes, so I've not had half as much opportunity to gain support from the drugs dependent unit as I have from CDP ...

For this long-term user, then, the primary significance of CDP has been as a source of practical (health) advice and of emotional exploration and support. The agency is available and ready to put in as much time and effort as the client, but exacts no punishments for lapses and lack of progress, preferring to seize positive opportunities as they occur - even if this is extremely seldom.

Angela - feminist community care in action

Angela had been referred to CDP by her new doctor when she moved from the South coast to Brixton.

I went to my doctor. I just signed on a new doctor's thing in Brixton and they told me (about CDP) - he didn't quite know what to do because he couldn't prescribe me what I asked for and didn't quite know what to do about it either but he thought that there was some help that I needed. So what he did was to contact - because he was only doing a four month stint at various doctors' practices - so he contacted the social worker at Brixton and she suggested CDP. So he - I'm not sure whether he made the appointment or got me to make the appointment. (That) must have been about five months ago ... it seems to me that this doctor - a very very good doctor but unfortunately he's moving on - is one of very few (who will use non-statutory services), and he's sort of open to - well he doesn't consider every drug addict that turns up, or anybody that goes there with a drug problem, is a waste of time - he's got an open mind. I think he's rare, very rare. But obviously the social worker that deals with the Brixton area, I don't know how large an area, she immediately suggested CDP. And that was her only suggestion as well. And he, in fact, the doctor, after I'd made my first appointment and came here, Lena told me that, in fact, he'd made an appointment and he came along to check it out. And so, he's an unusual doctor.

Before moving to Brixton, Angela had been living in Brighton and, despite her familiarity with the post-1960s remnants of the counter-culture which had produced some drug advice and counselling agencies on the south coast, by the late 1970s and early 1980s she knew of no such service anywhere in the area. The only help available was the treatment orientation of the local clinic, with no back-up social work support. Angela is a mother with a teenage and a younger daughter and a sensitive response from the clinic might have included the organisation of some sort of social work support. This, however, was not her experience:

> I was with the clinic. I was registered on methadone ... But I think that's all - the only thing offered there. And most of the people that go there - when I first went there I was using heroin and stuff as well as amphetamines - so I was given methadone. But they don't cope with any other problems. They don't consider anything other than heroin and barbiturates I suppose, to be a problem ... the suggestion they had for me in Brighton was the consultant - I think the top man there suggested I got a private doctor and another one suggested - not suggested - but told me he was going to enforce a section on me.

Angela did not know anybody else who was using CDP when she came to it. Not surprisingly, she was uncertain about what to expect.

> I met Lena straight away and she sort of sees - knows me - I see her regularly. Although I know the other ones as well. And I can remember being incredibly nervous, thinking that it was going to be yet another sort of, you know, 'we don't deal with people with your problem', and

instead, I found, although Lena said it was my 'amphetamine problem', that in fact it's not generally considered
a 'problem'...

I also wanted at that time, I wanted therapy, of a sort.
Because I'd previously had three years psychotherapy in
Brighton and at that time I thought it was - it had been
of great benefit to me - and my husband ... and it was
just an incredible relief actually to be able to just talk to
someone who wasn't sitting in judgement.

I was still very wary. I had trusted two doctors
previously in Brighton in the past, only six months before
I registered with the doctor in Brixton, and they had
come across as very, very sympathetic, but in fact it
turned out that they were far from being sympathetic
and just getting as much information out of me as
possible and then turning round and saying 'hospital'
without any consideration for me or my domestic affairs
at all.

In contrast, Angela found that she could build upon a
relationship of trust and realism in her sessions at CDP, and
that discussion could be usefully broadened out beyond the
treatment-orientated focus on her drug use alone.

For the first four occasions that I came here they were
very much concerned with (my prescription) ... the
doctor had finally written a letter for the clinic saying
that he thought that I should be given a maintenance
prescription and so they concentrated very hard at first
to try and get that but certainly after about the first
month and a half, when I came once or possibly twice a
week, the emphasis was off that and far more onto what
I was, you know, all the problems I'd got at home, so the
whole emphasis was taken off, especially now that I have
got a prescription, you know... I don't want to spend the
times I come here to talk about drugs, discussing other
problems, things that I want to do, so they sort of try to
... get me to write down, in order of priorities, the things
that I am interested in and want to do, and then they
work on those.

The way in which Angela's attention was directed away
from a focus on her drug use has been a very positive

diversion, not just in a psychological but also a social sense:

> For the last three years I've been pretty untogether. I
> more or less have been a hermit - I didn't leave the flat -
> and that was another important thing, it (visiting CDP)
> was the only time I ever left the flat and the only people
> I ever saw. If anyone came round to the flat, which was
> rare, I'd disappear ... and so I had no contact with
> anybody at all. I made no contact which is, you know,
> really horrific ... The doctor had seen in fact that I was
> in a far worse state than I thought I was and he got me
> to a point where I broke down ... and so actually getting
> here although, yes, it was difficult initially I suppose, it
> was also a relief, the fact that I was able to make
> contact with people and talk - I mean it's almost like a
> revelation which seems ridiculous really.

Angela's sense of self-worth was virtually negligible by the
time that she came to CDP. She had tried to stabilise her
life and drug use but somehow kept finding herself breaking
away, visiting contacts on the south coast and scoring drugs.
She felt, she says, 'completely worthless and useless', particularly in relation to her children. CDP's approach to
Angela and her problems clearly had to be sensitive but nonetheless realistic:

> I was in the wrong place at the wrong time, and they let
> me know that ... it was as though they sort of didn't
> minimise in any way the problems I felt, but let me know
> that I wasn't seeing them in perspective and that there
> was a lot more to me than what I'd thought. I see Lena,
> certainly, as far more of a friend. I mean, for me, it
> isn't *having* to go to Camberwell, or any of the things
> that I used to (feel about) drug clinics - all the 'Christ,
> do I look alright?. It's nothing of that, it's just com-
> pletely relaxed.

> I've come along here and I've ... rushed in the door in
> hysterics and tears - it doesn't matter, it's just being
> able to come and see people, and in fact Lena has, she's
> very perceptive, and she won't take any bullshit from
> me, none at all ... at first she didn't, but gradually now
> she knows ... my strengths and weaknesses I suppose -
> she knows where she can push me and where she can't.
> She won't let me do what I usually do which is create a
> diversion from the subject.

> Honesty is something - to be able to be honest and know
> that it's not going to be used against you ... to be able to
> go to a doctor for instance and say 'look, I have a
> problem and I need help', and there are all sorts of
> unrelated problems too. It isn't something that can be
> done normally. Because they take one step back to look
> at you and think, 'right, children in care, mother in
> hospital' and that really is the general attitude. And of
> course they encourage you to talk and be as honest as
> possible and all the time they have no intention of acting
> on your honesty in any way. And honesty has always
> been the most important thing for me. It's essential to
> aim for honesty in a relationship. And it's lacking in my
> life quite a lot and so I found any time that I was
> criticised by anyone here, it's constructive criticism.
> And so the honesty is something I welcomed.

Angela had only recently begun to consider the wider role
of CDP and so was unable to give an account of her
impressions of it other than in terms of her own relationship
with workers there. She had no idea how other clients might
have come to use CDP initially, assuming that like her they
would have been referred by GPs, 'though when I think about
it, I know that wouldn't be the case.

This particular client has obviously benefited greatly from
CDP's sensitivity to the whole situation of the person, and
she has nothing but praise for the agency. Whilst the long-
term outcome has yet to be consolidated in a positive way
(and whilst shortage of the various resources that Angela
needs to make 'stabilisation' a reality continues to militate
against a positive outcome), we can fairly characterise the
medium-term situation as a successful example of 'community care' and encouragement of self-help.

It is the belief of CDP staff and the impression of
the present authors that the staff's feminism is an integral
feature of this work. This illustrates a broader point
about social work and other forms of health and welfare
practice - that such practice cannot be reduced to a
set of technical casework skills, but is always enlivened
and directed by some broader 'philosophy'.

5 The Blenheim Project in the early 1980s

LOCATION AND PREMISES

As if all reaching the same stage of development at the same time, all three street agencies sought new premises during the period of our study. Of the three, however, only the Blenheim actually made a move in 1983; not a great distance, in fact only across the street, but in terms of the condition of the premises, certainly a great difference.

They are still at the hub of what remains of the West London (i.e. Portobello Road, Latimer Road, Ladbroke Grove) counter-culture scene and of the newer, greyer and nihilistic post-punk drugs scene that followed ten years later. However, their move from the crumbling block that they shared with other community agencies in Acklam Road to the new, concrete warren beneath the Westway seems to point to more significant changes. As an area known for its squatting communities, identified with a post-1960s bohemia of music, alternative arts, mixed cultures and a handy proximity to central London's West End, the Blenheim Project's North Kensington location had always been, and remains to a lesser extent, an attractive part of the city for young people. But the levelling of the squatting communities around Latimer Road and adjacent areas, the gentrification of housing and local shopping facilities, and the closure of many of the old alternative community agencies, has changed the locality - both physically and culturally. The Blenheim Project today is almost a new project in new premises in a new area. Indeed, what follows is very much an account of an agency during a period of transition.

As the potted history in chapter 2 indicates, the Blenheim has moved premises a number of times in the past, though always within the same neighbourhood. Its home at the start of our fieldwork was at 3 Acklam Road. Here it had the occupancy of a large sitting room/office, reception area, a small kitchen (occasionally turned over to intimate counselling sessions), a dusty room upstairs (used for counselling and the storage of old files) and, finally, the use of a toilet in which the light bulb never seemed to work. The heart of the project, however, lay in the orderly confusion of the sitting room/office. It seems best described in this way because the easy chairs, the old cast-iron fire place, the posters, carpet, the endless cups of coffee gave it a welcoming 'sitting room' feel for visitors to the project. At the same time as some staff tried to initiate or control conversations with clients in this atmosphere, others continued with ordinary office work - using the desks, filing cabinets, typewriters, phones and so on that also had to be accommodated in the room.

The project now occupies a large unit beneath the Westway in Thorpe Close, between Portobello Road and Ladbroke Grove. Outside the large windows, the Metropolitan line trains run above ground, monotonously drowning conversation when the weather demands that the windows be open. It takes some time for the visitor to realise that the constant 'swish-swish' sounds are from the traffic over-head, literally running over the ceiling. But these are really secondary impressions. What is really striking about the new premises of the project is the sense of space. It is light, open-plan and uncluttered. There is desk space for all the workers, new phones dotted around, and a wooden and glass dividing wall between the office end and a more casual room furnished with easy chairs where meetings can take place with visitors, the management committee and so on. Two small rooms have been constructed at one side of the office end to accommodate the more personal and intimate counselling sessions.

The old Acklam Road premises both shaped and reflected part of the nature of the Blenheim project; it will be interesting to see how the new premises look in a year or so. Ruth Hood knew the Blenheim Project as a staff member in the late 1970s and, as a member of its Management Committee today, she suggests a similar range of factors will be affecting its development in the future:

> The whole tone of the neighbourhood has changed. The squats that used to exist aren't there any more, several of the cafes that used to be shelter and warmth and gathering places don't exist any more. And all those new Carnaby Street type shops change the culture very much. I can't say how that changes the everyday sort of work - I'm sure it must have quite a big impact. And, of course, the project has changed premises, to more up-market premises as well, and I'm sure over the next six months or so, or year, that will have a big impact. (Ruth)

The agency is, in some respects, simply catching up with changes to which many of its local clients have already had to adjust (whether this involves upward or downward mobility on their part). Moving into new premises is therefore an opportunity to facilitate agency changes already in hand. However, not all these changes are directly tied to the agency's role vis-á-vis the immediate locality, since it has for some time been partially orientated to a much broader area of operations (as has the Community Drug Project (CDP) and, to a lesser extent, the Hungerford). As one Blenheim worker observed:

> I suppose that, in terms of locality, the locality of the Blenheim has become less important, in the sense that we are very much less centred on North Kensington as an area and what that means is, in fact, that if we are to do our job properly that gives us a much greater range of services that we need to be in contact with. Because it's not just the local probation office, say, it's the probation offices dotted all around West London.(Steve)

More emphatically and more broadly, Gwenda, at the time the newest Blenheim social worker, sees them offering a service on a national scale:

> I would say really that my work is certainly not particularly local. I mean, a lot of our work is literally national. I mean publications and so on, we send to Scotland, Wales, everywhere and I'm not sure that the local authority would pick up the tab ... Clients, they come from Beaconsfield, Cambridge, just to spend an hour here, for our 'drugs demystifying' process. So in actual fact we cover the whole of London. In fact, as far as Southern Ireland, Northern Ireland, we are sending our booklets. And I don't think that it's realistic to rely on the actual local authority. They just say, like a lot of other local authorities, 'we don't have a problem here particularly', but there's a problem not only in this area but all over the shop and we just try to meet needs as they arise, wherever they come from. So I think it needs to be looked at nationally, rather than locally, we are not community based.(Gwenda)

THE STAFF

As well as being the one agency that actually changed its premises during our study, the Blenheim also underwent staff changes. Barbara left after several years as part-time Administrator and was replaced in mid-1983 by Anne. Among the social work staff, Roger left after five years of working at the project, taking with him the street knowledge of an ex-user and the social work expertise built up in those five years. He was replaced by Gwenda. As our fieldwork neared its end, the other longest-serving Blenheim worker, Steve, also left the project. Thus the staff composition - and with it the approach of the Blenheim Project to its work - is in a significant phase of flux and transition. It is, of course, impossible to say exactly where this transition will lead, but some sense of the emerging priorities and guiding philosophies should become apparent from the account of the agency that follows.

We now describe those staff members who formed

the mainstay of the agency in the period 1982/3.

Qualifications and experience

Despite the fact that he left the project about a third of the way through our fieldwork, Roger's background is worth describing at some length because he was, at the time, the only street agency worker (though there had been a number of others in the past) who brought the knowledge and empathy of having been a drug user to the acquisition and development of social work skills. His personal reflections on the experience of withdrawal and rehabilitation are intrinsically interesting and are also illuminating about the work of and connections between various agencies.

Roger came from a middle class background, and in the late 1960s went on to University to study Computer Science, partly, as he put it, 'to get some financial independence and away from home'. He discovered that Computer Science held little other attraction for him and, studying near to London, he soon developed an alternative interest in the city's flourishing counter-culture of free concerts, underground music, arts venues and so on, 'for once not really thinking about what the futue was going to be whatsoever, living day to day, and enjoying it immensely'. Leaving university he had briefly joined a commune in the north of England and then taken a series of odd jobs. Following an introduction to drug use at university, he established a pattern of regular use of hard drugs and, by the time that Roger moved back to London to work, he was 'heavily into using'. He registered as an addict around the same time as taking the job. After a number of periodic but unsuccessful attempts to come off, 'things just fell apart'. He continues:

> I was registered at Westminster and they suggested that I went to ROMA. I can remember my total horror. It's something I try to recall in myself when I'm advising other people about things, that I felt, when I was sent, 'right, off to an institution'. Now, I do so glibly say, why don't you try this, why don't you try that, and yet at the same time it was a sort of horrific thing to me ... I waited nine months for a hospital detox bed. It was an absolutely appalling wait. Partly, it's Westminster's

policy that you should be kept waiting to check your motivation but, partly, it was the time of year - it would have varied over 9 months I suppose, but I mean it was just dreadful, I was ringing up, going to appointments at the Maudsley, going to St. Bernard's, all the various DDUs, because Westminster has only got one drug bed that they can use, so they are making referrals to other places and I can remember being absolutely horrified again at the sort of way I was treated, the questions they asked, they didn't accept what I was saying as the truth, they were just giving you a hard time basically, again, presumably to test your motivation.

I remember being really righteously indignant about it all, you know, OK, I wanted some assistance but there was no need to go to the extremes that these people were going to to check out whether it was going to be worth my while, or worth their while.

Roger feels that he was lucky throughout all this insofar as he had a concerned and committed doctor who (following up this connection) is now on the management committee of the Blenheim. On leaving hospital Roger would have been homeless but, through the Westminster clinic's contact with Elizabeth House (a drug-free residential half-way house) he was able to move into stable circumstances in which to consider what he wanted to try and do next. The policy of Elizabeth House encourages residents to go out to work and after a while Roger followed up a suggestion to do voluntary work with the Nucleus advice agency in Earls Court.

And this was when my whole world opened up. It was a real revelation. People like (my doctor at the clinic) had been saying to me what I should be doing is social work and I would say, oh, yeah, yeah, but ... partly, I think she was right. I think my dismissal of it was more dismissing it as a job, I just don't think I thought I was capable of doing it. Nucleus sort of slotted me into this whole network of things that I got really excited about and I became full-time information volunteer there for about 9 months, something like that, and began to see this as a sort of career option that I would be extremely interested in following up.

Feeling it would be sensible to move on beyond Nucleus to gain further experience Roger applied for and was appointed to a job at the newly opened Riverpoint night-shelter in June of 1977.

> I was there 18 months, and I think working in a night-shelter, especially somewhere like Riverpoint, gives you a really good ground knowledge of problem areas and what's available, especially having had a welfare rights background at Nucleus.

It was whilst working at Riverpoint that Roger first met workers from the Blenheim on their visits to the shelter. When they advertised two part-time posts in early 1979 Roger still felt that he had doubts about his ability as a full time professional social worker and so applied for this post. He was accepted for the job at a time when, as he says, 'the project ... was probably at its lowest ebb'. Roger's recollection of his job description indicates the priorities of the project then, as distinct from their development and change whilst he was with it. 'When I was employed it was homelessness first, drugs second, field work third ... or even field work second, drugs third ...'. From the point of view of social work practice within the agency, what is important to note is that this period of insecurity within the project meant the new workers could lay the foundations for changes in practice and approach. Counselling was developed and emphasised as an approach by a then new woman worker, particularly with what she identified as a neglected client group - single women clients who could be encouraged to come to the project alone if the atmosphere was not intimidating. This recognition was one which the Blenheim has followed through with striking success. Roger himself brought an understanding and familiarity with the workings and interconnections between a variety of non-statutory and statutory agencies in the field. By the time that he had settled in to the instability and insecurity of the project, the time was clearly right for a re-appraisal: 'That period was really good for us because we had to sell the project and look at what we were doing and it was remarkably successful ...'

Steve had lived in West London during his teens and gone to school in North Kensington, at one point doing a school project on various type so social services in the area which had first brought the Blenheim to his

attention - however briefly. Following later involvement
in local neighbourhood community groups he decided
that he would like to move into the social work field:

> Not having that much in the way of educational
> qualifications, I decided I'd go to college and do
> a C.Q.S.W., which I did ... The structure of the course
> was that it was a term in and a term out and I did
> various placements ... and when I was looking around
> for the third placement - I'd begun to develop an
> interest in drugs because ... I knew a lot of people
> that took drugs and things ... And there was an advert
> for a job at the Blenheim, and I thought, oh yeah
> ... I remember them ...

Steve was accepted for a placement at the Blenheim
and when, towards the end of his stay, one of the established
workers left, he applied for the vacant job. He got the
job and became a full-time staff member in August 1978.

Lin had developed what she now sees as a naive but
genuine interest in social work after going through some
bad times herself in her youth. Her first job in the social
work field had been a secretarial role in an agency finding
adoptive homes for mentally and physically handicapped
children. After travelling for a couple of years she returned
to London and took a job with Enfield social services
department, applying for a social work course at the
same time. She then took the course full time, developing
an interest in counselling approaches to social work.
She moved to the job at the Blenheim shortly after the
completion of the course, attracted to the advert by
the feeling that working in the drugs field would take
her into 'an area where I knew there wasn't an awful
lot done for women, which was the case at that time'.

At an early age, Gwenda had been labelled an alcoholic
and been in trouble for truancy and various other matters.
As she says, she then spent 'many years of trying to shake
off the labels that had been attached ... working, actually
having to prove that you were employable in commerce and
so on'. After working in business and then taking a course at
university she felt that she could make use of her background
in a positive way: 'The early idealism was replaced by a much

more professional attitude of 'where can I possibly be most useful and also finding the job interesting?'

Prior to joining the Blenheim staff she had worked with ex-offenders, some of whom had alcohol and drug-related problems, and had also previously done some voluntary work in mental health aftercare, and counselling with women with sexual problems. She heard of the job vacancy at the Blenheim through a client that she was counselling at the time and, as she puts it, 'thought that I might enjoy it (even though) there were areas that I had to learn'. Gwenda joined the project in early 1983.

Having introduced the staff, and before moving on to our account of the agency, it should be noted that the available background documentation and the additional interviews with former Blenheim staff who are still in contact with the project meant that we were able to draw upon a wider and deeper source of material in our account of the Blenheim than we were for the other two agencies.

Working philosophies

Reflecting his length of time with the project, Steve offered a quite extensive exposition of the nature of the project. His statement reflects most of the issues as seen by Blenheim staff with the exception of feminist concerns:

> Hopefully there is a basic philosophy about what goes on and that creates the framework for a creative environment in which people can contribute their own skills. But again it's one of these things that it's important to have a situation where you've got a fairly clearcut idea of what the central core of the work is and how people can then develop off that ... I've always taken the view here that the sorts of skills that are applicable in a place like the Blenheim are actually very very wide, because we're dealing with a very broad group of people, ranging from professionals in non-specialist agencies to parents and users, and with a wide range in terms of the problem. It's everything - legal, and medical, and social and personal and all the rest of it. So there is the capacity to have a really wide spread of skills. The

dangers in that, I think, are that it doesn't take a great deal for the central core of the thing to become 'unglued'. I think it's a lot easier in services that have a much more defined role and say, right, we will see anybody between the ages of this and this and with those particular problems because that is a structural core for the whole thing and people will either adhere to that or they will get out.(Steve)

As long as the central core of the agency remained 'glued together', then that is precisely what the Blenheim offered its clients - a fixed centre-point, a known location to return to when things got too bad or out of control. Whether this amounted to an efficient use of resources and time is something Steve is less sure about.

Blenheim in that sense was a kind of stability to a lot of people in the sense that they might go out of the area for three months or something and they knew that when they came back they could phone us up and we'd still be there. I think for a lot of people that was very useful just as that, you know, it was a bit like the hub of a wheel. I think it did help a lot of people survive on a day to day level 'cos they could come in and phone up and do all the bits and pieces they needed to do, talk to us and we'd try and help them out with practical things. I think it was useful, but in terms of our own satisfaction, and also in terms of the use of resources generally, I don't think it was a very effective way to do it, because we were wasting a lot of time hanging around in the office on the off-chance that someone would turn up. Or when they did turn up perhaps some days they'd have something quite dramatic they wanted to have somebody deal with, but other times there wouldn't be that much going on for them and they'd just want someone to talk to, which was fine, but we thought we could offer a bit more than that.(Steve)

As the agency approached its own internal feelings of the necessity for change, it looked outside itself and found that the area around it, and the drug problems it dealt with, were also changing. As a result the agency changed its methods and has made a major contribution to the resources available to help drug users through its development of self-help information materials for wider dissemination than just to visiting clients, and through adopting a clearer focus on drug-related problems as the direction that the agency would pursue:

> The area was changing anyway, we couldn't hope to track the same sort of people, and we noticed that drug problems were increasing, especially heroin, 'cos it was that '79 time when a lot of heroin was beginning to come in. We recognised that the sort of people that were using were changing as well and what we did was we decided that we were going to emphasise much more the drugs element of our work and that we were also going to have to say, well, we're not working in North Kensington as such, we're working in West London because people were much more spread out and that was the only way we could attract people in. And that begged a lot of questions about what we'd be doing. Fieldwork and things ... wasn't terribly relevant, you know, because we'd be going to pubs and whatever, and you might find just one or two people there and it's a bit of a waste of time, you know, nice to go for a drink but not terribly productive from a work point of view, and basically, that philosophy continued and things like the leaflets came out of that and that was the real turning point, I think, in terms of the direction of the agency.(Steve)

When Lin joined the project her own views on how she wanted to work fitted in well with changes in the character of the project that were already happening.

> Things that I wanted to do also fitted in with the Blenheim's own feelings about things that weren't working. For example, when I came it was almost a kind of day centre and there would be about twenty pretty stoned, pretty obnoxious men, just sitting around all day, talking at the workers, you know, it was always directed at us kind of. And for a start, women never came in, or if they did it was just as part of a couple; it just wasn't a very nice place for women to come. It wasn't a terribly nice place for anyone to come.

So with talking with the others about how this wasn't working, from the point of view of it not being a safe place for women to be, and from the point of view of it being totally unstructured ... (which I found really frustrating, and I think, the others did too, although we all had different reasons for wanting to change it). So we changed the system to appointments, and made the place nicer.(Lin)

Nowadays staff agree that the Blenheim works on several levels:

(a)   encouraging outside agencies to contact them about problems, approaches and resources available;

(b)   at a more 'formalised' level, in involvement in educational work, giving talks and so on;

(c)   developing longer term relationships with both clients and professionals who continue their contact with the project after the initial enquiry or visit.

Any working vision of the project, it is argued, has to incorporate these levels of its work.

I think what's quite important about the first two is that they give some indication of what our attitudes are to things, and I think what they do is they encourage people to look at things in a particular way and also to recognise that a large part of what is going on, either as a parent or as a drug user, has to come from themselves and that there is this place that is willing to help them sort a few of the odds and ends out around that.   But basically, that they do have some control over their lives.   And the other thing that I like to think that we do on a very general level is give people some hope that these sort of problems can be solved, because I think that's a commodity that's in a bit short supply really.   So there are a number of levels that it operates on. and they overlap of course.(Steve)

Division of labour

'Overlap' also describes the nature of the division of labour within the agency.

As Ruth points out, the agency has never worked out a formal division of labour and responsibility. Yet, as Roger indicates, a fairly clear informal division of labour has been apparent for some years:

> One of the ways that the project has not yet ever worked is to divide the areas of work up, and say, OK, you've got three members of staff, that member of staff will concentrate on housing, that one on drugs or whatever. It's never happened. And I think that's come out recently actually ... there was some comment that the project does not want to do that, that a lot of the strength of the project lies in the different workers doing the whole range, dealing with whatever turns up, whoever turns up at the door, or is on the telephone. But within that being able to develop special interests.(Ruth: past staff member, present management committee member)

> I hold on to my primary beliefs which are that primary care is incredibly important and, yes, that includes someone listening to you, but it includes very practical solutions to day to day problems. Well, I felt much happier dealing with that, much more competent dealing with social security than worrying about my ability as a counsellor, although now I do feel competent at counselling and know what I'm doing, but at that time I probably didn't.(Roger)

Such potential conflict of approaches - between counselling the individual, seeking policy changes through dialogue with other agencies, and emphasising primary care and a focus on everyday problems - can, not surprisingly, contribute to serious feelings of frustration within the agency:

> And it builds up - and you're always one person short, or the building's about the fall down and you know you are never working at your most efficient, and everybody's particular areas and interests are different, and you always think your area of interest is the most important the project should be concentrating on.(Roger)

In the division of labour whilst Roger was still at the
project and before he was replaced by Gwenda, the two
male social workers shared the male client caseload
whilst Lin saw the majority of women clients. In the
past, and in many other projects now, this might have
worked out equitably, but the policies of the Blenheim
brought their male to female client ratio close to 50/50
which meant that Lin was at one time carrying the heaviest
client burden. Many of the women clients would actually
all be visiting at the same time for the project's women-
only session but nonetheless, the Blenheim's achievement
demonstrated the need for more women workers. With
Gwenda joining the staff this need was partly met. At
the close of our fieldwork, prior to leaving the Blenheim,
Steve described the agency's division of labour in the
following way:

> What we were doing up to a while back is we were
> all doing more or less the same thing: Lin was obviously
> more involved with women and I tended to be more
> involved with the kind of policy-type issues, you
> know, management committees and that kind of
> stuff. And things like the public face of the Blenheim
> in terms of leaflets. Gwenda is trying to work out
> what her particular interests are. I would imagine
> that she would want to develop prison and post-release
> type of work. And what we've done recently is that
> the structure has actually changed quite considerably
> in the sense that we are getting a publication worker.
> We've got one year's salary from the GLC, and we're
> getting a worker to concentrate on publications
> and educational materials, to pull together the ideas
> we've got as far as leaflets are concerned and also
> to produce educational material for giving talks,
> and slides, and visual things and whatever.(Steve)

To summarise: all the social work staff work with presenting clients and telephone enquiries but women clients would
primarily be dealt with by Lin or Gwenda, whilst in the past
Steve and Roger would take male clients. Roger continued
some involvement with outside agencies (such as voluntary
work at Riverpoint and advice facilities at free festivals
through Festival Aid). Steve pursued his interests in presenting the public face of the Blenheim project through the

production of a video about the project's work, and involvement in meetings with other agencies. The administrator's
post, filled first by Barbara and now by Anne, is concerned
with the day-to-day administration of the project, liaison
with the management committee, the preparation of statistics and back-up support for the social work staff in dealing
with phone enquiries. Finally, in considering the division of
labour, it should be remembered that, uniquely among the
three street agencies, the Blenheim emphasises that it works
and makes decisions as a collective.

The interests reflected in the working division of labour
obviously reflect personal approaches to the kind of problems
that the agency deals with, but they also allow certain
unifying perspectives to be consolidated.   Perhaps the
most central themes here are the encouragement of
self-help and self-motivation, the utilisation of existing
community resources (whilst campaigning for better
provision) and the identification of hidden groups with
'drug-related problems' who may be coping in some way
but are vulnerable and can be given assistance to help
themselves cope more effectively. The social work staff
express these themes themselves:

> Our approach? I think, very definitely in all the
> work that I've ever done I believe very strongly in
> self-help and self-motivation and that fits in very
> well with the Blenheim. I mean when people refer
> people I actually tend to say, 'get them to phone
> up', you know, rather than having appointments made
> for them.   And the whole basis of counselling and
> looking for support in the community for whoever
> it is, whether it's men or women or parents or whatever
> ... is certainly a Blenheim approach.(Lin)

WORK WITH CLIENTS (AS SEEN BY THE AGENCY)

Steve suggested to us that the pragmatism of the Blenheim
approach partly grew out of Roger's street knowledge
of drug problems, his own awareness of the way that
self-help community organisations had worked, and the
agency's rejection of the 'specialist' mystique surrounding
work with drug problems (a mystique allegedly perpetuated by

the rehabilitation houses and the clinics). This approach
extends beyond making use of local resources within
the Blenheim's own neighbourhood, and has become part
of the response to any client coming from another area.
As Lin explains:

> Two years ago ... most of the people that came in
> were from this area, kind of drifting around the
> area, and that's really changed now. Now, we get
> people from all over London that have picked up
> our leaflets, seen our number somewhere, whatever.
> And so I think that I'm more engaged in looking at
> whatever the area is that someone's come from,
> actually researching what facilities, what support,
> and networks are in that area rather than this area
> specifically.(Lin)

Individual empowerment

To find further resources for people is not the same as
handing them easy answers on a plate; as the Blenheim
sees it:

> Our priorities really are to be what people actually
> need and not necessarily what ... they actually want.
> People often want us to be a body that actually
> supplies drugs and all sorts of things and give them
> a very easy way out.   The point is that we can't
> give people an easy way out.   The individual, it's
> all down to self, it's all down to the individual. We
> can only encourage, we can't do it for them.   And
> they often want some magic wand but we can only
> give them a very commonsensical view of what they
> can actually do.(Gwenda)

As Ruth put it, drawing on her impressions of the Blenheim's
approach in the past and present, the agency staff have
to 'try to work in such a way so as to leave a lot of power
with the client and try to facilitate their decisions and their
choices, rather than other ways people might have of working'.

An approach which has emphasised helping people
who are capable of coping and who may already be doing
so in some way had led the Blenheim to render assistance

to groups who are apparently 'hidden', who may be surviving psychologically, but who could cope far better with the aid of accurate information and support. Two principal groups here are parents, relatives and friends of people with drug problems, and women users. All three street agencies would emphasise that they extend help to the former group and all three approach it in much the same way, providing factual information to dispel myths and worries, giving advice by phone or in counselling sessions or just keeping in touch to give support. The leaflet on 'How to Help' produced by the Blenheim has rapidly become a major resource for all agencies to pass on to family and friends of drug users. It is with their making a priority of women clients, however, that the Blenheim has taken a singular and significant initiative.

Positive discrimination

In 1981 women represented 32 per cent of the Blenheim's clients. Throughout 1982-3 the project actively sought to encourage more women to come into the project:

> Our 'hunch' was that this was not indicative of the numbers of women of women on the streets, but rather a reflection of women's position in society, making them less likely than men to seek help from agencies such as ours. (Internal document for management committee on 'Progress on fourth worker', undated)

Through meetings with women in short stay hostels, links with local women's centres and other groups, and the establishment of the women-only afternoon at the project, Lin (with the support of the other staff) presented an image of the Blenheim as seeking women clients wherever such information might be passed on. Women now represent nearly 50 per cent of the Blenheim's clientele, and a fourth worker is required to consolidate this work. This would be a woman social worker with responsibilities to:

a)   extend the direct work of the Blenheim Project in relation to the needs of women;

b)   develop networks of self-help among women, specifically those drifting around London and those with drug related problems;

c)   encourage the growth of an awareness among
      other agencies in the field as to the special needs
      of women and to help develop services to meet
      those needs.

At present, the agency runs a regular 'group' for women
clients (not all of whom are necessarily using drugs or
alcohol in problematic ways). This group has grown over a
year or so through word of mouth contacts spread by staff
and clients. It has functioned as social support, organising
outings to the theatre and the seaside, and as information
bank, compiling a core of medical information concerning
women's health and drug use. The group adopts a feminist
perspective, seeking to place place the experience of women
in using drugs in the context of the broader social, cultural
and economic pressures on them. Its members have come
from a wide range of contact sources - from Homeless
Action, Riverpoint, various rehabilitation houses, community
groups, and so on. The aim has been to create an environment in which women clients would feel more comfortable
than in the traditional masculine atmosphere of most drug
agencies. The workers emphasise the necessity of this
approach because their view of the psychological vulner-
ability of women drug users who often feel that they have
lost their essential femininity, whereas male users reportedly
see some sort of masculine toughness associated with their
drug use, and rely on this as part of their assertion of their
sense of self. The supportive women-only nature of the group
has enabled it to explore these gender-related issues of power
and identity, and to explore ways in which women's experiences of sexual abuse have contributed to their dependence
on drugs.
      In this, as in other aspects of the project's work, it
is developing a perspective which is not restricted to
looking at drug 'addicts', but at ways that particular
social groups have of 'coping'. The Blenheim believes
that drugs are seen by many in the field, and by the general
public, as something quite apart from all the other problems
of life. Thus, for example, although therapy might be
very useful for some clients, the Blenheim knows of very
few therapists who would agree, most feeling that therapy
is appropriate for the general problems of life, but that
somehow drugs are a 'different sort of problem'. With

the women's group, and with much else in their practice, the Blenheim attempts to bring drug problems back into the realm of ordinary problems, back to a concern with access to community resources, and back to a realistic point of view where the power to do something about the problem rests with the client.

The project's involvement with women users has certainly increased over the last five years. In the latter half of the 1970s, suggests Kate (an ex-Blenheim worker), the breakdown of clients was an average ratio of 60 per cent males to 40 per cent females, aged between about 17 and 35 (with a few older clients), virtually all white and probably 75-80 per cent working class. By the time that Gwenda joined the agency in 1983, she was seeing a virtually equal ratio of male to female clients, most of whom were now middle class, although the age ranges and Caucasian origin remained unchanged. Maintaining a caseload with women clients has proved to be a task involving constant re-investment of staff time and effort (perhaps because of women's past experiences of state welfare agencies, and because of some feeling on their part that it is selfish or self-indulgent to claim time and help for themselves, instead of servicing the needs of others):

> Gender, that's really changed for us. I mean I think it fluctuates - I think one thing that we notice is that we're working very specifically to get lots of women to come in, but you can't just sit back and say, 'oh, that's it, they are coming in', because when you start doing that, they stop coming in and I've really noticed that. Women are really high up on our stats - but I think a lot of that's because we've also got a lot of mothers, and supporters (of people with drug problems) which, again, is a typically female role. You know, we don't get that many male 'supporters'. We do get some. We had one today. (Lin)

The bar chart 5.1 illustrates the rise in women clients as a proportion of all clients, as indicated by the project's records.

The division of labour, philosophy, and the priorities

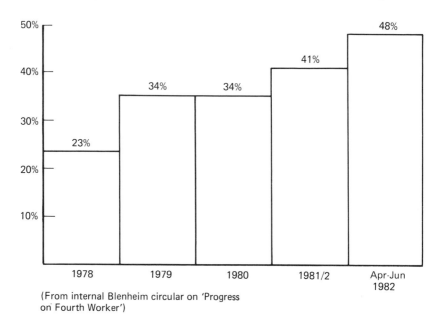

(From internal Blenheim circular on 'Progress
on Fourth Worker')

Chart 5.1: Women 'customers' as percentage of total

of the Blenheim are still changing as the effects of the staff
turnover manifest themselves.   The appointment of the
fourth, woman, social worker is still not a settled matter.
After a period of quite vigorous work these factors left
the Blenheim in a slight trough.   New workers must find
their feet, and the agency as a whole has to re-construct
itself around new ideas and approaches.   The process
cannot be complete until the issue of the extra workers
- a publications worker and women's social worker -
are resolved. However, so long as the baby is not thrown out
with the bathwater, and the clients to whom the Blenheim
has traditionally offered a service are still a part of its
priorities, there is undoubtedly a firm basis on which to build
a new staff team and agency identity.   Leaving these
developments aside, however, there will continue to be
certain constants in the everyday practice of the project,
which we now examine.

A highly variable workload

Client demand on the agency varies from a slow trickle
of enquiries on 'quiet' days, to a deluge of enquiries and
immediately problematic client presentations on others:

I remember one bloke ... lived on Portobello
Green for a long time, drinking cider bottles, and
taking barbs, and I can remember one time he came
into the office and I was the only one there at the
time, and he was absolutely out of it, he was legless,
and the building we were in was pretty dreadful, it
didn't inspire a lot of respect from people, towards the
actual premises, and he came and sat down and sat
around for a bit and then he stood up and walked like
out of that door there and there was a broom cupboard
just outside the door and he opened that door and I
heard the sound of running water. And I said, 'what
are you doing?' and he said, 'I'm pissing'; 'Are you
pissing in the broom cupboard?' and he said 'yeah'.
And he was totally befuddled about what he was doing
wrong. He thought he was just taking a leak. That
was No.3 Acklam Road.

And that actual incident catalysed a lot of things
for me. It just seemed to sum it all up somehow.
The dirt and degradation. Quite a lot of people,
apart from those people, quite a lot of others,
younger people using barbs, fooling about and
generally being quite unattractive. As I said
before, not so many using addicts, some, certainly,
but not so many as now and perhaps not so many
as previously, there was quite a long phase when
there weren't so many. A lot of quite young
people on the squatting circuit and quite a lot
of those with housing problems, abuse problems
of various sorts, drinking too much, popping too
many pills or whatever, across the range and
everything feeding into everything else. An
eviction taking place and then legal problems
on top of that. I'm thinking of people about late
teens, early twenties sort of age, in a mess, and
not knowing where to go, lots of social security
problems of course, lot of money problems, and
quite a lot of problems with the law, getting
picked up, getting nicked, getting banged up
for a few days and then out again. (Ruth, past
worker, present member of management committee)

Ruth's recollection of the client in the broom cupboard gives us a particularly sharp 'snapshot' of the vicious circles in which Blenheim clients have found themselves in the past. It is a no less accurate summary of the problems that are brought to the Blenheim today. We shall focus more upon the range of clients and the nature of their problems in a subsequent section. Here we hope to give some sense of how agency workers cope with hearing the sound of running water in the broom cupboard or, more broadly, what their concerns are, and what resources they can use in their day-to-day practice.

In discussing this third and final agency, it should be noted that all the workers in all three agencies were remarkably candid about what they felt they could actually achieve and also about how they perceived their use of time.

Within the Blenheim project, staff changes (occurring at the same time as they have attempted a major reorientation of the project to pick up more women clients and to develop their practical 'Help' leaflets) have made it difficult to assess their use of time. Our study was not, of course, a time and motion study - rather, it is to the credit of the three agencies themselves that staff time use is an issue considered seriously, both formally and informally. During the period September 28th to October 16th 1981, the Blenheim project conducted a 'Time Use Survey' to help plan future work. Naturally, this only represents work carried out during the three week period, and it is skewed by the fact that meetings, appointments and committees run in cycles so that, for example, 'consultancy appeared twice ... while a management committee does not appear', and holidays and sickness are under-represented. The results however did, said the Blenheim workers, 'fit fairly well with our impressions of what we do':

Unrecorded	12.79%	
Counselling/interviews	15.34%	
Desk duty	9.11%	-work with clients
Follow up	4.00%	28.45
Travel	4.24%	
Consultancy	3.03%	
General admin.	33.94%	(includes 100% of Barbara's half-time work)
Work with agencies	17.22%	

As Steve said, these are interesting results because most social work agencies think that they spend the majority of their time with their clients. Of course they do not, and indeed in order to function as agencies they probably never could. At the time that these results were presented to the project's management committee, one of its members was a senior officer at Kensington Social Services Department who agreed with this observation from the point of view of statutory agencies.

Street agency workers (and ourselves) are placed in an invidious position here, because there is undoubtedly a very serious demand for street agency services, possibly much of it untapped and unencountered because of the office-hours routine of the street agency service. But that demand, reflecting the client's needs, can be very erratic. Roger honestly comments on this dilemma:

> We're all terribly guilty that we're not as busy as we imagine ourselves to be. Some days it's absolutely crazy like the day you came in and had to sit in here and I was seeing people all over the place. But there are other days, like today, when there's just a few phone calls perhaps. (Roger)

This erratic take-up of services despite the existence of fairly continuous client problems may, some have suggested, have something to do with the hours during which the service is on offer. Workers in rehabilitation houses who see their residents having some sort of crisis not just between the hours of ten and five but in the evening, through the night and at weekends, find it a source of dismay that street agencies are supposed to be a point of immediate contact yet are not available when people may be most lonely and vulnerable. This is a serious failing in the service provided by all three street agencies. It is understandable in terms of pressure on staff and other resources but the low priority which it has received as an area for agency expansion is less comprehensible. Workers at the Blenheim have discussed this point from two angles - first, the opening up of the project as a resource to be available outside of normal hours and second, the justification of leaving clients to fend for themselves for weekend periods:

Steve and I discussed this a couple of weeks ago and we

did talk about whether we'd be willing to work in the
evenings. I mean we *do* if there's clients that are
working anyway, we stay on or go get something to eat
and come back. We don't turn anyone away because they
are working. And we have discussed this quite realistically. I think in conjunction with that, I'd like to see
groups here, we were going to have a partition in the
office, paid for by a charity, I would very much like to
see the other half of the office used for groups. Non-
users or ex-users groups. So that, in fact, we do have a
night life as well as a day life, but the staff aren't on
duty all those hours. And some of the groups might be
self-help or could be staffed at times by workers from
other agencies, you know.(Gwenda)

The feasibility of providing something approaching
a 24-hour service for clients has been discussed before
at the Blenheim, but has not resulted in any formal out-
of-hours initiative, partly because it is often more realistic
to respond informally, as the need arises. Staff agree
that weekends are a problem in the provision of a more
extensive service. 'Sooner or later somebody's going
to have to cope with the weekends, and in lots of ways
it's almost better that they do it straight away'.(Kate,
ex-worker)

Ethnic minorities absent

The problems that clients have can manifest themselves
in highly visible or in low profile ways. For example,
the Blenheim has 'a certain number of people (who have)
been busted or arrested, and there's a court case coming
up and they've been sent by probation officers'. Other
clients feel that their lives are in 'absolute crisis, they've
run out of money, relationships about to collapse, lost
their jobs', and so on.

But a lot of people whom the project sees are generally
coping with their problems in a fairly stable manner
- holding down jobs, but perhaps just getting to the stage
where they feel things might get out of control, and
so need some sort of support and help. For such clients
the anonymity of the appointment system in the new
Blenheim premises is far more appropriate than referral

to agencies, such as the Hungerford or City Roads, which are more evidently working with clients from the 'street' drug scene:

> We've had quite a few referrals from City Roads of people who phoned City Roads, who City Roads don't think are chaotic enough or on the scene enough, and it would actually do more damage to take them into City Roads, like the woman I saw this morning.(Lin)

Workers in all the agencies are aware that the subcultures surrounding drug use are very strong, and that there can be serious negative consequences of self-labelling for people brought into unfamiliar contact with a heavy drug using scene.   The subcultures of drug use can be very supportive, providing social networks and survival strategies; but they can also imprison people within subcultural expectations and values:

> The subcultural sort of thing is so strong and they '*must* be so different to everybody else' - that they *are* very different and *so* sensitive - therefore they need it.   But I'd be bloody sensitive if I'd been taking painkillers for a long time - I wouldn't want to face the world, you know.(Gwenda)

The boundaries surrounding particular drug using cultures are of course related to race, gender and community. Lin touches upon some of these interconnections in discussing the ethnicity of Blenheim's clients:

> Race is mainly all white.   Now I think that's for two reasons.   I think, first of all, we're in Notting Hill Gate, where there are lots of black people's information centres, Portuguese Advice Centres, Spanish Advice Centres, etc., and obviously people of different kinds of races or relevant groups go to specific places, which is right.   I mean why should they come to a white drugs project?
>
> I think also that their whole style of use of drugs is really different in different kinds of communities. I just think that we're the worst - white English people - totally isolated, you know.   In a real mess. I think the whole kind of family network and support thing is really different in, say, the black community.(Lin)

In the opinion of Ira (ex-Blenheim and CDP staff member and now a social worker at a DDU near Nottingham), very few non-white clients used the street agencies in the past, and the same is true of the whole of the drugs scene today, both in the agencies and the clinics.   In his experience, 'non-whites very rarely have problems with drugs, save cannabis'; Roger concurs, noting only some minor changes with young people of mixed race occasionally being brought to the Blenheim by parents concerned about their involvement in glue sniffing.(This was the position in 1983.)

A DAY OBSERVED

The Blenheim project opens its doors between the hours of ten and five, sharing a main entrance with a number of other agencies occupying the Westway complex. Clients are directed by paper signs to the Blenheim and in other directions to other agencies.   Clients are rarely really early birds; only occasionally may someone be waiting for the first worker to show up. In the past there might have been several, sitting on the crumbling wall by the steps leading up to the door of 3 Acklam Road. In their new premises, an up-market image seems to have dismayed some of the old chaotic clients who in the past might have appeared for an early morning cup of coffee after a night of sleeping rough.   The gradual acceptance of long standing practice, coupled with the air of efficiency suggested by the new premises, encourages other clients to adhere to the appointment system.
    Phone calls are sporadic this particular morning, irregularly spaced, variable in length.   Most are handled by Lin, though some are taken by Gwenda (slowly familiarising herself with the full range of clients, agencies and problems that come to the Blenheim).
    With only a few weeks to go before he leaves the Blenheim, Steve is 'phasing out', finishing up his involvement in various sub-projects (in particular, publicising a video film he has helped to make on the Blenheim's work). It is hoped that the film can be loaned to other street agencies to give them an idea of the work of a street

agency, and perhaps be taken to conferences and meetings and shown to participants who might otherwise have no opportunity to get an idea about the work of the Blenheim. This morning Steve is making arrangements to transport the video equipment and a TV set to ISDD later in the week, to show the film to the information officers there.

Gwenda is quite heavily involved in the Blenheim's contribution to the setting up of a local rehabilitation facility and spends part of the morning working on developments related to that. In particular she had attended a meeting the previous weekend where the various involved parties discussed progress and future plans. While the meeting had been 'useful', it was clear that the dynamics have still to be worked out, and she now has to ensure that it is understood by all concerned that responsibility cannot be shunted onto the Blenheim. The exact nature and extent of its involvement has to be emphasised, and Gwenda spends some time on this problem of diplomacy and policy.

A drop-in client turns up. He is not seeking help for himself but help with how to cope with his stepson, who is using drugs and whose mother is finding it difficult to cope. Steve approaches the problem with a sympathetic but detached manner, first seeking to put the nature of the drug problem into a context of factual information, describing what the drugs that the son is using actually do, the nature of their addictive potential, and so on. The father is also given information to take away to show his wife. They talk for over three quarters of an hour and the father seems relieved if only because he has been able to talk to somebody. Things seem more manageable, but it is emphasised that the agency can do nothing for the son unless he is willing to come into the agency himself.

Mornings seem to be set aside for paperwork and taking phone enquiries, setting up meetings, chasing resources - rehabs., clinics and so on - and for receiving professional visitors to the agency. For Lin and Gwenda the morning is taken up by these activities (with the exception of receiving visitors); the following morning was to be substantially taken up by the visit of SCODA staff introducing their new worker for Scotland to the London agencies. The

Blenheim are pleased that they do have the time to give to visitors, and emphasise what they see as their importance as a point at which expertise and information can be passed on to those new to the field.

The agency closes for lunch at 1 p.m. although workers may still be wrapped up in whatever they have been doing and continue to answer phones. Otherwise the ansaphone is switched on.

Afternoons at the Blenheim are structured around client appointments, which decreased slightly during, and for a short period after, the agency's move to new premises. This afternoon there are three counselling appointments, plus the same number of callers without appointments. Following each lengthy counselling sessions, the workers record in the client's files an account of what happened. These reports are inevitably lengthier and more detailed than their telephone enquiry records; it is important for workers to keep up to date with both their morning and afternoon report writing so that one day's work does not start to 'slip into' the next day. Special care must be taken to ensure not only the accuracy of information about the client's problems and personal circumstances, but also about the drugs that they are using. Street agency workers generally have a very good and clear pharmacological knowledge of drug formulae, terms, effects and so on - which should really come as little surprise given that such matters are central to the work that they do, and over the years the agency has collected several simple, straightforward medical guides to the range of available pharmaceuticals. This is much the same sort of resource as most GPs would have to rely on if they were interested in drug problems.

Perhaps, with some further training in this area, if only for one specialising worker, the street agencies could develop more of a role as 'local' - west, central and south London - information agencies offering the information about legal drugs and their effects. The anonymity which they can offer could perhaps encourage many who presently feel uncomfortable about asking anyone for advice, to use their services and closer links could perhaps be forged with GPs in their areas, perhaps by GPs advertising such a service in their surgeries.

TWO CLIENT CASE STUDIES

All the street agencies are aware that what they do, what they see and deal with, is a potentially unrepresentative tip of the iceberg of drug-related problems. Before we describe the range of clients and problems that the Blenheim project sees, we merely enter the caveat that although the three street agencies see a broader range of clients than many other agencies in the drugs field, their focus is still a narrow one, and does not necessarily yield a very clear picture of the real extent of drug use in society, even if taken in conjunction with impressions gathered from the clinics, GPs and other agencies. For a start many of the people who come to the street agencies have often been referred by another agency - in which case they were 'together' enough to seek out the help of some agency in the first place; or else they have come via the recommendation of a friend, in which case there would appear to be some degree of support, concern and care for them, provided by some sort of social network. The Blenheim, like the other agencies, is keenly conscious of the existence of other sections of the drug-using population who do not use the referral network in which they work.

As we have seen, the Blenheim Project aims to provide both a local and metropolitan service:

> The clients at the Blenheim always have, and still do, come from all over the place. Quite a lot of them are either temporarily or permanently local and a lot are not. A lot are drifting from borough to borough. A lot of them have ended up in London from somewhere else. ... it's always been seen as an agency that will deal across the board and it's always been seen as a strength of the project.(Ruth)

Despite some changes in the composition of clients coming to the Blenheim (certainly more women, perhaps more middle class backgrounds), this spread of geographical origin remains constant.

The principal drugs encountered, however, have changed. In the late 1970s these were mainly barbiturates, diconal and others available on the streets from prescription sources. But around late 1979 and early 1980, the Blenheim was seeing the consequences of an influx of Iranian heroin; as this drug established its 'trendiness' (Roger), more people were calling the agency, having discovered that they had a problem with the drug. This new source of drugs on the street market particularly affected the Blenheim because the key centres for dealing were in the Kensington and Chelsea area:

> There was a focus in Kensington and Chelsea for the Iranian population that came here and a lot of the dealing in places like Kensington Antique Market did affect our work.(Roger)

> Changes occur because of price, fashion, availability ... I suppose the two main phases that have gone through since I've been here, bearing in mind there is always a level of multidrug use, have been the barbiturate phase and the heroin phase. And the barbiturate phase was going before I started and lasted up to say 1979 and then dropped off quite dramatically, and it wasn't just to do with us picking up another group of people ... from that point there was a very steep rise in opiates and heroin.(Steve)

Perhaps the only real 'constant factor' in the Blenheim's work is its attempt to set some working parameters as regards the age range of clients. This tends to be late teens to early forties. The problems of early teen youth are often to do with solvents, a problem which it is often felt unsuitable to deal with in a project more generally concerned with 'harder' drug use. At the other end of their age range experience has suggested that most prospective clients over the age of forty tend to have, principally, an alcohol problem. Referral elsewhere is often more appropriate therefore. The adoption of such a general guide to the age range of clients at the Blenheim is in accordance with the practice of the other two street agencies. However, for none of the agencies is there anything absolute or fixed about age limits.

It is against this background - not dissimilar to that faced by other agencies in the field - that we now describe two case studies as described to us by the clients themselves. Obviously, theirs are two voices amongst many, but their accounts of how they use the service are at least as valid as any others. These sections then lead on to discussion of some issues in the referral system through which these and other clients find their way.

Marjorie - anchorage, centrepoint, mother

In her interview with us, Marjorie first of all described the nature of the problems which led her to contact the Blenheim:

> ...I'm married to him now but I was living with a man who was on heroin and we were having a terrible time. I went to a local hospital which did me no good at all. I was there for a year. And my son was also on heroin and I was in total anguish, really, you know, terrible. My son actually is thirty-odd but, you know, I felt totally responsible for the whole thing and then I started to use phisetone, so there was the three of us. And I'd heard of the Blenheim, quite a lot, and I thought 'well'. In fact, my son was going to court, and I was feeling absolutely desperate, and I just walked in here and I met Gwenda and she talked to me. She was very helpful, making me realise that the more guilt I felt about my son, the worse it was ... the support that I've had from Gwenda, she's not pushy in any way, she's just very receptive and very comforting and one feels that there is somebody there, you know, I can say anything to her, you know what I mean?

Marjorie's son was entering hospital for treatment and both she and her husband had recently given up drugs, but she still made regular visits to the Blenheim, seeing it as offering to herself and others a point of anchorage:

> These youngsters, I mean, they get into such a state, and if they could only get somewhere where somebody could say, 'well, there is this that you could do, or there is that you could do', do you know what I mean?

> So that they could attach themselves to some, you know, it's like having an anchor, they know they can come here, they know they can say anything and they are not going to be frowned on or be told 'you shouldn't have done that'. there is no pressure on them or anything else and that is the most helpful method to do anything, because obviously anything that happens, you've got to do it yourself, you know, nobody will do it for you. But to have a feeling that somebody is really supportive and cares about you, I think it's just essential, absolutely essential, that's what I think about the Blenheim.

She had heard of the Blenheim through the local hospital that she had attended but at first was unclear about whether it was a project working with drug users.

> But then I think someone told me. I heard it, you know, somebody did say they deal with drug problems, and I was only on a small amount of phisetone and I sort of thought I'm not quite sure if I'm the sort of person they deal with or not. They won't be able to help me. But I was, you know, welcomed, and they have in fact helped my family. You know a lot of people do know about the Blenheim, particularly in this area.

> (But) perhaps they don't get enough publicity so to speak, I mean, if the doctors were given information about it, I'm sure that would be useful because I'm sure they must have a lot of this. Because I know that these kids, you know, they don't dare tell anybody, if you see what I mean, so this is their problem, you know, I mean, I suppose I must have seen posters and things about the Blenheim Project.

By the time that Marjorie had decided that the Blenheim might be able to help her, she felt 'in a desperate state'. She approached the agency by just walking in - 'not knowing what was going to happen' - and began counselling sessions with Gwenda. She emphasises the trust that she immediately felt:

> I felt we were compatible. It's a sort of trust feeling
> and I feel that I can tell her anything and she's not
> going to sort of criticise me or I don't have to play
> cagey or anything, you know, I can be totally honest
> with her and she understands, it's a sort of communication
> thing. It could have been someone else and we wouldn't
> have got on, I don't know, but I feel that she is a
> friend of mine, not a doctor or a psychiatrist but
> a friend, that's the feeling. But I mean she's definitely
> helped me.

Marjorie's feelings about Gwenda and about the Blenheim
are in sharp contrast to her feelings about the staff that
she had encountered at the hospital she had attended:

> I found them all very pseudo, you know, very sort
> of tripped up by their expertise, do you know what
> I mean? I felt that they were being manipulative
> and using their training - you could feel this - that
> they were more interested in getting a kind of ego
> kick out of being clever about you, than you were
> getting out of the sort of humane approach which
> Gwenda has.

Marjorie felt that she had gained a sense of perspective
on her problems which she had been able to pass on to
her family - 'like a pebble in a pool, the ripples, you know
what I mean...?':

> You see, particularly if you are using anything (i.e.
> drugs) yourself, your sense of perspective goes.
> I mean, drugs do have the sort of effect of warping
> the judgement, so one needs somebody with a cool
> head and a very matter of fact approach, not heavy
> and dramatic, 'Oh, my God, you're schizophrenic', or you
> know what I mean. I mean, it's been an enormous help to
> me really. In fact, there's a girl coming now, here, who
> was in a terrible state and I was able to tell her to come
> and she does come, you know, I mean, lots of people
> don't, they go once and they don't bother to come back.
> But this girl, she's a friend of my niece, and she pops in
> to see Gwenda quite a lot and she's definitely been
> helped. So I think it's an essential, you know? ... it's
> here to help people who've got drug problems, isn't it? I

mean, there's an awful lot of bumph in this area, a hell
of a lot, it's an anchor, isn't it, for these people. Not an
anchor, what is the word I want? It's a centrepoint,
something they can grasp on to, you know, everything is
so chaotic in their lives they are scrubbing about, they
are trying to raise money for drugs, you know, it's like
having a mother you can go to. And it just sort of gives
them a bit of strength I think to help them to sort of be
able to think about their problem in a more relaxed way
instead of dashing madly, you know how they go, they
haven't got much time to think. To sit down here for an
hour you begin to be able to sort of talk about why you
do it ...

Claire - 'a real help in staying off'

Claire has been using the Blenheim on and off for two
years or so.   She first described how she sought help
with her drug use:

I first went to my GP in Hampstead, because I was
going to ask him for methadone. I was on heroin
at the time, and he said he is not allowed to prescribe
methadone, but they are, in fact, apparently. He
said he wasn't allowed to. But I found out through
some friends, drug users, about the National Temperance
Hospital. And I was there for about six months on
methadone. At the end of six months you have to
come off. So I went into a hostel for a couple of
weeks to come off and came out again. This is about,
over two years ago, this is. Got off the methadone,
came out of hospital, I was alright - back to using
drugs and everything and then I got myself into a
real - pretty bad state, using a lot.   Went to see
my GP in Westbourne Park, where I am living now,
and she referred me to try the Blenheim Project,
to go and see them and what they could do for me.
It was two years ago when I first came here ...

My experience of hospital was a bit heavy, making
you come off when you weren't ready to sort of
thing. I was a bit nervous about coming to the Blenheim.

That's when they were in Acklam Road. I remember feeling a tremendous sense of relief ... talking to them. They really did seem to understand. I felt I was more on the same wave-length with them than I would with a GP or one of the special drug clinics.

I was very determined to stay on heroin. And they then put me in touch, referred me to a private doctor in Croydon. He prescribes heroin and pills. It was right for me at the time. I was in a terrible mess. I couldn't afford what I was using but no way was I going to come off so they referred me to him. He was full up actually, he didn't want to take any more people. And I was recently told that he only took me because I had been referred by the Blenheim. So it's quite a good contact I think, between the Blenheim and doctor. So, I've been with him now for about one and a half years and decided about two months ago I wanted to come off, so I've been in hospital for about six weeks, been out about a week now and I just got into touch with the Blenheim again.

Claire had found that withdrawal was not as easy as she had hoped or thought, and felt that the Blenheim would be able to help her in some way:

I found it was not as easy as I thought it would be. I was worried about all the tranquillizers I was on, put on by the doctor. So I came here as a cry for help, really - what can I do? Can you offer me any help? I had a chat with Lin, oh, I can come in whenever I want for counselling and also they've given me addresses, given me various ideas, they've thrown at me, to try and help me get off the tranquillizers as well. I'm going to relaxation classes, maybe thinking of trying an acupuncturist, put me in touch with a psychotherapist if I wanted one, also got the Narcotics Anonymous numbers from them to try that.

Like many street agency clients, Claire was keen to contrast the approach of the Blenheim with that which she had encountered in clinics and elsewhere:

I went in to come off heroin and they treat you
as though you are a sick person, which one isn't really.
Not sick, taking drugs, that's bad but it doesn't mean
you are mentally sick.   And they put me on various
different   types   of   antidepressants,   sedatives   and
all that lot.   Which I don't really like because, I got
really emotional because I was coming off, crying
a lot and someone thought, you know, damp all that
down, put her on antidepressants, make her all cheerful
... prescribing pills and then getting stabilised on
your pills and then shoving you out.   Whereas here
it's more ... I have to get off my pills I'm on at the
moment, I was nervous about coming off them.

And someone's going to my GP and speak to her
- they need to have a chat with the GP themselves.
She doesn't want me to start cutting pills, (so we
have) to find out the best way of going about cutting
down slowly.

Claire had previously had little follow-up assistance
in staying off.   A social worker who had been attached
to the private doctor's practice had persuaded her to
take a place in a concept-based house in northern England
which turned out to be highly inappropriate, and Claire
left after two days.   She feels that the Blenheim can
offer a broader degree of support and assistance:

Basically, they are here to see people and decide
what's best for them, make referrals, rehabilitation,
doctors, or whatever is right for you ... They don't
push you into anything, they just feed you up with
ideas, and follow up ideas for you if you are interested.
Individually work out what is best for each person
rather than some drug clinics, methadone programme,
off in six months, you know, that's it, sort of thing
... the doctor tends to treat you as if you were mentally
ill and just prescribe something for you and doesn't
really want to get involved at all because I think
it worries most GPs, and drug clinics, they are very
much authority figures, not really talking to you
personally.

> Two years ago I got real help from them (Blenheim) and now I'm getting real, help from them in staying off drugs.

> Is it similar to the Hungerford? It is a street agency as well, isn't it? I think maybe they (the Hungerford) are more a street agency. They aren't always as calm and relaxed and interested, as the Blenheim is. I think there ought to be more street agencies rather than going to a clinic and being prescribed methadone.

Claire's final point about the difference between the Blenheim and the Hungerford is worth emphasising at the end of our survey of the three agencies. It is possible that some clients might favour the sort of streetwise, street-pressure type of environment that the Hungerford has to deal with, whereas for other people like Claire the quieter and calmer atmosphere of the Blenheim (without so many people dropping in all the time) is valued as safer and more reassuring.

Any description of the work of the three agencies therefore, has to take into account not only where they are located and therefore the people that call in off the street, as well as the formal philosophies and social work styles of the staff, but also the atmospheres of the agencies - which clients get to know, and which are relevant to their choice of one agency or another.

WHAT ELSE CAN BE DONE TO MEET CLIENTS' NEEDS?

In their development of new directions for the agency, the Blenheim staff suggest that they ask themselves 'What else can be done realistically?'(Lin). One possibility recognised by Blenheim staff is to attempt to correct what Steve identifies as an imbalance between client assessment and the development of new services to meet the needs uncovered by such assessment:

There is an imbalance between what I reckon is us making a fairly accurate assessment of what somebody needs and actually being able to deliver it. The way that I cope with that sort of frustration is to get more involved in what you might call the political with a small 'p' stuff, about the development of services and about trying to encourage a view among people that are in a position to make decisions about these things, that certain things are happening, and a response needs to be made, and that the responses being made at present aren't appropriate to people, and I think, for the street agencies in general, that they are in a very good position to do that and I don't think that should be at all underestimated as an important area of work.(Steve)

One of the practical vehicles for getting across the message about the need for a wide range of services to meet the range of client needs, as these crystallise at particular times, is education and training. There is much enthusiasm about the extension of the agency's 'How to help' series of leaflets and some talk of getting a full-time training officer to further 'demystify' the practice of working with drug users.

What else can be done realistically? I think the whole thing of education and training - getting rid of all these stereotypes - I think that can be done. We've certainly started to do that, as have other agencies. I think it's really important to go and talk to parents' groups, schools, colleges, nurses, to police, social workers, youth workers, all the people that anyone with a drug problem is going to come into contact with, that at the moment just throw up their hands in horror and can't cope with that. Because I don't think that a drug problem is a very specialist kind of thing that only specialist agencies can deal with. I think that's ridiculous. Because there are so few facilities, you know, you train everybody so that more people can work with people with drug problems. (Lin)

Finally, the agency's attempt to develop its own services so as to meet manifest client needs not being met elsewhere may take the Blenheim into their potentially most ambitious project and one which, if it comes off, should take up much of their resources - at least initially.

> The detox centre that we are planning to open here is going to be wonderfully exciting. It is much more for people who are working, women can go with kids, couples can go together, you can go with friends and family. Take a week off work, a weekend at both ends, (get involved in) art therapy, occupational therapists, all kinds of things, acupuncture. It's going to be different from the things that there are at the moment.

Should the detoxification centre and associated activities be successfully launched, then the project will in one sense finally and fully have turned the corner on the difficulties it faced in the mid-1970s in connection with its then Day Centre. The Day Centre was supposed to provide an environment in which users could maintain themselves physically and socially as such, and it was closed by the agency because the users were, basically 'taking over'. It has taken some years for the Blenheim - indeed for each of the three street agencies - to consolidate a new form of social work practice that takes advantage of clients' episodic readiness to change themselves. The availability of a new detoxification activities centre would help to provide some of the material prerequisites to an expansion of this service. But, looking back on the past history (described in chapter 2) it is clear that management of such a centre would be fraught with difficulty and this suggests that the Blenheim should be clear about the extent of its commitments and obligations to the centre. However, it is through confronting such difficulties that the street agencies have been able to develop a range of social work practices that would not otherwise exist in the drug field. It is in this ability to innovate, and to demand to have their discoveries (and the perspectives of their clients) taken seriously, that a significant degree of the value of the street agencies lies.

ISSUES IN THE REFERRAL SYSTEM

Who defines the problem, the service, and grounds for referral?

An operational dilemma for all three street agencies, no matter how settled they are in their view of drug problems as their principal priorities, is how far to extend their services to help with the range of other problems that they encounter.

In the case of the Hungerford the focus upon drug problems is clear, and attendant (i.e. drug-related) problems are usually referred on to other agencies once a certain stage of the agency's capacity to help has been reached. The Community Drug Project attempts to deal with 'accompanying' problems that arise within the context of an established long-term relationship with a client, but refers on in most other cases. The Blenheim, however, has had a broader base of concerns from its inception, and therefore experiences some understandable ambivalence about handing on problems other than those with a drug focus - such as housing, social security etc. This ambivalence is expressed in Roger's description of how the agency has come ot see itself and how clients have come to view its service:

> People are now seeing us very much as - although we're trying to counter that - that we'll deal with the drug side of their problem and they'll go somewhere else to deal with the other bits and sometimes if things are complicated we'll advise people to go to the CAB or Housing Advice Centre because they do have specialist skills that we've not got. As things have got more and more legalistic and complicated our specialisation has become drugs and we've lost out on the homelessness and welfare rights bit. We see ourselves probably as a coordinating centre, if someone's got some problems then we coordinate other people sorting them out as well as anything else...(Roger)

This is not only a legacy of the Blenheim's past; it is also a reaction to the attitudes of staff in the many agencies in the referral networks that the Blenheim either has used or has tried to use. Such attitudes (say Blenheim staff) perpetuate harmful stereotypes, short-circuit sensible and preventative paths of action, and often occur where staff should know better. Where the dominant stereotype is of the client as dishonest and unreliable then it is not surprising that in many cases the view becomes a self-fulfilling prophecy:

> Very inflexible attitudes towards drug users just doesn't do very much to encourage drug-using people to go in there. With any drug users, particularly with women, particularly when they are with kids. I think it's a real problem in clinics, you know, like women with kids are already frightened to go into clinics because the kids will be whipped into care possibly, or at least put on the 'at risk' register. That is what happens. And it's such a Catch 22, because if someone is chaotic on the streets, you know, all over the place, teh quality of parenting is pretty bad and if they go and get registered and stabilised in some way, that quality of parenting would improve, but because they are so frightened because of the kids, they won't do that. And also because people always ask, 'where do you get your money?'. Everyone's asked that, but it's kind of assumed that women are going to be on the game.(Lin)

It is particularly disturbing that criticism of this sort should be levelled at medical staff in the clinics and also the medical professional that may be the first point of contact for the worried drug user - the GP:

> GPs is a worrier. A lot of them are pretty ignorant. They don't really want to know. They have this picture of a stereotype quite often. Of Piccadilly bogs and things like that. And we have, in fact, only one GP locally who offers counselling facilities, symptomatic treatment, not methadone and so on.(Gwenda)

However difficult it may be, the Blenheim staff obviously wish to feel that they control the definition of the service that they give and the description of those to whom they give it. Unfortunately, one corollary of prevalent misinformation about drug problems and drug users is that people are often under a misapprehension about what the project does. We have already noted that some clients themselves appear at the project hoping for a benign source of prescribed drugs. But misunderstandings about the work that the project takes on also extends throughout the referral network.

> The people that are coming in a the moment are coming from quite a broad cross section and I think a lot of that has to do with people's misunderstandings of what drug problems are. Also people's understanding of what the project does, depending on what their interpretation of it is, then, obviously they send different people to us. Like there was some bloke that came in the other day, with a glue-sniffing problem, and the information had come via a church youth-worker, who'd got it from the Knights of St. Columbus newsletter, which had us down as dealing with glue-sniffing. Now, those kind of things, they didn't get it from us that we dealt with glue-sniffing. It's kind of, somebody does a directory or picks up some information, somebody else says, oh, glue, drugs, and they get strangely transmuted to something else.(Steve)

Apart from the fact that the Blenheim project does not consider glue sniffing a serious drug problem, and perhaps not a 'drug problem' at all, this particular example is fairly trivial. But as an instance of a commonly recurring event, it indicates breakdowns in communication among an inadequately informed and serviced network of agencies that could work more efficiently with more accurate information and the resources to process it.

Serious consequences can follow from inappropriate referrals if they are not immediately identified as such and dealt with accordingly:

> Although people do come in, and there isn't drugs anywhere in it, it's sometimes quite hard to say, look, go away, you don't come into our thing, so we do try and deal with whatever it is. But I suppose it gives us a get out if we just feel it's not kind of within us. I mean there was a bloke in here the other day actually, that did want to enquire about detox and things, and he was actually very psychiatrically ill, he'd been in and out of care for years, and he

was referred by his psychiatric social worker, it just seemed so much more appropriate for her to deal with it than me, because he'd have to go to the Bexley or one of the psychiatric hospitals, and you know, she knows him, she's with him in the day centre, I'm sure she knows much more about what's available than I do and it seemed really odd in a way that she sent him here.   But I had a chat with her and that was fine and we sorted it out, and I think that we are not always the best place for somebody and it's OK to accept that.   We don't have to feel that we can do it all really.(Lin)

Unsystematic, individualistic and regular referral links

It is important to note that, as with the other street agencies, the Blenheim recognises its own role in the general referral network and, also, within that role, recognises its limitations.

Perhaps more importantly, it also recognises the limitations of the referral network itself.   This is a rejection of any idealised vision of eagerly interlinking agencies, knowing their own capabilities and the capacities of others, with certain key and established agencies almost acting as brokers to keep the system smoothly inter-dependent and mutually aware.   The reality is a rather more piecemeal set of connections based, for all the agencies, less on systematic networking and more on coincidence, happenstance and circumstance.

So the way it's tended to develop in terms of relationships with other agencies has been in a fairly piecemeal sort of way.   Which means, in turn, that it's usually directed by the customers who are coming in, in the sense that if they have a probation officer in, say, Kilburn, then we will develop some sort of contact with Kilburn probation office and that, in turn, means the next time Kilburn probation office gets somebody with a drug problem they are more likely to contact us.   And so there is a kind of ideal of how Blenheim should be working with other agencies in terms of having fairly good contacts with a lot of them and being able to link into a lot of networks and suchlike, like hang between them.   But in actual

fact it's quite difficult to do that because the common
factor in terms of the agencies that we are contacting
is usually the fact that they are in contact with
us rather than plugging into a network which has
got all sorts of relationships between them. Like
if we were, say, all that clued up on what a local
probation officer was doing, then we'd also have
keys into all the sort of facilities that they use,
and their hostels and that kind of thing and we don't.
We don't in fact have that.(Steve)

Such realism about the way in which referral networks
evolve also extends to the agency's perception of how
it sometimes can and sometimes cannot work effectively
with other agencies on joint projects.   One example is
offered by Steve in discussing the fate of a project planned
with the Cyrenians and aimed at extending support to
clients who had recently left the Cyrenians' hostel and
were attempting to establish an independent lifestyle:

The Cyrenians we worked with for a while. We were
working with people that had left the Cyrenians'
hostel and moved on to their own accommodation
and we were seeing the need, and they were seeing
the need, because people tended to get fairly isolated,
a kind of difficult transition between living in a
hostel and living on your own.   But it was just a
completely different way of operating.   We did that
for a while and found that in the end the numbers
concerned didn't really justify what we were doing and
we came to a joint decision that we wouldn't do that any
more.   Which I think was great, you know, because I
think there is nothing worse than holding onto something
and having a lingering death with everyone too afraid to
say, 'look, this isn't working'. I think we were actually
fairly responsible about doing that.(Steve)

Such realistic attitudes have not always been a characteristic
of the Blenheim, or indeed of many agencies in the field,
and this undoubtedly allowed them - consciously or unconsciously
- to misconstrue what other agencies themselves do and
minimise the potential for cooperative work.   In the
past this was the case even with relations with the other
street agencies:

> I think when we were going through our crisis, we
> were very apprehensive and scathing of the work
> that was being done in almost every other agency
> in the country and I think part of that was to do
> with our own paranoia about our own position. Part
> of it was to do with our misunderstanding that they
> were seeing a different group of people to us, they
> were in a different area, and just because they were
> in this case another street agency, didn't mean that
> they were necessarily seeing the same sorts of people
> so we couldn't understand why they were working
> in a totally different kind of way. I mean, nowadays,
> I think we get on extremely well, we all work in
> different ways because the personalities involved are
> different and because the areas that people are working
> in are different, and having accepted that then you can
> make the jump into looking at some common factors and
> some common problems that come up.(Steve)

What this particular explanation of the changing conditions
which dispelled an atmosphere of distrust and the promotion
of mutual support and cooperation leaves out is the turnover
of agency staff. This should not be forgotten or underemphasised.
As we have noted, the street agencies, and indeed much
of the non-statutory and statutory sectors, have a staff
turnover which, at least in the younger stages of people's
careers, seems to go in three or four year cycles. The
staffs of the street agencies, as well as others, are not
the same today as they were before relations got better
between them. Importantly, the relationships which
exist between agencies *per se*, but are often relationships
between particular staff team compositions, or simply
fairly individual contacts between individual workers.
As a basis for long term cooperation and coordination
of provision, this situation obviously has its dangers.
This was a source of concern which Ruth had noted in
the past:

> I think what it boiled down to was, and perhaps still
> is, I don't know, individual contacts between individual
> workers, do you know what I mean? So that the
> link between the agencies would travel through the
> relationships between two individual workers. And
> if one of the workers left, then the link would break.
> And I was conscious of that at the time.(Ruth)

It is likely that the three street agencies themselves now feel sufficiently confident about their own complementarity and distinctiveness to have forged links with each other which will be sustained throughout periods of staff change and so on. However, this remains a point to bear in mind, especially as there are some indications that the three agencies, while all placing emphasis on their own desire that other agencies understand their priorities and ways of working, do not necessarily describe each other as accurately as they themselves would like to be described.

While the Blenheim does indeed take referrals from across London and beyond and, similarly, makes onward referrals on such a scale, it is fortunate in having good connections with a variety of services in the West London area specifically.

> We've got a fairly good relationship with quite a lot of local groups, the Citizens Advice, the Housing Emergency, a fair amount of contact there. Obviously where we've got the most contact is with the local groups, in this community, North Kensington, but because not everyone who comes in here is from this area, what's actually needed is to find out what local groups there are in their areas as we haven't got enormous lists of what the local groups are. Because we've built up relationships with groups here they are more likely to take people and that would not be the case in other areas.(Lin)

To a significant extent the development of such local contacts reflects the Blenheim's belief that alternative means of providing support for people to come off or cope with drugs must be found for those who would not find referral to a detoxification facility and concept house appropriate:

> The majority, or almost the majority of people we see, they don't want to go off to rehabs. They don't want to go off to detox ... basically, it's not appropriate for them to go off and live in a bubble for two years. They are basically staying here in the community and so that might mean finding local voluntary work in the community; if it's women, putting them in touch with women's groups; things

like evening classes, TOPS courses, or the voluntary
workers' bureau down the road, we have quite a
lot of contact with them.(Lin)

The long concern of the Blenheim with housing problems
has obviously contributed to the establishment of contacts
with housing advice agencies and also with non-concept
based residential projects.   The Cyrenians' hostels were
a frequent source and recipient of referrals in the past,
but no longer take drug users.   Good contact has been
built with other supportive communities, however, such as
Elizabeth House and the nearby Alwyn House for drug free
residents, and ROMA for notified users on prescription.
Perhaps less supportive but no less vital is the availability of
over-night bed space at Riverpoint which the Blenheim views
as its local nightshelter.

Steve describes the state of relations with the rehabilitation
houses, noting how some projects are developing and
(as we have noted above) presenting relationships between
agencies in terms of relationships between workers in
them:

The rehabs - as a rule we don't use rehabs that much,
but I think we've got fairly cordial relations.   But
there again, not on a day to day level, I don't think
any of us are particularly chummy with any of the
workers.   And not that we don't like them, just that
we don't come across each other.   Cranstoun, the
whole of the sort of EAPA (Esher Association for
the Prevention of Addiction) network, is beginning
to pick up on more people ... there is some sort of
tie-in there with things like the Leatherhead Association
for the Prevention of Addiction ... And the 235 Project,
we are beginning to have more contacts with them.   But
they are also in the position of spreading beyond being
just Cranstoun, they're moving out into areas of advice
through the Leatherhead thing, parents' groups, that sort
of contact.   I think rehabs, agencies in the non-statutory
field, in the drugs area, they recognise what we can do in
terms of running down the options for people.   So we get
on pretty well I think.   They are also kind of anxious, I
think, about some of the things we have been saying
about (their) approaches, and suchlike.   I think they're
beginning to pick up on that a bit.   City Roads also refer
quite a lot of people to us.   'Cos they tend to get people

phoning up at odd times or whatever and they say, well,
if you want to have a chat, and you happen to live in
West London, or whatever, give the Blenheim a ring, and
that's great.(Steve)

Apart from the rehabiliation, residential and crisis
intervention agencies, there are other specialised drugs
agencies with which referral contacts are strong. The
most obvious are the other street agencies, but there
is also contact with Release and out-of-London projects,
such as Lifeline (which stocks the Blenheim's leaflets).
The development of contact with various women's groups
has also been important to the Blenheim in recent years
in their efforts to encourage more referrals of women
clients to the project. While Roger was at the project,
he was involved in Festival Welfare Services, a link with
the Blenheim's counter-cultural past. Festival Aid provides
drugs advice and welfare advice workers for people attending
free music festivals which take place around the country.
The experimental drug scene of the festivals, no longer
bound together by the rules and understandings of the
1960s and 1970s 'counter-cultures', tends to encourage
chaotic use and the mixture of a variety of drugs. Through
this work the Blenheim have picked up a number of clients
that they wouldn't normally get, people who might be
put off going to the office of an agency in the city but
who might feel less intimidated about approaching a
tent in a field. With Roger leaving the project, however,
this particular aspect of the Blenheim's own brand of
'detached' work may not be pursued. As with some other
aspect of street agency work, the role may leave with
the individual. Relationships between the non-statutory
and statutory sectors are often forced or at least encouraged
by the intervention of law and the need to resolve legal
problems.

For the Blenheim, its relationship with the local North
Kensington Law Centre can be very valuable, and the
relationship is cemented beyond the regularity of mutual
referrals by the presence of a representative of the Law
Centre on the project's management committee:

The main kind of contact with the Law Centre is
care orders being slapped onto kids and, you know,
the parents going to a Law Centre to fight it and

the Law Centre sending them to us as well. So there's been like a three-way liaison on a few occasions between the social services, the Law Centres and us. But that has been only when it has involved kids, otherwise, it was always someone who was a single man or woman drug user, they wouldn't get a social worker anyway.

Specialist drug units and generic medical care

For all three street agencies past and present members of staff commented on the shift from a mood of suspicion to a mood of cooperation with which the statutory agencies had approached them. Speaking with past experience of work in both the Blenheim and CDP, and currently employed as a member of the social work staff of a regional drug clinic, Ira suggested that:

> There was always a lack of faith ... that the statutory
> agencies had in the voluntary agencies in the drugs
> field. Strangely enough, that has not been so in
> the alcohol field, where, I think, the voluntary and
> statutory agencies work far more hand in hand.
> I'm not sure why. I suppose it could be differing
> philosophies. On the whole, drug treatment units
> have seen drug problems as more a manifestation
> of personal inadequacy, while voluntary agencies
> have seen drug problems more of a manifestation
> of broader social problems and the result has been
> a philosophical conflict between the two. However,
> I think that recently there has been more of a merging
> of the two views ... And that's maybe why now the
> voluntary agencies are able to have closer links
> with statutory agencies. And I suppose as well,
> that voluntary agencies have been around long enough
> now, because after all, if you go back to 1968, there
> were virtually no voluntary agencies in the drugs field,
> and 15 years isn't a long time, but I think they have
> shown that they are permanent. That's an important
> first step. I think, however, there needs to be more
> cooperation, but that's obviously something the agencies
> need to determine between themselves.(Ira)

Steve describes the position today, observing that whilst boundaries may be blurring between the statutory and non-statutory agencies at some levels, the latter can and should still retain a partisan position.

> I think we've got beyond the stage where we are kind of at war with the statutory services in that sense, because I think, generally with voluntary organisations, the line between statutory services and voluntary services is a greyer area and I think people generally appreciate that ... But there is also still an element of feeling that street agencies, in particular, are run by a bunch of hippies who are trying to, you know, they happen to have got lucky enough to get paid for doing something they would probably be doing anyway. Sure, I think agencies like the Blenheim are more partisan in the sense that they've got less organisational restraints on them than say a statutory service has. But I mean, I think that's OK. You know, what's wrong with that? I think those workers in statutory agencies, they get worried that their motives are going to get misunderstood because I do think they tread quite a knife edge in that respect. You know, they are much more clearly than, say, we are, in a position of being between customers and general social policy decisions and having to be aware of the fact that they've got a social services committee that is scrutinising their work and that sort of thing. And I think it does make it difficult for them. I think in lots of ways that we are in quite a fortunate position insomuch as we can approach the whole deal without so much ambivalence.

This situation may allow street agency staff to feel less ambivalent about their work but it also denies them some of the statutory powers which they might at times prefer to have rather than having to bargain, plead and cajole for resources. This is not to say that the statutory sector can claim automatic access to what are, after all, extremely scarce resources, simply that in competing for them the street agencies can face a lot of frustration and disappointment. Lin describes how the successful referral of one client to a clinic can nonetheless be a frustrating experience for the social worker:

The people that were just in here before basically
wanted to go to a DDU, and they live in Fulham,
but Charing Cross just aren't taking any more people
at all. So I had to make out a case for him ... I always
feel like I've had to do this whole bit, because they've
got a two year old daughter, and his wife's four months
pregnant, and everything's on the rocks. And he's
self employed and ... has been keeping it fairly together,
but can't do it any more and I have to do this whole
big sob story and they said to me at the clinic, 'right,
what can you say to me, that will make me think
that we'll take him and not somebody else?' and
so I did it and after that $2\frac{1}{2}$ weeks they finally decided
that, 'yes, they would give him an appointment'.

I mean he was just saying to me now that most people
don't last for $2\frac{1}{2}$ weeks, they just disappear, you
know, and it's very few people that can, at that
stage, last out for 2 weeks. But I was just thinking,
he was doing the 'oh, thank you, you're so wonderful
bit', and basically, yes, I pulled a few strings and
got him in there. But all that means is that some
other poor sod's been pushed down to the bottom.
And I often just think, you know, I mean, what's
the point of it all.(Lin)

The role of the clinics is commented on more generally
by Steve:

The clinics I think basically are a very marginal
activity to what's going on in the drugs field, and
I don't think they have accepted that. I think they see
what they are doing as having a very much more central
role than it actually has and certainly our experience
here - I think we've got a much broader perspective of
what's happening in the drugs scene in general than a
clinic has, but we don't have the power to be able to
influence decision-making - and that's a real imbalance.
(Steve)

The Blenheim's view of the clinic system does not
in any way predispose it to oppose the provision of medical
assistance with drug problems. The agency is keen to
get clients who need such help to establish a relationship

with their own GP and the agency also disagrees with
a number of other workers in drugs agencies who oppose
the use of private doctors.

> If we get someone who is just on the brink of sort
> of going over the top, getting very dependent, if
> they are willing, we actually write a letter to their
> GP and suggest certain things to them and we hope
> they don't think we're being terribly presumptuous
> but, you know, it's often out of their line of vision
> ...(Gwenda)

> We need so many more different approaches around,
> so that at least there are choices. I mean, I'm against
> any kind of private medicine, of course I am, but
> at the same time, it's one more option. You know,
> it's there for non-drug users and it should be there
> for drug users too. And that's the reason why we
> sometimes use private doctors. But we don't advertise
> the fact that we have names, and we very rarely
> resort to them. But, as I say, some are OK and are
> ones that need to be there as a resort. As a resource.(Lin)

As was the case with the other two street agencies,
relationships with statutory social services seem to be
minimal, despite the fact that the local office is literally
down the road from the Blenheim. Steve feels that in
the past the social services have been reluctant to recognise
the existence of a drug problem in the area or among
the cases that they come across, but that this is now
changing. The Blenheim, like all the agencies seeking
to demystify social work practice with drug users, would
like the social services to recognise the problems of
such clients and principally deal with them as part of
the overall case of the client, or else in some cooperative
arrangement with an agency like the Blenheim. Hence
the role of the Blenheim in the referral network of the
statutory sector could, they suggest, place less emphasis
on any desire to be a competitive or even directly co-
working agency, and more on them being used as an information
and liaising agency. Describing a meeting with staff
from the local social services office, Steve suggests
how the Blenheim might view the development of their
work with statutory agencies like social services and

probation:

> A few months back I went and talked to all the seniors
> down at Westway social services, and that was interesting.
> In the sense that they were saying, 'well, surely
> we're going to come into conflict over situations
> like, for instance, care proceedings on a child whose
> parent or parents are using drugs'. And I think they
> felt a bit unsure about sharing work, in the sense
> that they saw what we were doing in some way as
> competition with that, because we were doing things
> like, 'this does not necessarily mean that if someone
> is using that they are a bad parent', and I think towards
> the end of the session they actually came to understand.
> And I said to them, 'look, what you've got to see
> is, if you phone me up about somebody and I say
> something, that is my opinion, you are still left with
> the decision. You've got the statutory responsibility
> to either decide to instigate care proceedings or
> not, but you should be doing that from a basis of
> the best possible information about that'.

> I suppose the basic principle for me is that if people
> are well enough informed then they will make rational
> decisions, you know, that's the kind of idea, and
> I think that that's something that needs to be worked
> on particularly with respect to drugs.

6 Complementarity in provision of a range of options

LESSONS FOR US ALL

The purpose of this concluding chapter is to overview our descriptions of the activities of the three agencies, and then to make some comments on possible future developments that are inherent in and emerging from their current work. Lastly we return briefly to broader issues of social policy (first raised in chapter 2) and discuss drug-related problems and responses to them within the context of the housing market, labour market, and other aspects of life in the 1980s. We hope that this admittedly rapid treatment of issues goes some way toward meeting the various needs of the street agencies and of the broader constituency of interested persons.

LOCAL RESPONSIVENESS AND LONDON-WIDE COMPLEMENTARITY

The services provided today by the three London non-statutory agencies described in this book are so diverse that it would be both difficult and misleading to attempt a summary in a nutshell. A decade ago, perhaps, the

services of each agency were rather more closely articulated
around one particular element (day centres - described
in chapter 2).   But today the day centres are no more,
and each agency has developed its particular mix of services
to other agencies and directly to clients, in response
to its location, history, referral links, local potential
clientele, and staff interests. Our feeling is that the information
that we have gathered (and the reader will appreciate
that we collected and recorded more than we could present
here) justifies the following statement:

> *The street agencies are best understood not as
> separate agencies but as complementary pieces
> in a wider jigsaw of response to drug-related
> problems.   They operate primarily on two levels
> - locally and London-wide - and in two main
> ways - services to individual clients and families
> and friends, and to other agencies (statutory
> and non-statutory: drug-specialist, generic, and
> specialising in fields other than drug problems).
> Services include telephone and face-to-face
> advice work (with drug users and with other agencies),
> counselling (sometimes over an extended period
> of time), referral of users and professional enquirers
> to other appropriate services, and education
> and training.   Whilst each of the three agencies
> covers each of these areas of work to some extent
> each also specialises in one or other aspect of
> work - probation work and training (CDP), publications
> and women's needs (Blenheim), pressing problems
> of street users (Hungerford).*

The extent to which the individual agencies operate
on one or another of these two levels varies with the
agency: the Hungerford, for example, works mainly in
the immediate locality whilst, at the other extreme,
CDP has very little local casework.   But this is not to
say that CDP has no walk-in self-referrals; nor that the
Hungerford does not operate at a London-wide level
- it does, but mainly in concert with the other two agencies.
The Blenheim falls in between these two positions, operating
at local and London-wide levels.

There is also the question of the extent to which each
agency or the agencies together can be said to have a
national 'presence'.

Of the three, it is perhaps the Blenheim that has, historically, been the most publicity-conscious and policy-orientated: and this agency publishes some practical guides on advice-giving, and on 'how to stop'. Lately, the three agencies have cooperated on press releases in response to government reports and other items of concern to them, and they also form a part (together with a small number of other agencies) of a 'street agencies group' which attempts to influence the policies of SCODA (Standing Conference on Drug Abuse, the DHSS-funded 'umbrella' organisation for non-statutory drugs agencies). This national presence has yet, however, to make itself effectively felt as far as policy-making is concerned. For example, none of the agencies were in any way involved as members of working groups drafting the government's Advisory Council on Misuse of Drugs reports on Treatment and Rehabilitation, or on Prevention. The Treatment and Rehabilitation report, which was published in 1982, is regarded by street agency staff as an inadequate document, biased against the voluntary sector generally, and neglectful of street agency experience in particular. It is fair to say that the agencies' direct influence on UK drugs policy is currently marginal (although the prospects for more subtle, longer-term contributions to policy making remain open). It is with these observations in mind that we restricted our summary statement above to the operation of the agencies at local level (where they operate autonomously from each other) and at the London-wide level (where they cooperate and are to some extent complementary).

In the following sections we reflect on some of the findings and implications of this study and offer some summary comments in respect of the organisation of work within each agency, relations between the three street agencies, relations between these and other London agencies, and the national picture.

INTERNAL ORGANISATION

The main practical day-to-day problems for the agencies is how to strike a balance between attention to funding, meeting the demands of other agencies, dealing with clients, and keeping adequate records on these activities.

There is necessarily a tension between these tasks,
even though each of them is a necessary part of the whole.
Full and clear records are, for example, important for
organising one's work with clients (particularly those
who keep contact with the agency over a period, or who
return episodically), and for assisting other agencies
with their drug-related workloads (in which case, records
on the aims, working methods, and drug-related information
needs of particular generic and specialist drug agencies
are particularly valuable). Also, full records - or at least
the appearance of full records - constitute an important
resource for applications for the funding necessary for
the agency to exist. But record-keeping can be extremely
time-consuming, with the result that other work (the
conduct of which is meant to be recorded) is disrupted.
A similar tension can occur between meeting the demands
of other agencies (phone enquiries, requests for visits,
training, etc.), and helping clients who present themselves
(or seeking out clients who could benefit from the service
but don't know of its existence and approachability).
On the one hand, working with other agencies may be
the most valuable long-term 'investment' (insofar as
generic agencies are enabled to cope better with drug-
related problems) but, on the other hand, clients have
quite pressing immediate needs which cannot always
be met by other agencies as they presently operate.
The resolution of such tensions is a constant problem
for the street agencies, and each comes to its (temporary,
still-developing) solution through an application of its
main resource (staff knowledge, experience and skills)
to the 'presenting problems' (ie. the mix of clients presentations,
other agencies' demands, and the current funding situation).
Because these circumstances differ from one street agency
to another, each strikes its own characteristic balance
between the various needs of the moment. The only
thing that is absolutely central to each of the three is
the need for funding.

Fundraising: continuing concern over agency survival

Fundraising was not something with which the staff of
most statutory services necessarily had to concern themselves
directly throughout the period leading up to 1982-3.

Statutory agency staff may concern themselves with the adequacy of manpower levels and material resources, such as buildings and equipment, and sometimes with the possibilities of getting funding for some specific project or new initiative: but the continuing existence of statutory organisations *per se* has not been in doubt. In the case of the three street agencies that we are discussing - and in the case of many other voluntary organisations - it is the very existence of the agency that is almost constantly in doubt. It is a rare year that allows the staff to say with confidence that they will be there in a year's time, because the whole agency is regarded by funders as a 'project', rather than an 'institution'. Hence the fight for survival tends to become the pivot around which other tensions and problems hang.

One possible response to this situation might be that routinely voiced by street agency staff themselves - the constant effort to raise funds from a variety of increasingly already-committed sources, and the staff strain and short-term prospectives encouraged by this rather hand to mouth existence, are detrimental to the agency and to its actual and potential clientele. Proper acknowledgement of the worth of the work of the street agencies should, this view continues, be matched by assurances of long-term rolling programmes of financial support, in which the state (at national, regional or local levels) underpins the continuing existence of the agency, leaving it free to concentrate on its work with clients and other agencies, and be able to support new sub-projects.

One argument against this view is that existing legislation does not provide a coherent framework for direct, long-term central government funding of local non-statutory projects. Such funds as government departments do make available to non-national organisations are generally channelled through regional and/or local administrative structures, emerging in the form of 'joint finance' (NHS funds with local government matching funds) or urban re-newal (DOE plus a proportion of local Borough funding). Only in particular instances does government directly fund local or regional projects, and then the emphasis is usually on so-called 'pump-priming' of new initiatives which are expected to be transferred to locally-available finance after a few years. The current DHSS 'drugs initiative' (£2 million p.a. for

3 years) is an example of this principle. Continuation of such
projects is premised upon the possibilities of there remaining
sufficient current account flexibility amongst the (potentially
rate-capped) local and regional Local Authorities, within NHS
Regional and District budgets, and/or within commercial and
charity budgets, to take up shortfalls in 1986-7. There are
few signs that the present government intends to trim the
directions of its general economic and fiscal policies sufficiently to permit the development of a general policy of
central government support of local or regional projects;
indeed the situation was similar under previous administra-
tions. Thus it seems realistic to consider as our main future
scenario a continuation of the situation in which fund-raising
is a central and continuing pre-occupation of the three street
agencies, and to discuss the future development of their work
within that framework.

Social and interpersonal prerequisites of agency survival

As we have already noted, fundraising is not the only
activity that the agencies have to maintain in order to
keep themselves ticking over as a working organisation
able to respond to clients. there are also administrative
tasks, book-keeping, compilation of records, production
of annual and other agency reports, correspondence not
only having to do with individual cases, relations with
landlords, responsibility for supply of heat, light, power,
tea, coffee, sugar, bisucits, etc. None of these tasks
(except the supply of refreshments) produces any immediate
benefits for clients - but the agency and its workers
would quickly cease to function without them. We can
therefore describe such tasks as being formal functional
prerequisites. Alongside these formal, technical prerequisites
are a number of informal, social prerequisites of street
agency work - such as joking and making cynical remarks
(as 'distancing' or coping responses to trying and upsetting
situations); giving practical and emotional support to
individual staff members as and when they need it; making
criticisms in an informed but constructive and non-threatening
manner; and defusing tensions within the agency. Such
social facilitation is as much a functional prerequisite
of work in a street agency setting as are the more technical

requirements for premises, telephones, etc.

From our contacts with, interviews with and observations of the agencies, it seems to us that the administrator, who is formally responsible for 'technical' services (including routine fundraising activities), also plays a key role in facilitating social relations within the agencies. The administrators are concerned with the business of keeping the agencies ticking over and it is they, especially, that have the most obvious affective roles within the agency. We can only speculate that their administrative responsibilities allow them to 'distance' themselves somewhat from the hectic day-to-day demands of social work practice (in a way more difficult for those staff members who are solely engaged in such practice), and to make helpful and occasionally critical remarks from a position that is not threatening (because the administrator/receptionist is not the 'senior'). We now attempt to place the administrator role in relation to other roles within the three agencies.

Discussion of a typology of agency functions and associated staff roles

In our Typology (Figure 6.1), we have contrasted this technical/social facilitation role of street agency administrators with three other roles that also seem to exist in each of the agencies. These are distinguished according to the degree to which each role is concerned with meeting immediate presenting needs of clients, and the extent to which it is concerned with the organisation's survival (and hence ability to meet client need over the longer term). The technical/social facilitation role that we have identified in agency administration can, for example, be rated as high in terms of its concern with organisational survival, and as relatively low in terms of its concern with meeting immediate client needs.

There are roles within the street agencies which we identify as being simultaneously highly concerned both with the organisation's survival and with immediate client need. (This is represented in the top right-hand cell of the ty-pology.) Some advice to other agencies falls into this category - when the contact is concerned with a particular client about whom he or she wants advice or support, and when the agency or individual advised is in a position to 'put

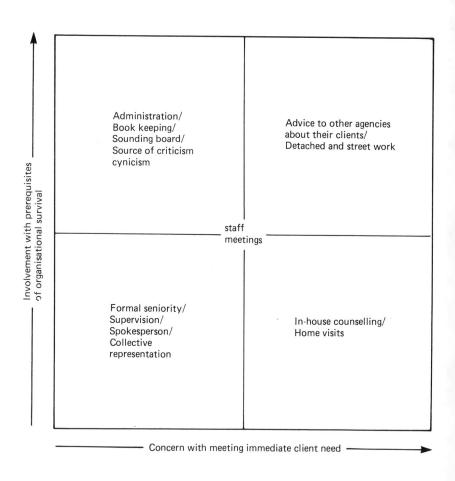

Figure 6.1:   Typology of four street agency functions and
              associated staff roles described according to
              degree of involvement with (i) organisational
              survival and (ii) meeting immediate client
              needs:

in a good word' with street agency funders (or potential funders). Detached work may also fall into this category, insofar as it is a method of making a worker immediately available 'on the streets' to those who want information or advice but who would not initially be disposed to refer themselves to the office; and detached work serves the longer-term function of organisational survival, insofar as it is a source of information about trends at street level, and also 'advertises' the agency's service to persons who may require its services at a future date. In each case, resources are being built up (contacts, information, goodwill) that may be used in the future.

The bottom right-handed cell of the typology refers to direct services to individual clients and their presenting problems (in the case of initial contacts) and emerging needs (in the case of repeated contacts or counselling). This role is highly concerned with immediate client care, and less concerned with organisational survival.

Lastly (bottom left-hand cell), there is the role of providing project leadership, supervision of other workers, spokesperson for the agency, and link with the management structure. In the case of CDP and the Hungerford, the position of Senior Social Worker exists, filled by Ronno and Jane respectively. It is our impression that, although the Blenheim operates as a staff collective, one person tends to emerge to take on some aspects of the role of the senior worker - being a vocal spokesperson for the agency. This is perhaps based on conscious (and unconscious) deference to experience and length of service with the agency, and *may* change as circumstances and staffing of the agency change.*

Whether such a *de facto* role is necessary, desirable, or just difficult to avoid is, of course, arguable. It does not seem necessary either from the point of view of organisational survival, or from that of direct responses to clients. One advantage of this lack of necessity is that there is a certain flexibility in the work-load of the senior worker, and this allows space for formal appraisal of existing services, and for development of new activities that are neither tightly organisational-survival orientated, nor client-responsive. This positive flexibility is most clearly

---

*By mid 1984 the situation in the Blenheim had changed, and staff were unhappy with our description.

seen in the case of CDP, where the relatively low client
demand has encouraged the senior to develop extremely
worthwhile initiatives, especially in respect of training
services to other drug-related agencies and to probation
services.

Each of these four roles - administrative/facilitatory,
advisory/detached work, intensive in-house and home
visit work with clients, and supervisor/spokesperson -
has its place in the overall functioning of the agencies
(though we must emphasise that the balance between them
differs between agencies and over time). Formal staff
meetings, and the more informal interaction that occurs in
the small teams as they go about their shared business, help
to hold these roles together and to provide opportunities for
sharing of the work. There is a high degree of flexibility and
work-sharing, and considerable scope for attempts either to
consolidate or to dissolve the division of labour between staff
in the street agencies.

Implications of this discussion

There are two reasons for attempting this perhaps rather
formal description of the division of work within the
street agencies. The first reason is that it may be helpful
to the agencies when they come to 'choice-points' in
their discussions about the organisation of their work,
responsibilities of individual workers and of the team
as a whole, and the appointment of new staff to replace
those who leave. Some degree of continuity is desirable,
and this can more easily be achieved if there is a clear
idea - shared by the staff and by management - about
the nature of the work and the qualities needed in replacement
staff. We hope that the preceding paragraphs provided
some thoughts that may be useful as an aid to discussion
in staff meetings - not only within the three street agencies,
but also within other agencies wishing to review their
working methods.

The second reasons for spending time on this description
in our concluding chapter relates to funding and to evaluation.
Firstly, prospective funders need to appreciate that 'direct
services to clients' measured in terms of client throughput
(i.e. through the office, and as recorded in a log of telephone
contacts) are simply a portion of the necessary work

of each agency. Each agency also has to have the capacity to do the other things described above, if it is to survive and function sufficiently well to help those clients whom it 'processes'. If the funders do not take that into consideration, then the street agencies will collapse - just as they did (to all intents and purposes) at points in the 1970s, when funding did not suffice to keep pace with the changing nature and expanding size of the drug problem in London (see chapter 2). Secondly, in relation to 'evaluation' of street agency services, potential sponsors and contractors of research need to appreciate that their studies must not focus exclusively upon client characteristics and upon client throughput, but must also take into account the value of the other tasks of street agency staff summarised above (and discussed in greater, qualitative detail in chapters 3-5). Insofar as external agencies' decisions on funding may (sometimes, rarely) be tied to their sponsorship or appraisal of evaluation studies, these two considerations are linked.

Summarising, we can say that future development of the agencies should take these issues of internal organisation into account. These remarks conclude our commentary on the internal organisation of work in the three street agencies.

RELATIONS BETWEEN THE THREE STREET AGENCIES

This and the following sections of this concluding chapter take as their point of departure the increasingly close relations between the three London street agencies, their tendency to cross-refer clients as and when appropriate (in terms of clients' needs) and feasible (in terms of agency workload, clients' domicile, etc), their cooperation around specific initiatives, and their mutual support and collaboration in the policy arena.

The question that we want to raise here is that of the extent to which, in the course of such cooperation, the agencies can and should specialise in a particular aspect of work (e.g. CDP in prisons and training; Blenheim in women's provision; Hungerford in street users and detached work). For this question to have any practical meaning it has to be related to one about funding.

Relationship between complementarity and funding

Only if funding is obtained from one or more regional
or London-wide sources (i.e. sponsors concerned with
areas larger than individual Boroughs or Health Districts)
is there any really practical basis for the agencies to
plan to share out metropolis-wide drug-related needs
between them. If funding were to be restricted solely
to very local sources, then there would be pressures to
focus on local needs (local clients, local agencies), and
this would militate against agency complementarity
on a metropolitan level. The street agency staff recognise
this situation and its funding implications:

> I think we have to be looked at as London-wide,
> given that there are only three agencies anyway,
> and I think that we are all metropolitan agencies;
> and to just look at ourselves in terms of a local
> agency raises lots of implications about funding
> and who is to use us and why. If we were local
> agencies, we wouldn't for instance be able to
> respond to somewhere as close as Lambeth, and
> yet we do ... If it were just the local borough
> that was pouring money into us, they would get
> quite stroppy because it isn't just their responsibility,
> it's a much wider responsibility.

Our own feeling is that the existing degree of complementarity
between agencies is useful, insofar as it allows each
agency to develop one or two specific services (to clients,
to other agencies) whilst maintaining the types of workload
that the agencies have in common with each other. Each
agency then remains a street agency in terms of its general
client-orientated social work, and builds upon this base
one or two specialisms (e.g. training), whilst not being
tempted to try to develop a wide range of services within
the confines of a narrow geographical area and funding
base.

This consideration implies a need for recognition of
the need for funding on a metropolitan basis. (NB: one
can say 'regional' instead of 'metropolitan' or 'London-
wide' as long as the first term is not taken to refer to
health service regions, four of which cover NE, NW,
SE and SW Thames, and would therefore need to co-fund

that proportion of street agencies' budgets corresponding to metropolitan services and administrative backup.)

Value of complementarity of services

Whether the tendency for each agency to develop its own 'specialist' services - such as training to other London agencies, developing the first strands of women-only provision in the drug/alcohol field (and discovering links between drug/alcohol problems and problems of violence against women, women's dependency on male support, etc.) - might go 'too far' as specialisation is a matter for discussion. Our own impression is that the development of specialisms by each agency and of complementarity between them is a very useful development that only becomes problematic if it begins to displace other essential functions of the agencies - and there are no signs of that happening at present. Where there are apparent gaps in the agencies' services to their localities (e.g. in CDP's lack of detached work and consequent lack of knowledge of local drug scenes), this is due to characteristics of the local area (where drug use takes place on estates, rather than on the street scenes more accessible to traditional methods of detached work), and to a lack of determination to initiate this service; such gaps in agency services do not seem to be connected to the agency's commitment to its specialist interests (prisons, training). In this particular case (of CDP) a community worker or similarly experienced person would be needed to generate the equivalent of detached work on local estates, and this would be a more productive line of development than another attempt at traditional approaches to detached work in that environment. Thus an undeveloped aspect of CDP's work (local knowledge, and trawling for clients) could be remedies alongside continuing development of its successful 'specialist' tasks (which are complementary to those of the other two agencies).

Summarising, we can say that the complementarity that has developed between the three London street agencies is useful, may quite possibly be an efficient use of resources on a London-wide basis, and seems to hold no immediate dangers. The street agencies may well feel that complementarity and specialisation should

continue, and probably develop further, funding permitting.
If regional or metropolitan funding seems inadequate
then consideration could be given to the possibility that
the innovative services that inter-agency co-operation
and complementarity facilitate might qualify for DHSS
Section 64 support as 'national experiments'. This seems
particularly apposite in respect of development of services
for women.

RELATIONS WITH OTHER LONDON AGENCIES

There are two main aspects of the street agencies' relations
with the wide range of London agencies with whom they
have some contact - for example drug dependence units
in the statutory sector; generic statutory services such
as probation, social services departments, GPs; non-statutory
services such as rehabilitation agencies and the one existing
crisis intervention centre.   These two aspects are first
what consequences the existence of the street agencies
may have on the perceptions of drug-related problems
and practices of other agencies, and secondly what these
other agencies think of the three street agencies (do
they think that the latter are useful, etc?).

Perceptions of the nature of 'the problem'

It is useful to refer here to a comment made in the closing
pages of the technical report on the evaluation of the
City Roads crisis intervention service. The Birkbeck College
researchers conclude that:

> What was an obscure and somewhat alarming
> problem of indeterminate dimensions, referring
> to people with relatively unknown characteristics
> and patterns of behaviour, has been clarified through
> the operation of City Roads. 'Multiple drug misuse'
> can now be seen to be a problem of manageable
> dimensions affecting people who can be fitted with-
> out much difficulty into the conventional recognis-
> able categories of 'deviants'; 'inadequate person-
> alities'; 'people with problems in living'; 'deprived
> people'; 'young offenders'; 'the homeless', etc. - over-

lapping categories, which overlap precisely because they are different ways of looking at the same people, which each single out and focus on specific aspects of a broader and more general pattern of living. (Jamieson et al, 1981; 59)

Similarly, the street agencies have helped to locate 'the problem drugtaker' within the context of 'a broader and more general pattern of living'. Right from their incepetion in the late 1960s and early 1970s, the street agencies have seen severe drug-related problems at first hand. As a result, they arguably have a more vivid impression of the problem and of its inter-relation with other problems than any other agency, statutory or non-statutory. In this book we have attempted to reflect the breadth of their experience and perceptions of the problem. In chapter 2, for example, we referred to the ways in which the drug problem may be shaped (in its qualitative as much as its quantitative aspects) by contextual systems such as the housing market, employment prospects, law enforcement, social welfare practices, policies and practices of drug clinics, and the availability of funds and methods of working in the non-statutory drug/alcohol/solvent agencies and community provision. One influence of the street agencies has been to encourage some staff in some of the statutory agencies to recognise these links, and hence to re-incorporate drug cases within their on-going social casework, advice and other services ('demystifying' drug-related work).

In attempting this task of institutional and professional re-education, the street agencies have faced an uphill task, as each new wave of public concern about drugs (amphetamine/cannabis/heroin/other sedative injectables/ solvent sniffing) has tended to redirect attention to specific substances rather than to elements of social welfare practice that can be applied to drug-related work in general. In this section we therefore want to give this aspect of the street agencies' work a helping hand, by quoting from three sources that support (in various ways) the idea that drug-related problems are about more than drugs and drug use. We present these quotations, without comment, as material for assimilation and discussion by readers.

On relations between housing and drug/alcohol problems in European and adjacent countries:

> Taipale's study reveals how structural changes in society and official measures have aggravated the problem faced by homeless alcoholics. The Second World War caused further housing shortages in Finland. Exceptionally rapid postwar structural changes, compounded by the process of urbanisation, placed a heavy burden on the housing stock, particularly victimising men without friends or family on the housing market. Strictly maintained public order, mirrored in an internationally high arrest rate for drunkenness, resulted in accumulated arrests among the homeless. Statistics on measures taken by the authorities have underscored the problems of the homeless. The large number of overnight boarding homes springing up in Helsinki after the Second World War acted to concentrate the homeless population in a specific few of these boarding homes. Investigating homeless drinkers as one part of the general housing shortage reveals that the low social status and discrimination on the housing market experienced by these alienated men prove to be the main problem. (Report of Finnish Foundation for Alcohol Studies)

The London street agencies acknowledge, both in their working philosophies and their social work practice, that the drug-related problems of some (probably a majority) of their clients are homelessness-related. The street agencies are amongst those agencies which emphasise that men are by no means the only ones at risk to such problems. The concept of 'hidden' drug problems amongst women (e.g. heavy tranquillizer, alcohol or illegal drug use in the context of being emotionally and economically tied to a damaging relationship with a man, and being unable to find alternative accommodation because the sexual partner and the housing market both act to prevent such independence) overlaps with the concept of hidden housing problems amongst women. Recent additions to the housing literature may therefore be of interest to those working in the drug field:

The traditional image of homeless single people tends to be associated with men - the most extreme version being that of the male tramp under the arches.   By focussing this study on women we hope to redress the balance.   Because fewer women are to be seen sleeping rough, there is an assumption that fewer women than men become homeless.   Rarely do we stop to question what this means.   Are there really fewer homeless women around, do women adopt different solutions to their housing problems or homelessness, or are homeless women simply forgotten or ignored?

The response of many people to these questions would be that there was indeed a smaller number of homeless women than men, and that is why homeless men are the ones who tend to be in the limelight.   The basis of this response hinges on the amount of provision for the homeless, and the numbers game.   There are more hostels for homeless men than for homeless women and more men sleep rough, so clearly there are more homeless men than homeless women - so the argument goes.   Researchers fall into the same trap.   They go to the hostels, collect statistics and come to the conclusion that there are fewer homeless women than homeless men.   The obvious point is overlooked: if homelessness is largely evaluated at looking at the provision for homeless people, for as long as there are fewer beds for homeless women than men, there will appear to be fewer homeless women than homeless men.   A vicious circle is perpetuated: the researcher justifies the lack of provision and the lack of provision pre-determines the outcome of the research.

But what of the possibility that women adopt different solutions to their housing problems such as staying with friends and that their homelessness is therefore more concealed?   Looking at the evidence on household structure, women's income and employment status, increase in marital breakdown, and the housing options available to low income single women, there are clearly many women on their own who potentially need housing.   Yet, with the lack of provision, their housing need remains unmet and unrecognised. Housing Advice Switchboard's (a housing advice agency for single people) statistics (1981) provide forceful evidence for this argument. They reveal that the number of single women telephoning the agency for advice in 1979 was virtually equal to the number of single male enquiries, and that the proportion of female to male callers appeared to be increasing. Other evidence of concealed households comes from the 1977 National Dwelling and Housing Survey which estimated that there were at least 1.3 million single adults in England unable to form an independant household, and sharing all their living arrangements with other people of necessity.

The evidence indicates that the numbers of homeless women are not truly reflected in the numbers of women using hostels, and that women's homelessness is to a large extent concealed.(Austerberry & Watson, 1983)

It is possible that the work of the street agencies provides elements of a 'bridge' between apparently different kinds of social and health problems (such as housing problems, problems around women's unmet needs, young people's needs in general, and drug-related problems).

On prevention of drug-related problems, the government's Advisory Council has said:

1.8 Previous studies of the prevention of drug misuse have often adopted the following framework: Primary Prevention (....) Secondary Prevention (....). Tertiary Prevention (...).

1.9 This framework has been applied to any medical and social problems, although it should not be afforded the status of a comprehensive model of the essential elements of prevention policy. No single category adequately decribed what we felt should be the scope of the report, and yet we could see no way of developing the framework without sacrificing its original purpose of providing a brief, simple analysis of preventative

measures.   We   were   therefore   unhappy   about
adopting   it   as   the   basis   for   our   consideration.
In its place, we decided that we should concentrate
on   preventative   measures   which   satisfied   two
basic criteria:

a)   reducing   the   risk   of   an   individual   engaging   in
drug misuse.
b)   reducing the harm associated with drug misuse.

(Advisory   Council   on   Misuse   of   Drugs   report
on Prevention, 1984)

Broadly   speaking,   the   street   agencies   engage   the   second
of these possibilities.   By helping clients and other agencies
to   re-assess   drug-related   problems,   and   by   providing
information,   advice,   counselling   and   referrals   to   other
services,   they   provide   opportunities   for   the   circumstances
of   the   drug   user   to   improve,   and   hence   for   drug-related
harm   to   be   reduced.   In   improved   circumstances,   some
users   are   able   to   re-assess   their   drug   use,   and   to   reduce
their   drug   consumption,   further   improving   their   position.
Hence the pursuite of (b) above can lead to the achievement
of (a).

On   treatment,   rehabilitation   and   'community   care',
a previous ACMD report said:

The aim should be therefore:

a) to enable problem drug takers to utilise personal
resources   and   so   modify   attitudes,   behaviour
and   skills   so   as   to   achieve   a   more   stable   and
fulfilling   life   with   minimal   or   no   drug   related
problems;

b)   to   provide   the   social   supports   and   agencies
required   to   facilitate   the   development   of   the
individual so as to establish or re-establish problem
drug   takers   in   the   community   in   roles   which
they   find   more   stable   and   fulfilling   than   those
related to their previous drug use.
ACMD, 1982;35)

The role of the street agencies relates strongly to both these aims. Of all the voluntary and statutory drug agencies, they probably have the keenest appreciation of the need to work with generic agencies so as to make these aims achievable in the context of the problems indicated in the preceding quotations.

Need to promote street agency perspectives

We come now to the question of the extent to which other agencies regard the street agencies as fulfilling useful purposes. Of all the agencies with whom we conducted face-to-face interviews, the majority were positive in their appraisal, and the remainder were of no firm opinion owing to the tenuous nature of their relations with the street agencies. In general, we found it difficult to elicit negative views of the street agencies (only one observer of the street scene made very critical comments, but these were not generally shared, so we shall not repeat them here).

One remaining problems seems to be that, whilst those staff members in other agencies who had worked with a street agency valued the service, this positive evaluation seems in most cases to have remained with the individual concerned, and not been generalised to other staff in that agency or to its senior and policy-making staff. Most staff in most generic health and social welfare agencies and departments in London neither know of the street agencies, nor of their work, nor of their perspectives on drug/solvent-related problems. The street agencies' training, education and 'policy' involvements have a long way to go, in these respects. Perhaps more attention to printed material - cooperatively produced and/or distributed by means of more aggressive marketing techniques (rather than passive filling of the occasional order) could improve the situation. It might also be useful if street agency staff were to write more articles for the social work, community work, education, probation and health practitioner journals, in order to generalise their experience and perspectives. Perhaps there is a role here for some other agency/agencies to assist them rather more than is being done at present; some of the more ambitious publication plans of individuals in and around the street agencies have floundered in the past. Again, here, there are funding implications, since street agency staff cannot produce written or audiovisual material and also meet the immediate demands of clients and other agencies.

Summarising, we can say that the potential scope of the education-by-example role that the street agencies might service in relation to the variety of statutory (and non-statutory) agencies in London and the surrounding area is very great; and that the street agencies have so far only been able, for financial and other reasons (including their youth) to begin to take on this important role.

THE NATIONAL PICTURE

A street agency staff member gave the following reply when asked for his observations on the work of the agency in the context of national problems:

> I do believe there should be more street agencies running. No matter what type of agency, we'll say CDP, us, or Blenheim, there's nobody could say we don't serve a purpose, and if they did they're actually blind. But, we've had somebody down from Drugline in Birmingham and just talking to her, it's obvious that what's needed up there is a street agency first. And then maybe to act as a pressure group, saying we are seeing so many opiate users who have nothing to do or we are seeing so many people who need rehabiliation, and I think if a street agency was founded and started monitoring what people were coming in and using, then they could actually have the power to say, 'We need this in this area, because we exist and we see the problem'. Take a place like Bradford - my predecessor did detached work in Bradford. he used to be a user in that area, so he knew it really well. He went to the social services up there and said, 'God, you've got a drug problem' and they said, 'No, we haven't', and he said to them, 'Well, why do you think you haven't?' and they said, 'Well, we don't have a drug squad, therefore we can't have a drug problem'.

So, that's what I'm saying, there should be street
agencies and similar type agencies all over England.
I think there's a drug problem in Glasgow. I know
there's one in Edinburgh.   There's one in Leeds.
There's one in Birmingham, we've got to know
that, there's one in Bradford. So if street agencies
were started off, they could act as a monitoring
thing to see what the problem was, a good research
unit, then a pressure group maybe to say there's
this and this has to be done.

The street agencies' own staff members' appraisals
of the value of their work and of the need for it to be
extended to other areas of the country are unequivocal.
The street agencies also have views about the distribution
of recently-released central government temporary funding
of drug projects:

Two million pounds - that's just ridiculous.   I
mean I'm really worried that that's all going
to DDUs, particularly some that shall remain
nameless. And I think that what is really important
is that there should be new options, different
options, and not just repetitions of what there
is.   Which actually isn't working for most people.
So what's the point of making more?   I think
there have been some new innovative ideas going
in there and I just really hope that they are going
to get some money and it's not just all going
to go to the big clinics.   It's not enough money
- there needs to be lots more.   And there needs
to be more of everything.   I mean new things
like ... more help places for women, more street
agencies, more detox places...

It should be noted that one obstacle to a proliferation
of street agencies and other similar agencies nationally
is the lack of a base of experience in drug-related problems
and skills in applying for funds, outside the statutory
sector.   We will have to wait until the three-year period
of DHSS 'Drugs Initiative' funding is completed and assessed
before it is possible to see to what extent street agency
type work has been facilitated.   The picture is complicated
by the short-term nature of this funding initiative.

Summarising our overall impressions of the three street agencies described here - and they must remain, frankly, impressions rather than research conclusions - we want to say that we think that more street agencies, constituting a nation-wide system, would have beneficial consequences locally, regionally and probably nationally (in terms of likely influence on public debate and government thinking in this and adjacent policy areas). But we see few signs of a national network of street agencies being an immediate possibility. This is regrettable, since the range of options (for clients and for other agencies) that have developed around the three London street agencies may well provide a relatively cost-effective form of response to contemporary patterns of drug-related problems.

In assessing our views, the reader may like to reflect upon one possible limitation. Although published fairly promptly after the completion of the study, we have to acknowledge that in one respect this book is already out of date. As we describe, working in these agencies is a difficult and demanding job and staff inevitably reach a point where they feel they must move on. The three agencies have all undergone substantial staff changes. this may mean that present staff feel that what we describe no longer accurately reflects the agencies. This may be so; we believe that we offer an accurate description of their recent experience. Making an account of that experience more widely available is the purpose of this book and its importance lies precisely in highlighting the development and renewal of practice in a neglected arena of social work. Britain's drug-related problems are becoming more serious and there is, therefore, a serious need to share what understanding has been gained on ways of helping drug users.

PROSPECTS : DRUG-RELATED SOCIAL WORK IN THE 1980s

We began chapter 2 (on the histories of the three London street agencies in the 1970s) by introducing the reader to four aspects of the context in which the agencies matured. These aspects were trends in drug-related provision in the N.H.S., in non-statutory drug agencies and in law enforcement as it impinges on drug users; housing and employment circumstances; developments in the broader field of social work; and the financial circumstances of the three street agencies. We presented a model, presented as Diagram 2.1 on page 12, within which the development of the Blenheim, C.D.P., and the Hungerford (and other similar agencies) could be described. Essentially, we showed how developments between the four important areas (noted above and in the diagram) affected the possibilities for various approaches to drug-related social work and care by the street agencies in the 1970s, rendering their Day Centres inoperable because of the 'compression' of wider social problems and conflicts into too small a social space, and putting too much pressure on the staff. This is the historical background to the closure of the Day Centres and to the subsequent development of the three agencies on the basis of a mixture of 'drop in' and appointment systems, offering advice, counselling and referral services to clients or 'customers', and also advising other agencies. Later, the agencies developed experience and skills in respect of training and publications, provision for women, and working in co-operation with each other and with a wide range of other agencies (statutory and non-statutory). This has led to a situation which we describe as service 'complementarity'. These are the circumstances in which the three London street agencies have developed (or at least, had done up to 1983, when our study was done).

But what of the circumstances that the three street agencies and others doing drug-related work face as we move into the second half of the 1980s?

In this final section of the book, we want to step back from the detail of the work of each agency (as described in chapters 3, 4 and 5) and take a more panoramic view of the circumstances with which we must somehow come to terms in 1984 and beyond. These circumstances are very crudely summarised in the Venn diagram 6.1 (which can be compared to that presented in chapter 2).

Summarising paragraphs to follow, we can say that at the present time an increasingly complex net of care, training, treatment and control is being woven around a variety of social groups in the inner city, and that the street agencies are caught up in the centre of this social

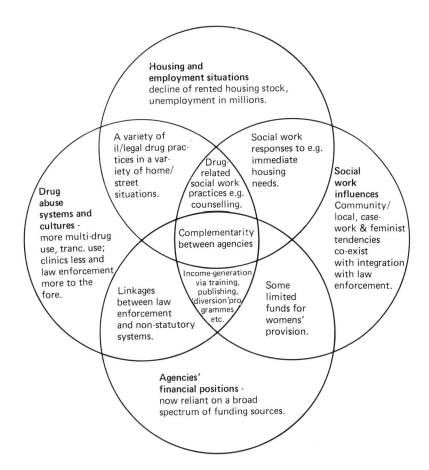

Housing and
employment situations
decline of rented housing stock,
unemployment in millions.

A variety of
il/legal drug prac-
tices in a var-
iety of home/
street
situations.

Drug
related
social work
practices e.g.
counselling.

Social work
responses to e.g.
immediate
housing
needs.

Drug
abuse
systems and
cultures -
more multi-drug
use, tranc. use;
clinics less and
law enforcement
more to the
fore.

Social
work
influences
Community/
local, case-
work & feminist
tendencies
co-exist
with integration
with law
enforcement.

Complementarity
between agencies

Income-generation
via training,
publishing,
'diversion'pro-
grammes,
etc.

Linkages
between law
enforcement
and non-statutory
systems.

Some
limited
funds for
womens'
provision.

Agencies'
financial positions -
now reliant on a broad
spectrum of funding sources.

Notes on how to read the Venn diagram Please read the diagram from outside,
inwards. The four overlapping systems/circles produce particular results;
e.g. the solidification of N.H.S. drug clinic practice around a general
policy of minimising opiate maintenance prescribing (left-hand circle),
together with the deployment of social work as a form of 'diversion' of the
individual from custodial aspects of the criminal justice system (centre
of diagram), plus swelling numbers of unhoused/unemployed persons and
responses (top), leads to a variety of new approaches to non-residential
and residential provision (centre of diagram). The street agencies are well
placed, because of their history & recent experiences, to encourage other agencies
to respond constructively to those complex problems (see text)

Diagram 6.1 From 'street agencies' in the 1970's to complementarity in social work practice in the 1980s:
influences upon the agencies from professional
social work, the drug abuse control system, the
housing market, etc, and available funding

drama, making their own distinctive contributions. Let us look at the situation as summarised in Diagram 6.1, taking each aspect in turn.

As far as drug-specific health provision and law enforcement policy is concerned, current indications are of a long-term drift from a primarily health-based response (albeit with legal underpinnings), to a law enforcement-based response. The Drug Dependency Clinics are now even less keen to prescribe injectable drugs than they were in the late 1970s and quite often see oral methadone as inappropriate for the bulk of multi-drug users who characterise today's street and housing estate drug scenes. For other problematic drug users, such as those having trouble with tranquillisers, the DDUs are of course not very relevant (nor were they ever supposed to be). Generally speaking, the variety and number of drug users outstrips and outflanks the so-called 'British System' of opiate control (see chapter 2), as is implicitly recognised in recent reports (A.C.M.D., 1982) and in recent research (Smart, 1984, b). Whilst there are some signs of a slight expansion of the clinic system and of its influence over non-clinic doctors (such as GPs), there is no sign of any general 'liberalisation' of clinic practice that would attract a large number of drug users (and keep them). Nor, on the side of law enforcement, is there any great liberalisation, indeed the reverse is true. Convictions for drug offences (possession and supply) are increasing, and Home Secretary Leon Brittain's December 1983 speech reclassified supply as a 'serious offence', disqualifying offenders from parole. It remains to be seen if importation, diversion and illegal supply of drugs will now decrease. (See Auld *et al.* on *Heroin Now* for discussion of the situation as of mid-1984).

Trends in statutory health and law enforcement practice are most interesting when related to the current development of social work and allied trades in the statutory and non-statutory sectors. The expansion, first in the United States and more recently in Britain, of schemes for 'diversion' of persons from the criminal justice system has been extensively discussed in the crimonological, social work and social policy literature, and most readers will be broadly familiar with the mainpoints. The familiar form of diversion is in the youth social work field, where it constitutes part of Intermediate Treatment (I.T.). It is quite widely acknowledged that whilst such schemes may divert some potential young criminals away from the unnecessary familiarity with more hardened cases in places of confinement (such as borstal), I.T. may also suck into the 'soft' end of the 'control continuum' (Cohen, 1979) a number of boys and girls who would otherwise simply have been given a cuff on the ear and a good telling off. I.T. has now become a model for diversion of a broader age range of criminals and potential criminals, including some who are found to be drug users. Instead of putting such offenders 'inside', the courts, probation service and non-statutory agencies may co-operate to offer the option of entry into a rehabilitation programme, such as those run on residential and non-residential bases by a variety of non-statutory agencies. (The Lifeline Project in Manchester is the NACRO 'flagship' in this regard.) For those offenders who are not diverted from prison, there may be opportunities for drug-related counselling whilst in prison, given by probation officers and/or staff of outside agencies (such as CDP). The overall result is a strengthening of links between the law enforcement system and welfare/health systems.

Taking the two preceding paragraphs together, we can suggest at present, control of drug users is characterised by their continuing displacement from limited health system facilities towards social work and law enforcement.

The situation is more complicated than this, however, partly because of concurrent tendencies towards 'community' or local 'patch' social work strategies (Barclay Report), which are themselves related to concepts of community care that tend to place primary responsibility upon women. (Finch, 1984, gives a critique of this tendency and discusses the difficulty ine volving alternative, non-sexist forms of community care.) Feminist approaches are relatively highly represented in the three street agencies, and probably in the non-statutory social work sector generally, compared with their profile in statutory social work; this may be partly a functionof age differences of the women working in these sectors, as well as of other circumstances. The inter-relations in practice, between these various tendencies in health care, criminal justice, social work, community care and women's provision are extremely complex, crystallising

in a variety of ways in the practices of differing agencies
and individuals: any generalisation would probably not
be warranted, as many readers will be able to confirm
from their own experience.

The other two main sets of circumstances providing
a context for street agency work are the material circumstances
facing the clients of agencies, and those facing the agencies
themselves (see Diagram 6.1). In both cases, these circumstances
have to do with accommodation and sources of income.
In respect of the clients, it is important to recognise
that drug use is most likely to be converted into severe
drug-related problems when it occurs in the context
of an extended biography involving housing problems,
employment problems, and attendant problems. Housing
problems may, as chapter 2 to 5 indicate, involve a lack
of permanent housing, social isolation and confusion
related to lack of a home and neighbours, lack of alternatives
to accommodation with violent or otherwise unsuitable
partners, and/or health problems related to the above.
Employment problems may include low wages or none
at all, causing a lack of financial independence and a
lack of adequate housing, diet, recreation and social
contacts. Both these aspects of clients' material problems
- housing and income prospects - have generally worsened
since the 1970s, providing a potentially more hazardous
context for the drug use of many of the street agencies'
clients. It is possible that, within this context, increasing
numbers of people might experience problems with their
drug use, even if the total number of users were to remain
constant (which seems not to be the case). Additionally,
drug users are confronted with a system of care and
control in which the emphasis has been shifting from
the former to the latter, and with greater linkage between
the two. This is the context in which the street agencies
and other agencies and individuals seek to help drug
users in the mid-1980s.

But the material circumstances of the street agencies
(and of some other social welfare agencies) are also
shifting. In spite of the increasing financial insecurities
of this decade, the street agencies are arguably no worse
off now than they were previously, and this is one aspect
of the various policy shifts noted above. Generally, the
street agencies have found their funding bases have shifted

from the health system *per se* towards a variety of funding sources and rationales available to them in the 1980s. Broadly, these sources of potential funding can be characterised as having interests in work (e.g. the London Boroughs Association, as long as it continues to exist as a viable entity), in the criminal justice system (e.g. Home Office and linked DHSS and D.O.E. funding interests), in feminist approaches to women's provision (e.g. the G.L.C. and some charitable sources), and in training and production of printed information and advice materials.

These shifts result in the street agencies looking rather less like informal adjuncts to statutory health services (which is, roughly, how they operated in the 1970s). Today, the agencies look more like providers of a variety of services related to the broad mix of material problems (e.g. housing and income) facing clients, and to the various social policy concern (self-help, law enforcement and associated social work styles, and an uneasy relationship between community responses and feminist approaches to social welfare). The variety of street agency practices is considerable, reflecting the complexity of health-related and social problems as experienced by broad swathes of the inner city population, problems that may often be exacerbated but are rarely initiated by drug use.

Summarising, we might refer to the oft-heard saying that drug use is a 'symptom of deeper problems': we would modify this, saying that whatever drug use *per se* may be motivated by (and we suspect that desires for pleasure and to pass the time may be amongst the motives), drug-related *problems* are indeed indications of 'deeper problems' around housing, money, relationships and so on that are very familiar to all social work practitioners. Most readers who have experience of other aspects of social work practice will find that the same sorts of problems recur in the drug field.

So, social work practice, advice-giving and referral in the drugs field is like other forms of social work practice insofar as it involves both responding directly to the immediately most problematic aspect of the presenting problem (e.g. responding to overdose or danger of it, to confusion due to intoxication, to lack of a bed for the night, to lack of access to basic health care) and then trying to build a relationship with a client (or helping another agency to do this) that will help him or her to grapple with underlying aspects of the problem. This difficult juggling act (immediate response/longer-term casework) is at the heart of all social work practice (not just drug-related), as is the problem of how to employ 'theory' in tandem with practice, each illuminating the other. As a street agency staff member put it, 'there's a balance there. You've got to do some learning and then get some theory, and then go back into the practice situation'. In other words you have to be prepared to get your feet wet, and then reflect upon your experience and to relate it to the thinking and experience of others (which is all 'theory' is). We have done our best to describe how this is done by the staff of three London street agencies, and now it is up to the reader.

7 Sources of information, materials, support and consultancy

ADVICE IN RELATION TO DRUGS, ALCOHOL AND
SOLVENT-RELATED PROBLEMS

ISDD (Information service, reference library on drug
misuse, development of education and training materials,
and research), 1-4 Hatton Place, Hatton Garden, London
EC1N 8NI.

Alcohol Concern - the National Agency on Alcohol Misuse
(replaces three previous non-statutory agencies), 3 Grosvenor
Crescent, London W1.

SCODA (Standing Conference on Drug Abuse - coordinating
body for non-statutory drug agencies), 1-4 Hatton Place,
Hatton Garden, London EC1N 8NI.

PARTICULAR PROFESSIONS AND WORK-SETTINGS

Central Council for Education and Training in Social Work (information service on training), Derbyshire House, St. Chad's Street, London WC1H 8AD.

Health Education Officers at District Health Authority Level.

Health Education Advisory Teachers in some Local Education Authorities

Lifeline Project (day centre for drug users in and around Manchester), Joddrell Street, Manchester M3 3HE.

National Association of Youth Clubs, 70 St. Nicholas Circle, Leicester LE1 SN7.

National Childrens Bureau (has information service, journal and other publications), 8 Wakely Street, London EC1V 8QE.

NHS Training Advisory Group, Hannibal House, Elephant and Castle, London SE1 6TE.

National Institute for Social Work, 5 Tavistock Place, London WC1.

National Youth Bureau (information, publications, training, etc.), 17-23 Albion Street, Leicester LE1 6GD.

Release (useful for legal aspects, women's rights), 1 Elgin Avenue, London W9 2PR.

Alcohol Counselling Service (has video on women and legal drugs), 34 Electric Lane, London SW9.

SCODA (for non-statutory drug-rehabilitation, social work, and advice projects). Address above.

TACADE (Teachers Advisory Council on Alcohol and Drug Education), 2 Mount Street, Manchester M2.

Report to SCODA, 1974.
Open Door - Or Appointments Only, Annual Report for 1974/5, 1975

'Brain Committee', first and second reports of:
Ministry of Health and Department of Health for Scotland, *Report of the Interdepartmental Committee*, London, HMSO, 1961.
Ministry of Health and Scottish Home and Health Department, *The Second Report of the Departmental Committee*, London, HMSO, 1965.

Burr, A., 'The Piccadilly Drug Scene' in *British Journal of Addiction*, 78,1,pp.5-19, 1983.

Central Statistical Office, *Social Trends*, London, HMSO, 1982.

Cohen, S., 'The Punitive City' in *Contemporary Crises*, 3, 4;pp.339-63, 1979.

Community Drug Project, various reports of:
Annual Report, 1969.
Third Report, 1972.
Report covering period July 1975-November 1976, 1976.
Seventh Report, 1979.
Annual Report 1980-81, 1981.

Crow, I., Pease, K., and Hillary, M., *The Manchester and Wilshire Multi-facility Schemes, A Research Report*, London, National Association for the Care and Resettlement of Offenders, 1980.

Dorn, N., and South, N., 'Sociology and Dangerous Drugs - Coming Full Circle': A review of J. Ditton and K. Speirits, 1981, 'The Rapid Increase in Heroin Addiction in Glasgow during 1981: Background Paper Two' in *British Journal of Addiction*, 77,pp.322-5, 1982.

Finch, J., 'Community Care: developing non-sexist alternatives' in *Critical Social Policy*, 9;pp.6-18, 1984.

EDUCATION AND TRAINING METHODS

Health Education Council, 78 New Oxford Street, London WC1A 1AH, & local HEOs.

NACRO (National Association for the Care and Resettlement of Offenders), 169 Clapham Road, London SW9. Runs training courses, some of them drug-related and is the managing agency of Lifeline.

TACADE (address above) publishes *Working With Groups, Drinking Choices*, and other training materials.

ISDD (address above) publishes *Drugs Demystified training pack*, a boxed set of materials for planning, conducting and following up local multidisciplinary training courses consisting of up to five evening sessions. The pack includes course convenors, guides to planning and running courses, reference materials on drugs, speakers' printed notes, and a variety of handouts for participants (pre-course reading, course discussion, and post-course application of learning). Price: £16.50 plus 20% postage & packing. Send SAE for full publications, list of leaflets, booklets & packs for practitioners.

By 1984 two projects were developing training services on a regional basis. Both began by concentrating on training for those in specialist drug agencies, but are expected to adopt a broader role: North West Regional Drugs Training Unit, Prestwich Hospital, Bury New Road, Manchester; and South West Regional Drugs Training Unit, 29a Southgate, Bath. You can contact them direct or via SCODA, who will also be able to tell you of training services that are developing in other regions and localities.

WHERE TO START

Of these various agencies, your first ports of call might well be ISDD and SCODA. ISDD carries the largest range of printed materials and SCODA is in the position to give the most comprehensive and up-to-date advice on agencies in your region or area that may be able to advise you.

REFERENCES

References (other than internal papers of the three street agencies) that were cited in the text are listed below. Additionally, a number of books and papers were read for background information but not cited, and these are listed in Appendix A6 of the lengthier reference copy, *Street-Wise*, lodged in the ISDD library.

Advisory Committee on Drug Dependence, *The Rehabilitation of Drug Addicts*, London, HMSO, 1968.

Advisory Council on Misuse of Drugs, *Treatment and Rehabilitation*, London, HMSO, 1982.

Advisory Council on Misuse of Drugs, *Prevention*, London, HMSO, 1984.

Auld, J., *Marijuana Use and Social Control*, London, Academic Press, 1981.

Auld, J., Dorn, N. and South, N., 'Heroin Now', in *Youth and Policy*, 2, 4, Spring 1984; see also same authors' article 'Irregular work, irregular pleasures', 1985, in Mathews, R. and Young, J. (eds), *Confronting Crime*, London, Sage (in press).

Austerberry, H. and Watson, S., *Women on the Margins: A Study of Single Women's Housing Problems*, London, City University, Housing Research Group, 1983.

Barclay, P., *et al.*, with National Institute for Social Work, *Social Workers: Their Role and Tasks*, London, Bedford Square Press, 1982.

Berridge, V., and Edwards, G., *Opium and the People: Opiate use in Nineteenth Century England*, London, Allen Lane/St. Martin's Press, 1981.

Blenheim Project, various reports of:
Annual Report, 1966
People Adrift: A report on the Activities of the Blenheim Project up to 1973, 1974.

Finnish Foundation for Alcohol Studies, *Report on Activities*, Helsinki, no date, Alkoholitutkimussaatio. For the original report on the study cited, see Taipale, I., 1982, *Asunnottomuus ja alkoholi. Sosiaalitaaketieteellinen tutkimus Helsingista vuositta 1937-1977*, published by the Foundation, ISBN 951 9192 17 4.

Home Office, *Statistics on the Misuse of Drugs in the UK 1981*, London, Home Office, 1982.

Hungerford Project (managing agency - Turning Point formerly Helping Hand), various reports relating to:
Hungerford Day Project, *Annual Report* (1970-72), 1972.
Helping Hand Organisation, *A Report*, 1972.
Hungerford Project, *Annual Report 1977-78*, 1978.
Helping Hand Organisation, *Drug Use in London - and responses to it*, no date.

ISDD, *UK Official Statistics Relating to Drug Abuse*, London, Institute for the Study of Drug Dependence, 1980.

Jamieson, A., Glanz, A., MacGregor, S. and Culshaw, P., *City Roads: An Assessment*, London, DHSS/Birkbeck College, unpublished (and see forthcoming book by these authors), 1981.

Judson, H., *Heroin Addiction in Britain*, New York, Harcourt, 1973.

Mitcheson, M., 'Total number of patients receiving opiate prescriptions 1977-9 broken down into percentages of heroin, injectable methadone and oral methadone, from 14 NHS clinics', London, University College Hospital, unpublished (copy in ISDD library), 1979.

Mitcheson, M., Davidson, J., Hawks, D. *et al.*, 'Sedative abuse by heroin adicts' in *Lancet*, pp.606-7, 21st March 1970.

Office of Population Census and Surveys, *General Household Survey 1978*, London, HMSO, 1980.

Rolleston Committee, report of:
Ministry of Health, *Report of the Departmental Committee on Morphine and Heroine Addiction*, London, HMSO, 1926.

SCODA, *Barbiturate and similar drug misuse among London drug users*, London, Standing Conference on Drug Abuse (8 pages), 1973.

SCODA, Dorn, N., Ettorre, B., Glanz, A., Hartnoll, R., and Pearson, B., *Record-keeping and assessment of utility in drug-related agencies: A practical guide*, London, DHSS, unpublished (12 pages), 1983.

Smart, C., 'Social Policy and Drug Addiction: a critical study of policy development', in *British Journal of Addiction*, 79, 1,pp.31-39, 1984.

Smart, C., 'Drug Dependence Units in England and Wales. The Results of a National Study', London, Institute of Psychiatry (unpublished), 1984(D).

Winter, I., Thesis on the Blenheim Project, unpublished draft (see Appendix A6 in *Street-wise*, the reference copy of this book, for an extended annotation).

Yates, R., 1981 *Out from the Shadows. Lifeline Project 10th Anniversary Report*, London, National Association for the Care and Resettlement of Offenders.